"Drawn from Mark Nepo's many years of teaching, this book offers a transformative journey that helps us to connect with and explore the eternal part of ourselves—our spiritual nature, our essence. Falling down is part of the human journey, but Mark shows us how it can become a path of spiritual transformation."

—Baptist de Pape, author of *The Power of the Heart*

"Mark Nepo shares a lifetime of hard-earned wisdom through his moving, heartwarming vignettes that are like songs for the soul taking us home to ourselves. I hope you will find a way to read this book slowly, deeply, and let it nourish you with its gentle, wise, and heartfelt guidance."

—Michael Brant DeMaria, PhD, four-time Grammy-nominated recording artist and author of *When All Is Lost*

"Nepo leads us with stories, poetry, metaphors, significant questions, and lessons he's gleaned from the wisdom of authentic teachers. All this has a ring of deep truth. I recommend this book with unreserved enthusiasm."

—Justine Willis Toms, cofounder and host of *New Dimensions* and author of *Small Pleasures*

"Mark Nepo returns. Hallelujah! Our ever-enfolding, always-growing, supremely astute sage of our times sings to us once again, and I couldn't be happier! You'll want to clutch this one close to your heart, to make it a part of you."

—Kris Ferraro, international energy coach, speaker, and author of *Your Difference Is Your Strength, Manifesting,* and the #1 Amazon bestseller *Energy Healing*

"Amid this luminous new collection of wisdom, Mark Nepo offers one of the most robust and tender teachings on grief I have come across. In Mark's hands, pain becomes poetry and enlarges our hearts enough to carry what we may have thought we couldn't."

—Mirabai Starr, author of *Caravan of No Despair* and *Wild Mercy*

"Mark Nepo has led workshops at Omega Institute for many years. His classes are like a gathering of travelers at an oasis, a nourishing stop on a long journey. Now, in this treasure of a book, we all get the chance to experience the magic Mark creates—the learning, the beauty, the healing. This new book is sublime."

—Elizabeth Lesser, cofounder of Omega Institute and author of *Broken Open* and *Cassandra Speaks*

"Mark has traveled into the depths of what it means to be human and brought back this book for all of us. When you fall, and you will because we all do, this book will be an outstretched hand helping you to stand again, and take the next step."   —Beth Kempton, bestselling author of *The Way of the Fearless Writer*

Falling
Down
and
Getting Up

Also by Mark Nepo

Suite for the Living
Acre of Light
Fire Without Witness
God, the Maker of the Bed, and the Painter

EDITOR
Deepening the American Dream

RECORDINGS
Surviving Storms
The Book of Soul
Flames That Light the Heart (video course)
More Together Than Alone
The One Life We're Given
Inside the Miracle (expanded, 2015)
Reduced to Joy
The Endless Practice
Seven Thousand Ways to Listen
Staying Awake
Holding Nothing Back
As Far As the Heart Can See
Finding Inner Courage
The Book of Awakening
Finding Our Way in the World
Inside the Miracle (1996)

Falling Down and Getting Up

Discovering Your
Inner Resilience and Strength

Mark Nepo

ST. MARTIN'S
ESSENTIALS
NEW YORK

First published in the United States by St. Martin's Essentials,
an imprint of St. Martin's Publishing Group

FALLING DOWN AND GETTING UP. Copyright © 2023 by Mark Nepo. All rights reserved. Printed in the United States of America. For information, address St. Martin's Publishing Group, 120 Broadway, New York, NY 10271.

www.stmartins.com

The Library of Congress has cataloged the hardcover edition as follows:

ISBN 978-1-250-90994-7 (trade paperback)
ISBN 978-1-250-86263-1 (ebook)

Our books may be purchased in bulk for promotional, educational, or business use. Please contact your local bookseller or the Macmillan Corporate and Premium Sales Department at 1-800-221-7945, extension 5442, or by email at MacmillanSpecialMarkets@macmillan.com.

First Edition: 2023

10 9 8 7 6 5 4 3 2 1

The dirt that packs
the plant is the beginning of beauty. And
those who haul the piano on stage are the
beginning of music. And those who are
stuck, though they dream of soaring,
they are the ancestors of our wings.

For those who are stuck.
—*MN*

THE GREAT WATERS

*In the beginning, I thought I was
going somewhere. I thought we all
were. But falling in while trying to cross,
I finally understood, the journey is to follow
the river. All the rivers, especially the ones
no one can see. The soul is a fish whose
home is in those rivers. So I can take you
across, if you want. But the secret is to go
everywhere by going nowhere. And I will
be here when you fall in. Which is not
a failure but an awakening.*

—MN

Contents

PART 3: THE JOURNEY TO WHERE WE ARE

All Things Are True

The Work of Integrity

On the Precipice of Growth

Being a Bridge

The Depth of Life

WHEN MEDIEVAL MONKS were asked how they practiced their faith, they said, "By falling down and getting up." This is the human journey from which no one is exempt. We are constantly challenged to get up one more time than we fall, to open one more time than we close, and to put things together one more time than we take them apart. The Japanese proverb *Nanakorobi yaoki* puts it this way: "Fall down seven times, stand up eight."

This rhythm between fragility and resilience informs the practices that keep us human. Yet no one can give these practices to you. Each of us must discover and inhabit them for ourselves. This is why the heart of my teaching has always been a commitment to introduce you to your own gifts and wisdom. And so, drawn from decades of teaching, this book explores the perennial choice-points we all face such as surviving and thriving, managing risk and enhancing risk, opening and closing, giving and receiving, living a balance between solitude and community, enlarging our sense of things when pain and fear make us small, and the never-ending practice of course-correcting and tuning as we go.

My aim here is to explore the archetypal rhythm inherent to every life. While no one likes to fall down, it is how we grow. From a longer and deeper perspective, falling down and getting up is the inevitable rhythm of transformation. In fact, each step we take forms a dance of falling down and getting up. This book focuses on the individual's transformative journey with all its ups and downs and twists and turns. In essence, how do we learn the dance of falling down and getting up?

The Hindu Upanishads offer the image of how a caterpillar bunches up before moving forward as a symbol of this kind of growth. Similarly, a nurse, who prompted me to get up and walk immediately after surgery, announced, "Two steps forward, one step back!" This is the rhythm of life we are asked to accept in order to live. *Falling Down and Getting Up* explores these timeless rhythms and the essential skills needed to fully live our lives.

To this day, each time I teach, I pause before the others arrive and say to everything and no one, "If this is the last time I have to be with others, let me give my all and hold nothing back. Let me offer all I have been exploring with as much love as I can." Then, the friends I'm about to meet come into the room. And we begin.

My want here is to have this book simulate, as much as possible, the magic and synergy that occurs in those circles, which I have been blessed to convene all over the world. Through the practices of question, journaling, and dialogue, and through the unpacking of metaphor and telling of stories, I hope to lead you further down the path of awakening where you can have the life you want by being ever more present to the life you have.

Eventually, everyone will be dropped into the depth of life. It may happen because of some life-threatening illness or sudden loss, or from being loved unconditionally for the first time, or by the sudden beauty of grace. But once broken open, the deeper, relational journey begins by which we truly know that we are alive.

Along the way, we all experience fear, pain, and grief. Each can be overwhelming. In addition to this, we, as human beings, suffer the tendency to inflate or deflate our sense of self and the nature of our experience. And so, much of our spiritual practice centers on learning how to see things as they are. While this can help us move through fear and pain, grief is another matter. Regardless of what we may lose that is dear, such a ripping away is life altering and there is no going back. These deeper teachers will all find us in time. Our challenge has always been to help each other face what is ours to face, so we can be as alive as possible for as long as possible in the tender journey we call love.

This book tries to uncover and personalize pathways that allow us to right-size our pain and fear in our journey to be fully here. And to help us move with our grief from the old world to the new, working with all that life unearths in us. To be sure, fear, pain, and grief are inevitable teachers, and together, we must try to understand their language and their lessons.

My hope is that this book will help you befriend your fear, pain, and grief and not be crippled by them. My hope is that you will discover one or two specific ways to move forward in your journey toward a blessed and authentic life.

So, to you who have opened this book, I thank you for your commitment. Not a commitment to *my* work but to *the* work. Not to my books or to working with me in person, but for your devotion to the deeper journey of being an awakened soul on Earth. Essentially, I see my call as an inner explorer, breaking and marking trails through the inner wilderness, which feeds everyone though no one owns it. For it is our common devotion to explore the depths of our inner nature that is so life giving.

The ways of Spirit may seem abstract and distant until, during difficult climbs, like now, we pick them up and use them. For every spiritual tradition offers tools and resources to repair what has ruptured between us. In this turbulent era, the world has fallen down, and we must help each other up and begin again. That is the aim of this book—to help each other up and begin again.

Let me invoke this journey with a recent poem of mine that encapsulates our recurring work in being human.

It's called "Anthem":

> *Yes, you fell down.*
> *I feel for you, for I have*
> *fallen many times.*
>
> *Now, you must get up.*
> *I know it isn't easy.*
> *I know it will take time.*
>
> *Remember, the seed*
> *can't imagine breaking*
> *ground. And the fledgling*
> *can't imagine flying.*
>
> *And so, your broken heart*
> *can't imagine finding its way.*
>
> *But life is this repeating journey*
> *from sleep to wakefulness,*
> *from blindness to sight,*
> *from fear to love.*
>
> *No matter how many times*
> *we fall, we are just beginning.*

PART 1

The Way of Learning

When chickens or dogs wander away, people know enough to search for them, but when their heart wanders away, they don't. The Way of Learning is nothing other than this: searching for the heart that's wandered away.

—Mencius

. . .

When I was boy, my father sat me at the tiller of our sailboat and had me steer by following a compass. He must have sensed my ability to stay focused. I quickly learned that, even when on course, the needle of the compass never stands still. Even when on course, we must maintain our focus and effort. Always a little to the left, a little to the right. The work of staying on course is never done. This can serve as a metaphor for the way of learning and the ongoing work of meeting choice-points in the journey of being alive. There is never one fixed answer or direction in life. We are always making our way through some fog or choppy water and course-correcting. Being a spirit in a body in time on Earth requires that we course-correct by staying in conversation with life and by entering the choice-points we are given.

In this part of the book, we will explore many stories about learning, including: how time unfolds, how no one is watching, how to fall and how to get up, and how to navigate the corridor of aliveness. We will explore the places where we remain teach-able. For it is under our endless want to count and compare that we can settle into what is enduring. There, in the truth and grip of our feelings, we wake close to the bone, like fish thrown into the turns of a wild river. Only you can run the river. Only you can ride the stream of aliveness that calls for each of us.

Our Conversation with Life

We're with the push.
We're not the push.

—ROBERT MASON

My Life as a Teacher

Teaching is a noble ferrying between
the ports of knowing and not knowing.

—MN

I come from a family of teachers—my father, my brother, my wife, my aunt. In the Jewish tradition, teachers are revered, learning is revered. *Rebbe* means "teacher." In the Jewish way of learning, questions lead to relationship and embodiment more than a catalog of answers. The reward for learning is more an enduring sense of knowing than a storehouse of knowledge.

Abraham Heschel confirms that:

In the eyes of the Ashkenazim [Jews of Eastern Europe], knowledge was not a means for achieving power, but a way of clinging to the source of all reality. In the eyes of Hasidim, study for the sake of acquiring scholarship was considered a desecration. The aim was to partake of spiritual beauty.

For me, the effect of being a lifelong student and teacher is that such a commitment has made my heart strong. In Hebrew, *lev tov* means "good heart." In this way, learning and teaching, together, evoke the practice of a good heart. My life as a poet coincides with my life as a student and a teacher. For the poet's call is to reveal how the source of all reality empowers a good heart to sustain the Web of Life.

Surviving cancer in my mid-thirties only deepened my life as a teacher. By surrendering to the miracle of life in order to survive, my sense of learning and teaching was transformed into an ongoing covenant of care. But my sense of learning at a deep level goes back to my child-hood. When eight or nine, I fell in the schoolyard, skin-ning my knee badly. While flat on the ground, I was forced to listen to the Earth itself for the first time.

Not long after that, I found myself on my father's thirty-foot sailboat listening to the sea as it carried us. I was instantly a student of this massive, clear, flexible ele-ment that was holding us up. These early experiences of listening directly to life taught me that strength and re-solve are always restored through the complete surrender of our naked attention.

Once on the other side of my cancer journey, I realized that the things we suffer and the things we love provide us with an Inner Curriculum. When we least expect it, it is working with what we're given while staying close to what we love that is a constant teacher.

Some of the thresholds I have been drawn to learn from and speak to over the years include:

- awakening to the paradox and true gifts of suffering,
- seeing obstacles as teachers,
- having the life of poetry and the poetry of life continue to blur,
- understanding creativity as an expressive form of healing,
- exchanging the want to be great for the great chance to be,
- understanding how giving attention is more essential than getting attention,
- learning from the acceptance of our limitations,
- and awakening to how we need each other to be complete and useful.

Each of these thresholds presents a choice-point that each of us must personalize, if we are to live a full life. So, through journaling and conversation with a friend or loved one, I invite you to explore each of these reflection-points over the next few months, one at a time, in an effort to better understand your particular place in the Universe:

- Describe an interior space that suffering has opened in you.
- Describe one obstacle and how it has changed you.

- Describe one experience in which the boundary between you and another has blurred.
- Describe one form of expression that has been healing for you.
- Describe one experience that allowed you to be, rather than achieve.
- Describe what getting attention has done to you and what giving attention has done to you.
- Describe your struggle to accept a limitation.
- And describe a recent experience in which you needed the presence and help of another in order to feel more whole.

Often, giving ourselves over to the life of experience yields the next phase of our Inner Curriculum. For each of us has our own language of wisdom, the way every tree casts its own pattern of light and shadow, though they all draw on the same Source. With every heartbreak, discovery, and moment of joy, with every lift of presence that touches us where we didn't think we could be touched, with every cut and confusion, another letter in our alphabet of wisdom is decoded. Take a step, learn a word. Feel a feeling, decode a sign. Accept a truth, translate a piece of the Mystery written in our heart. Day by authentic day, we learn our inner language. To be conversant in the web of relationship that our authenticity reveals is the work of every soul.

In the Jewish tradition, the word *sabbath* literally means "the one day we don't turn one thing into another." Perhaps,

the quintessential learning position is a form of receptive-
ness through which we relate to things as they are without
turning one thing into another.

Humbly, after a lifetime of teaching, I've come to see
that you can't change anyone. So, what am I doing in
the many circles I convene all over the world? Well, I've
come to see that being a teacher means serving as a green-
house: providing light and warmth to the living things before us so they can grow in the various ways they are meant
to grow.

If I am invested in changing you, that assumes I know
what you should be changed into. This is presumptuous
and dangerous. In the realm of transferring knowledge,
there are definite and precise things to learn and skill sets
to master. But in the deeper realm of knowing, there is
no such arrival point. There is only the constant becoming of our soul on Earth, which no one can prescribe or
schedule.

As a tree grows from the imprint of its seed, each life
grows in the world from the imprint of its soul. We can
only water the seed for each other and care for each other's
growth. In this regard, our being directs our doing. So, I
encourage you to water the roots of your being so it can
grow its gestures into the world.

In a modern age that commodifies everything, our challenge is to grow from the inside out, letting every holy calling find its own expression within us and between us. After
decades of listening to the stories and struggles of others, I

can bear witness that teaching, in its most profound form, is not moving a life from here to there, or from effort to achievement, or even from chaos to order. Rather, teaching is creating the enduring environment in which the seed of the soul can know itself and blossom.

With this in mind, I invite you to consider the vantage point from which you relate to your students, no matter the size or shape of your classroom: What are you looking for when you look into your students? What are you listening for when you listen to your students? What are you hoping to grow in the garden of their minds? How will you prepare the soil? How do you know when you should *not* turn one thing into another? How do you know when you *should* turn one thing into another? How can you best help each of your students by meeting them where they are?

Recently, I was teaching online, exploring the topic of "Heart and Path" with 542 eager students in China. As they were journaling, I quietly watched this honeycomb of lives unfold through the tiny, square windows that were connecting us through Zoom. I was looking into home after home, from living room to bedroom to dining room table. The fabric of humanity was being woven before my eyes. And there, I chanced to view a woman at her kitchen table journaling. She was perhaps in her late thirties. Behind her was an elderly woman who was combing the younger woman's hair. I imagined it was her mother.

I was opened deeply by the softness of this moment. The tenderness of this mother and daughter embodied all I was speaking to. I was in southwest Michigan in my study and 6500 miles away, in a small kitchen, these two gentle women were living their lives. It was a privileged glimpse of life loving itself, like a small flower opening along the forest floor. There is always an unexpected instant when I teach that brings me more alive. And here it was.

Like a biologist who talks endlessly about the conditions that allow for molecules to join, who is at a loss for words when seeing the very atoms of life pulse beneath his microscope, I was speechless to witness the very atoms of love at work three continents away. And while I wanted to cry out in affirmation of all I can't explain, I remained silent, like a bird watcher, not wanting to disrupt the small beauty that had landed before me.

After the session ended, I sat for a time in my study, replaying the image of the aging mother combing her daughter's hair on the other side of the world. It flickered like a candle in my mind that helped me find my way back to the source of all reality.

Moments like these, which can never be planned, affirm, yet again, that teaching is pointing toward all that makes life possible, toward all that helps us go on, while praising the living presence that no one can live without.

The things we suffer and the things we love provide us with an Inner Curriculum.

Questions to Walk With

- In your journal, describe the smallest thing a teacher did that helped you or changed you or led you to who you are.
- In conversation with a friend or loved one, tell the story of an unexpected moment that brought you more alive. How did you come upon this moment and what did it bring forward in you?

As Time Unfolds

What happens when people open their hearts?
They get better.

—Haruki Murakami

In the last chapter, I mentioned teaching online with a large group of students in China. It was a five-week course and the whole process was a gift. To prepare for the sessions, I worked very closely with Joy Huang Xiaoyu, whose depth of understanding in both Chinese and English is remarkable. With Joy as my translator, we entered a beautiful journey, unraveling words to their very fiber of meaning.

I wanted to open one of the sessions with a poem of mine called "Disrobing in Time." The poem affirms that the only power we have when feeling powerless is to admit the truth of our experience. By this act of acceptance, we disrobe ourselves of all excuses and denials until we stand naked in our being.

After discussing the poem in more detail, Joy exclaimed, "We have a perfect word for this!" Then, she introduced me to the Chinese word 蜕变 (t-way be-yan), which means "taking off all coverings to become one's true self as time unfolds." The ideogram literally means a snake taking off its skin to have a new skin, or a caterpillar breaking through its cocoon to become a butterfly. The word implies growth and transformation.

I was stunned at the depth and breadth of this one word. We have no such word in English. The word serves as a threshold. It reveals a theme, a vow, a practice central to the inquiry we are exploring throughout this book: How do we take off all our coverings to become our true self as time unfolds? In essence, this question is at the heart of all my work. For this is how we endure and remain more than what is done to us. This long, slow gesture that lives between effort and grace is at the center of all inner practice.

Being introduced to this notion by Joy made me think of what it means to be a Spiritual Warrior. In my book *The Book of Soul,* I discovered that the word *war* derives from the Indo-European word *wers,* which means "to confuse, mix up." All war and conflict stem from confusion. And so, a Spiritual Warrior is one who remains committed to the removal of confusion within us and between us.

In truth, healing often begins by removing what's in the way within us, while justice often begins by removing what's in the way between us. The ever-present question for a Spiritual Warrior is: What can each of us do, now, to inhabit this twin practice? How can we serve healing by clearing the confusion within us and removing what's in the way inside us, and how can we serve justice by clearing

the confusion between us and removing what's in the way
between us?

These are lifelong practices worth dedicating ourselves
to. Each of us can be a Spiritual Warrior by staying devoted to these constant ways of learning:

- how to take off all coverings to become one's
  true self as time unfolds,
- how to serve healing by clearing the confusion
  within us and removing what's in the way inside us,
- and how to serve justice by clearing the confusion between us and removing what's in the way
  between us.

These devotions are always interlaced and dependent
on each other. In serving justice, I can remove what's
wrongfully in the way and open the door of your prison,
but only you can walk out of that prison. Likewise, if I am
pinned under some weight of oppression, you can help remove that weight, but it is my work to stand again.

At their deepest, healing and justice work together the
way we need two good legs to walk and two good eyes
to see. And somehow, we grow, even when what matters
seems out of reach. Consider that while plants and trees
can't exist without light, it is their botanical call to grow toward the light while underground when that light is out of
reach. In just this way, we can't exist without the light and
warmth that informs all things, though it is our human call
to grow toward that light even when it seems out of reach.

To be broken by the elements or time is natural, and to be broken by each other by accident is human, but to intentionally break anything is cruel. We are capable of all three, which is why we need each other to heal one more time than we are broken. We need each other to remove confusion and to rely on each other to remove what falls in the way. In equal measure, healing and justice are the opposite of fear and confusion. And the opposite of gravity is the emanation of Spirit. We have no choice but to stay devoted to these fundamental forces that bring us together and keep us alive.

How do we take off all our coverings to become our true self as time unfolds?

Questions to Walk With

- In your journal, describe a confusion that exists within you and how you might begin to clear that confusion. Then, describe a confusion that exists between you and another and how you might begin to clear that confusion. Note the different kinds of effort required to clear inner confusion and outer confusion.
- In conversation with a friend or loved one, begin to tell the history of your journey in taking off all your coverings in order to become your true self. Where are you now in this lifelong process?

No One Is Watching

I need you to whisper
to your heart
before you speak.

—Michael Mejia

It took almost dying for me to realize that no one is watching. This doesn't mean we are alone but that no one is out of view judging us. From an early age, we are taught by parents, family, society, and various traditions that our actions are being judged. If we fail or come up wanting, we are censured by others to some form of living hell. Once we've internalized the watcher, we carry this living hell inside our minds.

The Argentinian writer Jorge Luis Borges has a poem called "The Watcher" in which he laments his hell for never being free of this inner critic. Once a pattern of criticism is knit in our mind, the watcher voice can appear as shame, guilt, regret, or perfectionism. Yet while we are always accountable for our actions in the world, we are not under the watch of some moral tribunal everywhere we go.

For true responsibility comes solely from the hard work of actual relationship, the authentic push and pull between honest, caring souls.

The struggle to free ourselves of the watcher is part of our initiation into the realm of a true self. At first, we are trained to seek the approval of these voices in order to comply with the expectations of others. However, when governed by the watcher, our entire perceptual field is misguided. For appeasing these voices is not where lasting peace comes from. In time, only great love and great suffering can silence and even break the grip of the watcher until we are left with a bareness of being that is irreducible.

After my journey with cancer, wrestling this poem into being marked my first felt understanding of our direct, irreducible experience of life. It's called "The Music Beneath the Music":

> *I have tried so hard to please*
> *that I never realized*
> *no one is watching.*
>
> *I imagined like everyone at school*
> *that our parents were sitting*
> *just out of view like those*
> *quiet doctors behind clean mirrors.*
>
> *I even felt the future*
> *gather like an audience,*

ready to marvel at how much
we had done with so little.

But when I woke bleeding after surgery
with all those mothlike angels
breathing against me, I couldn't
talk and the audience was gone.

I cried way inside and the sobs
were no more than the water
of a deshelled spirit
soaking ground.

Years have passed and I wait
long hours in the sun to see the birch
fall of its own weight into the lake
and it seems to punctuate God's mime.

Nothing sad about it.

And sometimes, at night,
when the dog is asleep
and the owl is beginning to stare
into what no one ever sees,
I stand on the deck and feel
the black spill off the stars,
feel it coat the earth, the trees,
the minds of children half asleep,
feel the stillness evaporate

> *all notions of fame*
> *into the space*
> *that waits*
> *for light.*

Yet, even knowing this doesn't prevent me from feeling the press of the watcher to this day. Here is a humbling example. My father was a master woodworker and a master teacher. However, when teaching his sons, he was persistent in his standard of perfection and endlessly critical. His constant judgment made me insecure about fixing anything. I feel thoroughly bereft and incompetent to this day.

Recently, my wife, Susan, and I were replacing coat hooks in our entryway. The old ones had pulled out of the wall. As we were removing them, I began to caution Susan, "Be careful, we don't want to make the holes bigger. Be careful. If the holes get bigger, it will be a mess."

My critical caw escalated until Susan said, "Why are you talking like this?" I grew defensive: "I just don't want us to ruin the wall." She stopped and said directly, "I don't know who's speaking here, but stop spilling it on me." Suddenly, I realized, after all these years, that this was the watcher voice of my father, now curated in my mind. Unaddressed, I was projecting his criticism—through me—onto Susan.

It is relentless how the inner critic, if allowed, will prod us to get on with it, to get things done, not to linger. But when I move too fast, I can't seem to focus or see clearly. And once unable to see or hear clearly, I am entangled in the web of watcher voices that keep me from living my life. The pattern just worsens.

In the Swiss legend of William Tell, the marksman is compelled to shoot an apple from his son's head to save his life. Secretly, Tell prepares a second arrow, in case he misses, to kill the one who compelled him to such a test. If allowed to rule our way in the world, the insidious claim of the watcher or inner critic is that we often empower a second watcher within us who carries a second arrow, ready to shoot us, if we should miss or fall short. With the second arrow of judgment, we ensure that we will not escape the web of watcher voices surrounding us.

Over time, I have learned that being preoccupied with the watchers in our mind keeps us from being present to ourselves, those around us, and the life before us in any given moment. In fact, the part of our mind occupied by the watchers is not available to perceive, understand, or experience truth. As the part of our heart occupied by wounds is not available for the full feeling of love and life, the part of our mind entangled with our watchers is not available to truly perceive ourselves or others.

Yet, it is not as simple as skipping over the wounds that occupy our heart or transcending the web of voices judging us. To be fully alive, we are required to disengage our watchers and to heal our wounds by committing to the inner work necessary to regain the full, complete use of our mind and heart. This unending, honest work is the practice of being a wakeful human being.

The truth is that we can never completely eliminate the

web of watchers or the scars of our wounds, but we can grow and evolve by quieting these voices and reclaiming the full expanse of our mind and heart. The challenge is not to judge ourselves for the appearance of these difficulties. Rather, it is the work of self-awareness to recognize the space they take up within us. Then, it is a form of heartwork to address these difficulties so we can be fully alive again.

All the meditation practices from various traditions offer us the chance to be still until the watcher voices are silenced. We can also create our own practices to till this psychological terrain, which is filled and preoccupied, like the buildup from erosion that covers mountain paths and diverts rivers. In the face of all impediments, it is the engagement of truth that clears the way. As the visionary educator Parker J. Palmer says, "To teach is to create a space in which obedience to the truth is practiced."

The work of quieting our watchers and healing our wounds is part of the ongoing, inner practice of truth. Accepting this led me to retrieve this poem, called "Where We Need to Be":

> *It isn't long after we arrive*
> *that everyone starts pointing*
> *and telling us where we need*
> *to be and what we need to do*
> *to get there. There's no time*
> *to really ask why. Soon, things*
> *happen and we're thrown off*

> *course and now there's all this*
> *effort to win their approval. If*
> *lucky, love will distract us more*
> *than suffering. If blessed, we're*
> *broken of everyone's plans and*
> *regrets and thrown like a hooded*
> *bird into a sea of light. If trust-*
> *ing the fall, we find our wings.*

When present enough and authentic enough, we hear a different kind of voice that comes from within, which is less derivative and which more directly imbues us with the emanation of life-force that we are born with. In *Chatter: The Voice in Our Head*, the psychologist Ethan Kross speaks to both the perils of the watcher voices as well as to the deeper, less derivative voice that brings us more into our lives.

Kross explores how marathoners deal with pain in the latter stages of running. Some try to distract themselves from the pain by focusing on anything else, while others choose to focus on the pain, to get inside the pain by being present to it completely. Studies show that those who are present to their pain move through it more quickly and are less impacted by the pain than those who distract themselves.

Kross also reports how self-talk that names our own person in an encouraging way touches into that less derivative inner voice that connects us directly to our inner resources. In fact, studies show that calling on our own person in our own voice improves our strength, resilience, and performance.

This brings us to those lasting voices that affirm us rather than judge us, voices that bear witness rather than watch. Voices like my grandmother who told me as a boy that I am more than enough, as long as I keep learning. These voices, which lead us back to our deepest, truest nature, do not drain us but open us to life. If blessed, these affirming voices can buoy us for a lifetime, outweighing the watcher voices.

Painfully, if we don't address the residue of other voices that keeps us from living, we will, in turn, become the watchers of those around us. As I did in replaying my father's criticism on my wife, Susan. By disempowering the watcher voices, each generation is challenged to break the patterns of imposition we place on one another, no matter how well-intended.

Under our unwanted influence on each other, there is nothing more restorative than true, honest companionship on the journey of life. When we can reclaim the humble position of a beginner, not pretending to know where any of this is going or how to get there, then, we truly walk together, lifting what is in the way and building what needs to be built.

When free of the watcher voices and wounds that I've accrued along the way, I am, however briefly, in awe of the power and majesty of life itself to enliven us and keep us going. Feeling this led me to write this passage, called "Drinking from Center":

> *Some say there's a fire at the Center of our Being. How does anyone know? Though I believe it. Sometimes in dream, I go there, and it's not some hell. More like a lake of light that drinking from heals. And healing is not erasing what life does to us. Rather, drinking from Center knits all the scars into a fabric that can't be torn. Regardless of how we get there, no matter what is broken or lost, the weave binds us. We call its pattern beauty.*

Ultimately, removing what's in the way reveals the pattern we call beauty. The fact that we are repeatedly covered again by voices and wounds is less a failure and more like a window that accumulates its film of dirt. It is just in our nature. Perhaps, so we can have the recurring blessing of discovering beauty, again and again, each time we help each other remove what's in the way.

> *The part of our mind occupied by the watchers is not available to perceive, understand, or experience truth.*

Questions to Walk With

- In your journal, identify the largest voice inside your head that is not your own. Tell the story of how this voice has come to take up so much space and authority in your life.

- In conversation with a friend or loved one, tell the story of an incident that allowed you to realize that no one is watching. How did this opening of perception affect you?

How to Fall and How to Get Up

You fall down a hundred times,
you get up a hundred times,
you learn a hundred lessons.

—Mike Tyson

After taking a hard fall when just a boy, my father sat me down and said, "You have to learn how to fall. If you sense you're about to fall, just go with it. Don't resist. Otherwise, you'll make it worse." Years later, I read chapter 64 in the *Tao Te Ching* where Lao Tzu encourages us to be like water because everything brittle breaks. So, what does the practice of falling involve and what does the practice of getting up look like? How can we be like water and not make everything worse?

At eighty-four, my dear friend Don is having to relearn how to fall and get up. Last summer, while pulling a broken bough of an elm off his garage, he fell on his side and bruised a rib. It took months to heal. This winter, while fetching the mail, he slipped on the icy mouth of his drive-way and landed on his chest. With nothing broken, he told me, "You have to fall with grace." He went on to say, "I don't mean that we should be graceful when falling, but to fall *along with* grace."

Don was suggesting that we fall the way a leaf falls in the hands of the wind. In the deepest sense, we are challenged to align ourselves with whatever current is causing us to fall. Contrary to being willful, we must learn to go with the force of life that is overtaking us and forget where we are going. Once taken over by the force of life, resistance will only break us further.

In the martial art of aikido, students are taught the art of falling, known as *ukemi*. Falling techniques in the martial arts help practitioners avoid injury while getting quickly back on their feet. *Ukemi* is a Japanese term that means "to receive." And so, the way to move through a fall is to receive it. Therefore, the central principle of the art of falling is *not* to break your fall but to tuck and roll.

When frightened by the suddenness of a fall, receiving it seems counter-intuitive. But to receive a fall is more aligned with Lao Tzu's notion of being like water. Paradoxically, receiving what befalls us is the way to work directly with what we're given. And working with what befalls us, we begin to apprentice in an inevitable law of spiritual physics, which is that the only way out is through.

The transformative questions remain: What are the inner corollaries of *ukemi*? How can we mentally and emotionally get back on our feet? What does it mean, inwardly, to receive the fall and tuck and roll? How we apply these skills to trauma, loss, illness, and grief determines the depth of our resilience.

If we look more closely at the techniques of *ukemi,* a fall is further softened by releasing the energy of impact with the slap of an open hand at the point of impact. Again, we're asked *not* to hold on to what happens to us, but to release its pointed energy, as best we can. The emotional equivalent of *ukemi* is the art of authenticity, whereby we meet and feel whatever befalls us openly and honestly. We don't avoid what happens but we don't resist it either. Our authenticity releases the energy of impact.

I want to introduce another aspect of the art of getting up, which involves re-establishing our connection with everything larger than us. Earlier, I mentioned scampering in the schoolyard when in elementary school. I tripped and took a hard fall, scraping my knee. I felt the sting of open cuts, but something in being flat on the Earth stopped me. I had never been this close to the Earth. Without realizing it, I received the fall and tried to hug the Earth. For the first time, I had a sense of the planet chugging along beneath us.

When I stood up, I took that bit of consciousness with me, not taking the Earth for granted. This sense of being carried by things larger than we can easily comprehend deepened my understanding of life. It changed the context of all my falling and all my getting up.

To summarize, here are some ways to practice falling

down and getting up, that we each must personalize when meeting adversity:

- to *not* resist the fall, but to go with it
- to be like water, to work directly with what we're given
- to fall *along with* grace, to align ourselves with whatever current is causing us to fall
- to receive the fall, *not* to break our fall but to tuck and roll
- to release the energy of impact
- to re-establish our connection with everything larger than us

While these practices derive from the physical acts of falling and getting up, there is enduring value in finding their inner equivalents, which help us to live in an embodied, integral way, facing what is ours to face and feeling what is ours to feel. For just as columns of water at sea never stop swelling and crashing, we never stop falling and getting up. Falling is only tragic when the motion is viewed separately from the larger cycle of living, in the same way that getting up is only heroic when that motion is viewed separately from the seamless motions of life.

Ultimately, falling down and getting up are continuous forces like night and day or exhaling and inhaling. When skilled at both, a deeper, more expansive understanding of life is possible, indeed, inevitable. To be clear, being more adept at falling down and getting up will not eliminate the harsh reality of falling nor the effort in getting back up. But experiencing their place in the larger rhythms of life will free us from being thrown about by the sudden tides of life. Like sleeping and waking, like listening and speaking, like giving and receiving—falling down and getting up are just larger steps we take to walk and make our way.

Inevitably, one of the gifts in being human is that it takes falling down to realize that there's nowhere to go.

Working with what befalls us, we begin to
apprentice in an inevitable law of spiritual physics,
which is that the only way out is through.

Questions to Walk With

- In conversation with a friend or loved one, tell the story of a time when you were too brittle in response to a fall in life. Then, tell the story of a time when you were able to receive the fall and be like water. How do you understand the difference?

- In your journal, describe a trauma, loss, illness, or grief that you are struggling with and apply the practices of falling down and getting up to what you are facing. How can these approaches help you get back up: to not resist the fall, but to go with it, to be like water, to work directly with what you've been given, to fall along with grace, to align yourself with whatever current is causing you to fall, to receive the fall, not to break your fall but to tuck and roll, to release the energy of impact, and to re-establish your connection with everything larger than us?

Traveling Again

The Chinese word *hsien* means "profound serenity and quietness." It immediately conjures a sense of stillness, the aim of all meditation, through which we can see and feel the world of being more clearly. The ideogram for this word renders the moon shining through an open gate or a tree standing alone within the gates of a courtyard. These root images suggest that the deep being of life will both penetrate us, opening the gates we create, and exist within us, despite the gates we keep closed. For being—like the moon and the tree—ignores gates, opened or closed.

There is another Chinese word, *tzu-jan,* which means "the constant unfolding of things." This word literally means "self-ablaze" and refers to the natural emergence of being through our unfettered heart-movements in the world. It describes the spontaneous expression that comes from living wholeheartedly in the open. When we are one with the life around us, our deeper self begins to blaze in the open, flickering like an unrehearsed flame.

So, there are many ways to experience the depth of life. And while the term *hsien* refers to the appearance of being through deep stillness, the term *tzu-jan* refers to the appearance of being through authentic and spontaneous doing. We must become skilled at both.

Both being and doing, if entered wholeheartedly, will let us drink from the pool of deep presence that underscores all life. I experience this mix of both every time I swim. While I started swimming as a form of low-impact aerobics, it quickly became a moving meditation for me. As such, I swim slowly, at the pace of what is real, aiming to move through the water without disturbing it. It feels like a spontaneous and submerged form of tai chi.

I was circling these notions while swimming and, as often happens, the teacher is near at hand. Coming up for air, I realized that the relationship of being and doing is very akin to these movements through the water. Since being is the domain of the deep and doing is the domain of the surface, we are most graceful and productive when in balance between the two. Too much out of the water, out of being, and we strain. Too much in the water, out of doing, and we are stalled. Too much either way and the life of resistance increases. So it makes sense to look to the world but to keep facing the deep.

I also feel this mix of being still and spontaneous, of being quiet and ablaze at the same time, while traveling. For, in the heart of travel, I feel wonderfully alone but joined to the crowd, deeply connected to the life around me while feeling anonymous—one fish in a school of fish following the patterns of light that surround us.

After almost two years at home because of the pandemic, I finally ventured out again. I was overwhelmed just ordering the Uber to the airport. I needed to reclaim that in-between space while traveling, that space where I am both still and spontaneous, quiet and ablaze. Once the driver, Christopher, dropped me off, I was back in the stream. But as soon as I got to the counter, I was delayed and would miss my connection. My mind began to spin. Could I still get to Denver tonight? Would I have to go tomorrow? Should I just rebook now? The delay threw me off and I was tight.

I was rebooked through Minneapolis. It all worked out, though I didn't arrive in Denver till after midnight. In texting my wife, Susan, I almost wrote, "Something went wrong." But I stopped myself, caught by an earlier flight deplaning. Dozens of passengers scurried out of the arrival gate, like bees scattering from a hive, buzzing about, intently focused on the countless choices suddenly before them.

Each person carried an entire world with them. It was then that I realized—all travel, including dream, is an approximation. And when something doesn't go as planned, which is inevitable, that unexpected change isn't wrong, just different. In the unexpected, we find the deep stillness. In the unrehearsed, we come ablaze.

After witnessing this truth, I texted Susan and said, "I am delayed. This is beyond what I expected." This made me less intent on arriving anywhere and I watched my fellow travelers, humbled that so much of this life—in all directions—is beyond what we expect.

We aim, we miss, we learn from where we land, and try again. It is presumptuous to assume we will always get what we want or land where we aim. I sat at gate A28 remembering how almost every gift of love and grace has awakened me when I've fallen off course.

I looked around at all the other bees in the human hive, of which I am a part. Now, I wished unexpected blessings for each of them. I hoped the lonely seeker would miss her flight and meet her love. I hoped the agitated builder would lose his way and stumble on the one thing he was born to repair. I hoped the father estranged from his daughter would be so delayed that he would have to soften, after hours in the terminal, and finally find a way to call her. And now, I hope that I can outlast my frustration and welcome whatever searing angel is waiting in disguise to pull me deeper into life.

Both being and doing, if entered wholeheartedly,
will let us drink from the pool of deep presence that
underscores all life.

Questions to Walk With

- In your journal, describe an experience of profound serenity and quietness that came upon you like the moon through an open gate. Describe the part of you that is the moon and the part of you that is the gate. In that moment, what caused you to open your gate?
- In conversation with a friend or loved one, describe a moment of spontaneity in which your heart felt like it had come ablaze. In that moment, what caused your heart to come alive in this way?

The Give and Take of Life

Life is a perpetual surf, covering and uncovering, softening what is hard, hardening what is soft, stirring what is buried, burying what won't stay still. All the while, the heart gives and takes, the mind opens and closes, and our sense of fear and safety expands and contracts. All the while, truth comes into view and seems to disappear. And our ability to perceive beauty comes and goes, while everything keeps growing and shedding at the same time. Though we see this constant covering and uncovering as trouble, we are constantly being given something while having something taken away. This deep and wearing action is how life keeps shaping us relentlessly until only what is essential and unbreakable remains.

Though we resist, the things that cover us wear away. This is how we uncover the miracle at the center of everything. We are worn till the things that don't matter crumble in the face of what is elemental—like sand before surf or hearts before time. Till the pearl forming within us is revealed. This is the purpose of experience.

Having been worn to what is elemental, I am always amazed, but no longer surprised, at the deeper order that moves under all trouble. In these brief moments of unimpeded perception, it is clear that as the unseen wind moves from the azalea to the young willow, the unseen force of Spirit moves from you to me and on to those yet born. Still, the azalea doesn't become the willow, even though they root in the same soil. In just this way, you stay you and I stay me, though we are informed by each other, just by virtue of how Spirit moves through all things.

Under the circus of existence, all forms are knit into a barely perceptible weave of being that spans from the stars to the endless drip in the darkest cave. And though the star never touches the cave, the light and dark inform each other. We carry their essence. As I carry you, though we have never met. I carry the dream you are about to wake in. And you feel my sadness as a sudden cloud blocking the light. We arc in a dynamic elegance that no one orchestrates, though no one can come alive without feeling its pull.

Yet we are the only creatures who project our limitations onto the world. Whatever we can't see, we declare as unknowable rather than admitting it is beyond our knowing. Whatever unfolds outside of our worldview, we see as chaos rather than of an order we can't yet comprehend.

When afraid, we cast the world as an untenable and fearful place rather than working with our incapacity to meet experience beyond our fear. Our challenge is to wait with courage until the aspects of life beyond our understanding come into view.

The answer to perceived chaos is not to impose some form of order, but to wait long enough for the inherent order to show itself one more time. For the inherent order of life is constant, even when imperceptible. It is we who come in and out of our clarity of being. Too often, we disenfranchise the depth of life, like a radio operator who when losing the signal remains convinced that the signal has vanished, rather than exploring how his means of reception has broken down.

But regardless of our limitations and stubbornness, we steadily unfold like a river, heading against our will to join a deeper sea. In this way, being alive is a turbulent and humble journey whose relentless blessing is hard to grasp when in the throat of it. Yet only when accepting that life is messy and mysterious can we stay tender and thrive. Only when accepting that we are more than what we gain and more than what we lose can we be illumined by the presence and wonder that allow the stars to push back the dark.

We arc in a dynamic elegance that no one
orchestrates, though no one can come alive
without feeling its pull.

Questions to Walk With

- In your journal, describe something you've recently gained from life and one thing life has recently taken away. How do you understand the give and take of life?
- In conversation with a friend or loved one, discuss one covering you've been forced by experience to give up and what you discovered in yourself waiting below this covering.

Choice-Points

I cannot think myself into a new way of living,
I have to live myself into a new way of thinking.

—CLAUDE ANSHIN THOMAS

Through the Sea of Days

In the outer world, we can *resolve* problems brought about by circumstance. But in the inner world, in the intangible world that informs everything tangible—the way the unseeable nutrients in soil inform everything that breaks ground—we need to *inhabit* the field within us and around us in order to let the deeper nutrients of life bring us alive. For ours is not to control life but to honor it.

Given that all things are true, we are constantly asked to withstand and, in fact, dialogue with the tension created when more than one thing is true at the same time. This is the work of paradox. So, try as we might, we can't resolve or solve the seeming dissonance between multiple truths. We can only let everything in, so we can absorb and integrate more than we currently understand. Until a deeper logic of Spirit reveals itself. In this way, we don't reconcile difference, we let it be our teacher.

While I can reconcile my checkbook, I can't reconcile the tension I carry between fear and safety or doubt and clarity or insecurity and my innate worth. I can only inhabit these tensions of paradox, which are thresholds to deeper levels of meaning that can help us live.

The word *reconcile* offers a spectrum of meanings. The most inclusive meaning is "to reunite, to bring back together, to restore friendly relations, to restore harmony between, to make peace between." This effort is at the heart of the South African Truth and Reconciliation Commission convened in 1995 to uncover the truth about human rights violations during the dark period of apartheid with the aim of restoring the humanity of all involved. This marks the best use of will, to work through our wounds in order to restore a larger natural order.

The next level of meaning for the word *reconcile* is more transactional and pragmatic. This level of reconciliation means "to resolve differences, to bring to terms, to pacify, appease, placate, to win or gain favor, or to mollify." Here, our will starts out with good intention but can be degraded to manipulate others in order to circumvent trouble or conflict and to gain advantage in a situation.

The most passive form of reconciliation offers a shadow version of acceptance, meaning "to resign oneself to, to come to terms with, to learn to live with, get used to, make the best of, become accustomed to, to acclimate oneself to, or to grin and bear it." This form of will can introduce us to the gift of acceptance but slip all too easily into the morass of resignation and acquiescence.

The origin of the word *reconcile* goes back to the Latin *reconciliare,* which means to bring back together with intense force. And this is the inherent problem with trying to solve life rather than inhabit it. When trying to solve life, we often use our will to force conditions into being, while the deepest engagements with life only come about when we have the patience and courage to let what is near in, so we can be transformed by the myriad forces of life. In this ongoing practice, we don't force order, but discover Oneness. In the realm of things that matter, our will is opened to cooperate with life in an authentic way until the larger natural order comes into being through us.

Rather than ask, "How can I reconcile love and suffering in the world?" which remains unanswerable, I think we are asked in each incarnation to open our heart to its utmost depth and breadth until the intensity of suffering is mitigated by the embrace of our love. To do this, we need our will to be a sail in the wind. To do this, we need each other to make it through the sea of days.

> *We don't reconcile difference,*
> *we let it be our teacher.*

Questions to Walk With

- In your journal, describe a time when you tried to resolve a situation by being transactional rather than inclusive, when you tried to force an outcome rather than let the situation be your teacher. What challenges arose? What did you learn from this experience?

- In conversation with a friend or loved one, describe a time that you learned to live with a situation when you might better have worked to restore authenticity in the relationship. What led you to resign yourself and what would it take for you to be more authentic in what you face? How do you understand the difference between resignation and authenticity?

To Chase or Ground

As great a tool as the intellect is, the mind chases, while the heart grounds. And so, a liability of the mind is that it seduces us to believe that life is always over there. But through great love and great suffering, the heart discovers, again and again, that life is always where we are—always here. This sometimes painful and sometimes tender realization grounds us in our lives and in life itself.

We are ever called to live from the heart with the mind's support and not the other way around. In Jack Kerouac's classic novel *On the Road,* the main character, Dean Moriarty, is modeled after Kerouac's friend Neal Cassady. In a deep way, their bond is knit around a common vow to chase the infinite, ephemeral moment. This is the initiatory aim of all transcendent artists and seekers, to find the mercurial portal through which the soul can taste of the

Universal Spirit that is its home. But this noble quest is often distorted into an addictive thrill ride for what always seems out of reach.

In *On the Road,* such a moment of chase arises when Sal Paradise, modeled after Kerouac himself, and Moriarty are hired to drive a 1947 Cadillac from Denver to Chicago. Dean drives most of the way, reckless, pushing the car, often speeding over a hundred miles per hour. They shed the car more than deliver it in a broken-down state. Yet despite the rush and high of the adrenaline-ridden trip, neither feels any closer to the truth of their lives.

So much depends on whether we lead with the heart or the mind and whether we are wholehearted or halfhearted. The great Austrian poet Rainer Maria Rilke frames a recurring choice-point for all of us in one of his poems when he says, "I am too alone in the world, and yet not alone enough to make every moment holy." Rilke speaks to the hesitation that keeps us from living life, lodging us in the in-between state, neither totally here nor there. When we can break this tension and inhabit life thoroughly and completely, however briefly, that complete effort allows us to taste the holiness in every moment.

We are always faced with this choice: to chase life with our mind, trying to navigate our tangled search for happiness through time, or to ground ourselves completely in the human experience, welcoming everything until life offers its depth to us through our opened and softened heart. Once grounded, there's nowhere left to race to, nothing left to pine after, and no more imagined perfections to fall short of. It is a constant and imperative practice to discern whether we are chasing our imagined versions of life or grounding ourselves in the authentic but flawed experience we are living.

The mind chases, while the heart grounds.

Questions to Walk With

- In your journal, describe a time when you felt compelled to chase after something. What were you after? What did the chase do to you? Was the journey worth your effort?
- In conversation with a friend or loved one, tell the story of a time when you looked elsewhere for comfort or meaning only to find that comfort or meaning was where you were all along. How did you discover this and what impact did this revelation have on you?

To Speak What We Know
to Be True

Integrity is telling myself the truth.
And honesty is telling the truth to other[s].

—Spencer Johnson

In one of my webinars during the pandemic, a brave soul who stammers asked, "What would you say to someone who hides because of their struggle to speak while finding comfort in the deep space of listening?"

This struggle actually frames a recurring aspect of everyone's journey. For through the depth of our listening, we all receive the deepest things from the fire of aliveness and they are all difficult to express. In truth, we all stammer and stutter. It is part of the human journey. One of the noble challenges of being alive is that, despite the impediments, we have to speak what is true. The stutter, whether physical or internal, between perception and expression is an innate reminder that it would do us good to pause and reflect before we speak. Yet we all have to resist the pause that leads to hiding.

And regardless of how awkward or raw we may appear, it is the heart of what we say that matters more than the ease or flow of our speech. A legendary leader who spoke to the world through his stammer was King George VI, who reluctantly became King of England during World War II. By working publicly to overcome his stammer during such trying times, he became a symbol of fortitude and resilience for an entire nation. There is also the compelling, humane example set by President Joe Biden who also suffers from a lifelong stammer.

More deeply, the story of Moses carries an archetype about listening and speaking that we all must face and live with. Of all his brethren, Moses was closest to God. Indeed, he climbed Mount Sinai to receive the ten commandments and heard God directly. But due to an accident as a child in which his tongue was burned by a hot coal, he stammered greatly. All his life, he suffered an inability to easily speak what he knew to be true. Though he listened to God directly, he couldn't convey what he heard to others.

Inevitably, this is everyone's fate when crossing from the inner world to the outer world. We all have trouble speaking what matters and yet we must try. Often, we are misled to think that falling short in how we convey the truth is a failure, when it is not trying at all that damages us. For even light through a crack is illuminating.

Like it or not, there is always a crossover from inner to

outer, from the urge of heart to the reach of hand, from the feeling rising in our throat to the tumble of words that spills out. Just as you can't swim in the deep till you make it through the surf, you can't move from inner to outer without crossing the surf that exists between our being and our humanness. This is one of the constant struggles in being human: to endure the refraction of all that is holy as it moves through us into the world.

We all receive the deepest things from
the fire of aliveness and they are all difficult
to express. In truth, we all stammer and stutter.
It is part of the human journey.

Questions to Walk With

- In your journal, describe one truth you perceive clearly, but which you have trouble putting into words. Try to describe the feeling of this truth. Try to associate a piece of music with this truth. Then, try to create an image for this truth.
- In conversation with a friend or loved one, discuss the difficulty in crossing from inner to outer that we all experience and try, again, to express the truth you journaled about above. Discuss what is clear and what remains unclear.

The Felt Realm in Between

As humans, we are often pulled to one extreme or the other: feeling mired in our humanness, entangled in the grit and circumstance of our days, or we try to bypass the pain of being human by being conceptual and hiding in the big picture. The challenge for us, as spirits in bodies in time on Earth, is to inhabit both: to let our particular and felt life be informed by the larger context of the Living Universe. To let both inform each other is what it means to fully be here.

A small poem of mine speaks to this. It's called:

SUGAR IN THE TREE

As someone sitting beneath a tree
can imagine the Earth from above
the trees, a heart encumbered by
reality can know Eternity.

Our mind always wants to get an aerial view, while our heart wants to put our hands in the soil of whatever is at hand. We live in the felt realm in between. We live most fully by being completely present to what's above and below.

From the moment we are born, we each carry this unimaginable life-force that wants to come out into the world. But, if not felt and contextualized, the power of life will whip us around. When younger, my own creativity was such a force. I could be so intoxicated with it that I would follow that voice anywhere. It would say to me, "Keep going! Don't stop! You don't need to eat! You're so close! Isn't this great?"

Well, in the moment it feels great, but this is where blind obedience, even to creativity, can trip us into addiction. The turning point, for me, was in acknowledging that I mistakenly thought that this creative force, this passion, would bring me something I was lacking. This urge in me dissipated when I could accept that we lack nothing, that we are already whole. There is nowhere to go.

Lifted and dropped enough by life, I finally put down the yearning that kept prodding me with the misperception, "If I could just get over *there,* then I would be fully alive." I am already fully alive. You are already fully alive. We all are. By following our passion, we just become more of who we are. We just brighten like the sun, which doesn't go anywhere. We are not chasing truth. We are becoming truth.

Humbly, I can't possibly contain or control all the Spirit that wants to come through me. No one can. There is an ancient story in the Jewish tradition that says that the light of life was even too strong to be held or contained by God. And so, God's initial container broke as the light of life burst into existence. And we and all forms of life are the shards of light that burst through God's initial container to create the world. Ever since, we have been remaking the vessel of God's light in our time on Earth through our care and creativity.

All this leaves us with the invitation to become more intimate with our own light. In time, we come to see that we don't have to pursue our light, but simply inhabit it. Even when that light feels gone, it's still there. It's just that I, for the moment, am not able to be in touch with it, or see it, or hear it. If I believe my light is gone, then I will do desperate things to find it. But if I accept that I have fallen out of touch with my light, then self-awareness becomes a practice of becoming more intimate with my own nature, one more time.

Ultimately, I am called to refind what is right here within me, rather than search for something that is lost. This is part of everyone's practice: how to wake when asleep, how to hear when muffled, and how to see when things are in the way. And we just keep doing this, again and again and again. Because this is what it means to be human.

In the fall, I was with a group of wise souls at Harmony Hill, a loving retreat center on the Hood Canal, south of Seattle, Washington. For more than thirty years, this nonprofit haven has been a refuge for cancer patients and their families. If you can make your way there, your stay, for you and your loved ones, is free. I return there annually to lead retreats.

This recent group showed their tenderness and resilience as we listened to each other's journey on a rainy day. One said with a quiver, "I was told that I don't deserve what matters." Another admitted, "The stories I've relied on don't serve me anymore." And the strong one who swims in the ocean every day whispered that her son won't speak to her. Then, the gentle one—whose home burned down, whose son was murdered, who lost her dear husband after thirty years—declared, "I wouldn't change one thing. These forces have shaped who I am." The entire time, the sun was alight on the tops of clouds, though the rain was steady. Just as the tops of these glorious hearts were alight while their tears flowed.

Each of these kind souls was modeling how to inhabit our light. Each was an example of imagining the Earth from above the trees while sitting beneath their own particular tree. This is the dynamic point of fullness we stumble into in which we feel thoroughly alive. In such moments, I admit that I somehow feel, paradoxically, both unique and common.

And so, I encourage you, with each passing day, to hold nothing back. Give enough light and attention to yourself, so, like a flower, you can be both delicate and resilient. Give yourself completely to the spirit rising in the mire of your humanness, until you feel both unrepeatable and eternal.

*In time, we come to see that we don't have to pursue
our light, but simply inhabit it.*

Questions to Walk With

- In your journal, give voice to three guiding questions you can return to every day that can't be answered but which will help guide you through life with a deeper perspective. Then place the questions on your refrigerator and start each day by reading them and assessing where you are in relation to them.
- In conversation with a friend or loved one, tell the story of a time when you felt the need to pursue who you are and the story of a time when you realized that you simply need to inhabit who you already are.

The Corridor of Aliveness

Throughout the years, I have been led to uncover and engage several choice-points in our human journey, places we have to navigate between extremes in order to stay in a pulsing corridor of aliveness. I have explored these choice-points across my books as perennial practices we each must personalize and inhabit to be fully here. In this chapter, I try to crystallize and integrate these learnings. Each of these choice-points opens a skill set we must somehow learn, if we are to keep getting up when we fall down.

Surviving and Thriving

Everyone alive must both survive and thrive. If we only survive, what's the point? Yet, out of fear, we can make a god of precaution, which sidelines us to watch life rather than live it. We are all bounced about by circumstance, forced to steer our way between being careful or full of care, between remaining outside of things or inside them. If we follow fear, we can slip into a recalcitrant and cautious way of living, which we can mistake as being judicious and prudent, when the original definition of *prudent* goes back to the word *provident,* meaning "to tend to the present, to see, as a way to prepare for the future." This is quite different from withdrawing from life in order to avoid possible outcomes.

The question to keep asking ourselves is: To what degree am I withdrawing from life to avoid what might happen rather than tending to life in order to inhabit what might happen? When we tend, we thrive. When we avoid, we increase our distance from life, which, in the end, drains us of life-force. Being overly cautious gives us the illusion of protection, when it is the continual infusion of life-force that truly brings us into those unexpected moments where surviving and thriving are one and the same.

In his poem called "Self-Protection," D. H. Lawrence raises the question: Is the best self-protection being who we are or hiding who we are? Periodically, it helps to reassess what it means for you to survive and what it means for you to thrive, and how these efforts inform each other. This gives us a fresh start with nothing between us and the moment we are living.

Managing and Enhancing Risk

Years ago, I was asked to lead a retreat for corporate bankers. Initially, they were resistant to spending time with a poet. The first session was awkward. So, I called for a long coffee break. We went to a nearby room and I listened, one by one, asking each executive what they did and why. To a one, each said, one way or another, that their job was to manage risk for their investors. Whether clients had a lot of money or very little, they saw their purpose as protecting whatever resources their clients brought to them.

I immediately understood why our conversation was awkward. Their gift is managing risk, while my gift—as a poet, mystic, and teacher—is to enhance risk. We reassembled and I spoke about this, inviting us to share our gifts and learn from each other.

From that day on, I realized that each of us is called to both manage and enhance risk in order to live a full life. They are complementary skills. In the outer world, it is important to manage risk. If we were having this conversation without paying attention while crossing the street, we might get hit by a truck. So, managing risk is crucial as we move through the outer world.

But, in the inner world, we only grow by enhancing risk, stepping from what we know into what we don't know. We only come alive by taking the chance to embrace what is new.

It is easy to confuse these callings. When we take needless risks in the outer world, we court danger and chance.

When we over-manage risk in the inner world, we are stalled in our growth. Without valuing both these qualities, we can dismiss each other, as the bankers and I had done upon initially meeting. The truth is we need to be skilled at both managing risk and enhancing it. They need to work together, the way two good legs help us to walk.

Opening and Closing

Just as there is something in us that feels compelled to get up when we fall, there is something equally powerful in us that needs to open, if we are closed too long. From biology to geology, the quality of aliveness depends on the rhythm of opening and closing. As I write this, the valves of my heart are opening and closing, as are the bronchia in my lungs. And over eons, the plates of the Earth open and close, shaping oceans and rivers. Likewise, how alive we feel depends on the rhythm by which our mind and heart open after closing. For life, at every level, must have some corridor to move through. Otherwise, we become dense as a stone. Like wounds that need air to heal, if closed too long, we become infected. When too self-contained, we become ill. Health resides in opening.

Giving and Receiving

Together, giving and receiving are how we put our care and attention to work. Like inhaling and exhaling, giving and receiving are supports to life.

Yet, most of us have a hard time receiving. During my cancer journey, I was humbled to receive the most ordinary things: orange juice or milk or thread to sew a button. Often, I would cry just to ask for what I needed—simply, without any guardedness or pride. I was so grateful, and cleansed by the pure act of give and receive. After such tender and raw need, I learned in time how to give more completely in all directions—to old uncles too stubborn to ask for what they need as well as to strangers in parking lots.

Years later, I was in the Caribbean, sitting at the mouth of an inlet, stunned by what it was teaching me. For an inlet by definition must give and receive. It must have water enter it and leave it in order for the inlet to remain fluid and useful. Similarly, every soul on Earth must both give and receive, must let life in and let life out. Ultimately, when we can stay open to how all things are connected, we discover that receiving is just giving in another direction. Ever since, I try, when pressed, to be like an inlet: to let things in and let things out, to let the deepest waters merge in my heart.

Solitude and Community

In solitude, we affirm and renew our direct experience of thorough, undeniable presence. But life is so much more than our individual experience. And so, through relationship, we absorb and integrate the experience and presence of others.

Whales and dolphins are great teachers in how we move from solitude to community and back. These mammoth creatures are air-breathing, which is quite miraculous. And though they can stay submerged for long periods of time, they must surface to breathe or they will die. But they can't stay on the surface indefinitely because they must be immersed in the deep or they will die.

This is a helpful metaphor for how we, as souls in bodies, must continually submerge ourselves in the deep, only to break surface into the world. The only question is: What is your personal rhythm between depth and surface, between solitude and community? How do we make a practice of breaking surface to serve the world and diving in the deep to renew our soul?

To Lean In

An ongoing challenge we each face is to lean back into life after the difficult passages push us away from all that matters. In truth, this is how pain, fear, and grief say hello, by pushing us away from our aliveness. It is our constant work to lean back in, again and again.

This is inwardly like the push and pull of surf and undertow. If you can, watch a crab be tossed back and forth by the tide along a shore, and you will see how it scampers to get back into the deep, only to be tossed on the sand. Over and over, it struggles to return to the deep, only to be churned and tossed back on land.

This is inherent to our life on Earth. We are ever scampering to return to the deep, only to be tossed ashore. The task is not to choose the shore or the deep, but to stay committed to the endless movement back and forth.

This enduring cycle of leaning in and being pushed back is akin to the plight of the Greek king Sisyphus who was compelled to roll a rock up a hill, only to have it roll back to the bottom where he would roll it up again. This was his task for Eternity.

But, as Albert Camus so strongly suggests in his essay "The Myth of Sisyphus," we must love the struggle of being pushed back, so we can lean in, for this is the enduring plight of human beings. Once we accept this, then falling down and getting up are not random incidents but an endless and even noble dance.

The Friction of Being Visible

One of the recurring struggles of relationship is how we steer our way between the friction of being visible and the cost of being invisible. If we are able to be who we are everywhere, we will inevitably encounter some form of conflict. For being visible and authentic, we can't possibly meet everyone's expectations. We will, at some point, be misperceived and misunderstood. This is the friction of being visible in the world. It helps to remember, though, that it is the continual, minute friction that causes the pearl to grow inside its shell.

The other side of this struggle arises when we retreat from being who we are in order to avoid conflict of any

kind. In an effort to please everyone we meet, we become invisible. While this may make the river of circumstance smoother, the cost can be greater. For hiding who we
are becomes corrosive. We begin to vanish. Once pretending
to be dumb, we lose our perception. Once pretending to be
obedient, we lose our sense of discovery. And once pretending that we have no opinion, we lose our voice.

Either way, there is a cost. Yet breaking out of the cycle
of being hidden is a difficult passage that everyone who
ever lived has had to face. It is beautifully rendered in the
Viking myth of Kalavalah. Here we find a woman who is
under the spell of a cold, demanding wizard. For nine hundred years, she is bejeweled constantly and dresses solely
to please him. One day, as he bids her to put on yet one
more thing to please him, she begins to undress, breaking
the spell. Soon, she stands naked before the cold wizard,
saying, "This time not for you, but for me." As she turns
away from him, free for the first time in almost a thousand
years, she becomes a salmon and, shimmering, swims up-
stream into her destiny.

This luminous story says a great deal about breaking
the pattern of being hidden. It carries the challenge we
each must face at some point in our lives: When do we
stop dressing for others? This refers to more than actual
clothes, but how we dress and cover our mind and heart.

When do we take the risk to be visible in all our strength
and frailty? When do we finally stand naked and declare,
"This time for me"?

If we refuse this challenge, we end up under a spell,

serving the wrong god. To personalize this more deeply: Who is the wizard you serve? What is the spell you find yourself under? And how can you begin to undress your compliance?

The Four Trusts

How do we break the spell of being hidden? One way is by practicing the four trusts:

- *Trust in the common presence of all things.* When living in the open, authentically, we begin to feel our kinship with all things. This gives us access to the net of resilience that all things in existence share.
- *Trust in the fact that no matter how we are split, we will regenerate and heal.* As a worm cut in two will grow into two worms, the mind cut in two will grow another mind. And the heart broken apart will grow back stronger and twice as loving.
- *Trust in the blessing that true intimacy will open us to Oneness.* It is a law of spiritual physics: love one thing deeply and you will learn how to love all things. This is the apprenticeship to Oneness.
- *Trust that what churns up our bottom only deepens our flow.* Some rivers deepen as they age. As the rush of water gets stronger, the river bottom is churned up. As the water flows deeper into the

newly opened space, the current continues to get stronger. The same thing happens to souls that deepen as they age. What churns us up only deepens our flow.

And so, I ask you: How do these four trusts appear in your life? Which are your strengths? Which need more attention? What is your history with the four trusts? How can trust help you break the cycle of being hidden?

To Look or Not to Look

In addition to our struggle whether to be seen or not, there is a corollary struggle whether to look or not. The Greek myth of Orpheus and Eurydice conveys the heart of this choice-point poignantly.

Orpheus was given an extraordinary ability to play the lyre, an ancient form of harp, so beautifully that creatures and gods alike would soften and go still to hear a single note. Eurydice was his love. They were incredibly happy. Until Hades, the god of the Underworld, fancied her. He took her from life to sit by his side. Orpheus fell into such unprecedented grief that his heartbroken laments on the lyre became unbearable. Even the gods become despondent. They went to Zeus to complain.

Zeus summoned Hades and demanded that he fix the situation. And though Hades would never disobey Zeus, he found a way to trick the mournful lovers. Hades, in turn, summoned Orpheus, telling him, "You can have your love. It will take you three days to bring her to the surface you call life. You must carry her on your back. But if you look at her once, she will be lost and be mine forever."

Orpheus steeled his resolve not to look Eurydice in the eye, though he couldn't wait to see her. But secretly, Hades told Eurydice the opposite. He warned her, "You can return to your lover. It will take three days for him to bring you to the surface you call life. He will carry you on his back. But you must look him in the eye, once, before you reach the surface, or you will be lost and be mine forever."

The two lovers struggled painfully on their way back to life. Their tragedy was impossible and inevitable. They failed and Orpheus lost Eurydice forever. Yet despite the sad ending, this myth reveals the innate positions each soul carries within it. Just as our biology carries X and Y chromosomes in which all of life is encoded, we each carry our deep yearning to look and not to look.

Each of us has a deep, feminine quality that believes, I must look or I will die. And each of us has a deep, masculine quality that believes, if I look, I will die. The questions remain: Which of these inborn qualities is pre-eminent in you? And how can you inhabit each with integrity?

When I learned of this myth and the capacities it reveals, I understood the profound dissonance that existed between my parents and me. Born in the Great Depression and being children of the Holocaust, they believed, if we look, we will die. If we look, we will not be safe. If we look, harm will come our way. And strange irony, they had a mystical poet for a son, who believes in his bones the opposite.

I remember coming home from college, ecstatic that I was beginning to see the Unity of Things and how the web of relationship held everything together. In my excitement, I tossed the glimpses I was seeing on the kitchen table, exclaiming, "Look!"

To my surprise, they cringed and backed away, as if to say, "How dare you ask us to look?!" And so, we pushed each other away, sadly for much of our lives. Though they have died, I try now to honor these different impulses with others, so we might learn about Wholeness from each other.

Yet how does this archetypal call reveal itself in our daily lives? How does the urge to look and not look besiege us as we walk through the world? Well, when we don't look when we need to, we fuel our fear. For fear gets its power from not looking. Without the courage to look at what is ours to face, not looking begins to murder our life-force.

And when we keep looking when we no longer need to, we fuel our worry and doubt. By over-looking and over-analyzing, we dilute our resolve. Over-looking can also murder our life-force. This is the cautionary tale at the heart of Shakespeare's play *Hamlet*. The gifted young prince, who is traumatized by the murder of his father, knows in his heart the terrible truth of all that has transpired. But every time he summons his will to act, he over-considers his choices and unravels his very understanding of reality. Until we famously find him holding the skull of the court jester, Yorick, who made him laugh as a boy. And there, he questions whether he should even exist at all, uttering, "To be or not to be, that is the question."

So, make no mistake, when we fall too far into fear or doubt, we are dragged into the Underworld at the mercy of Hades. We each must become more intimate with when we need to look and when we need to stop looking. This rhythm of deep perception, when inhabited precisely, will save us.

Effort and Grace

One final choice-point is our movement between effort and grace. The best way to understand this is to imagine a surfer working hard to paddle through the breakers in order to catch the most sublime wave when it appears. Then, the surfer rides the wave as long as possible, only to paddle back to shore or to paddle out and wait for the next wave.

This is an apt way to understand the rhythm between effort and grace. Effort is how we ready ourselves for grace, which we can never plan or foresee. When the wave appears and carries us—this is grace. And for the brief moments that the surfer rides the wave, he or she is one with the wave. In a parallel way, the merging of the seer with what is seen and the merging of the singular heart with all that has ever been felt—this movement is grace.

I often think that effort is revelation in slow motion. And so, even in my writing, I push the pen until it pulls me. I paddle out into the depths of consciousness until the wave appears. In the duration of the wave, I become one with what I feel and perceive and what I record there becomes the poem. And the reward for grace, no matter how brief, is that our complete effort of love allows us to become life itself. So, our call is to work for grace without intention, loving the work and surrendering to the wave whenever it appears.

What Needs Your Attention?

Let me summarize these perennial choice-points as questions, so you can personalize the areas of inner living that need more of your attention:

- Are you surviving instead of thriving? Is your caution thwarting your life-force?
- Are you balanced in how you are managing risk and enhancing it? Are you minimizing danger while expanding your chances to grow?
- Are you spending more time closed than open? Are you committed to opening one more time than you close?
- Are you balanced in your efforts to give and receive? How can you let more things out and let more things in?
- Are you by yourself too much or in the company of others too much? What is your rightful balance between solitude and community?

- Are you leaning back into life after the difficulties of life push you away?
- What is the friction of being visible for you? How does it compare to the cost of being invisible?
- Which is stronger in you, the need to look or the need not to look? How can you engage these impulses healthfully, so you can minimize your fear and worry?
- Are you too isolated by the walls you maintain? And in what ways do you give yourself away by having no boundaries?
- And where can you increase your effort, so you can be ready to accept grace?

Tuning as We Go

A great elucidation of the art of living comes from the work of Beethoven. In composing what was his last quartet for chamber music, known as opus 131, he stretched the common structure of four movements to seven. The musicians of the time felt ambivalent toward the great composer. How can anyone play seven movements in one sitting? And yet, they wondered, can we do it?

In addition to this innovative structure, Beethoven removed all the rest stops in opus 131. Classical musicians typically retune their strings during rest stops, as it is nearly impossible to play four movements, let alone seven, without your strings going out of tune. In playing opus 131, the frustration can be maddening.

But the deaf and life-weary Beethoven seemed to be saying, "No! You won't have time to tune! Like life—you must tune as you go!"

Indeed, for all our study and preparation, our music will not be perfect. We will, at times, be out of tune. And yet, how marvelous that the corridor of aliveness never rests. We must tune as we go!

We have to navigate between extremes in order to stay in a pulsing corridor of aliveness.

Questions to Walk With

- In your journal, describe one way that you are fueling your fear by not looking at something you need to look at. Then, describe one way you are fueling your worry and doubt by looking too much at something you don't need to look at anymore. How can you adjust your efforts?
- In conversation with a friend or loved one, describe a choice-point you are currently facing between surviving and thriving and what you need to do in your practice of opening and closing, and giving and receiving, to help you make your way.

The Anthem of Our Day

This chapter was written during the height of the pandemic.

Some time ago, under all the noise and crisscross of commerce and traffic and the endless buzz in the human hive, as we were all trying to keep up and get ahead, somewhere in the middle of China, in the silent microscopic fabric that no one could see, a miniscule atom shifted under all our noise to link in a dark way with its surrounding atoms—and COVID-19 was born. Ever since, the silent germ has been infecting the world at lightning speed, challenging us to spread our care and good will just as quickly and freely in order to help each other survive.

This is a hard-to-grasp lesson—that light must move as quickly as dark, that care must move as quickly as disease, that give must move as quickly as take. And nothing less than everything depends on this giving in all directions without hesitation.

No question, it is hard and yet imperative to feed more than our fear. For powerful moments in human history have begun with small courageous efforts that changed the world. Consider Gandhi's first steps alone on his march to the sea, and Rosa Parks quietly and steadfastly keeping her seat on that bus, and Nelson Mandela singing while being beaten on Robben Island where no one could hear, and Clara Barton stitching the wounds of a Civil War soldier into the night long before she was visited with the vision of the Red Cross.

Of course, in order to give this freely, we have to be still and dive deeply. We have to bring up what matters in order to affect what is. This is the kinship between renewal and resilience. It is no accident that the pandemic has forced us to be still; though the truth is that there has never been anywhere to run, though we have run for centuries. And so, love must emerge as quickly as fear. For since the beginning, light has met dark, not in a battle of good and evil, but in the torque of life-force that keeps the Universe going.

The times are hard and unexpected. They always are. But the river of being that carries us is always life-giving, if we can reach it. But this, as ever, requires diving where we are, not running from what is. We must be brave and must beware, mostly of ourselves. For the mind is like a spider. It will weave many webs. But the heart is like an arrow of light. It will pierce a hole in the dark that life will fill. Along the way, we stumble in the dark. Our fierce and tender honesty and love, the lamp we swing between us.

Growing in Place

It seems that, as we shelter in place, we need to keep growing in place. One way to do this is to try to remove everything between us and life. This is a lifelong practice. All the traditions speak to this and have for centuries. We need to remove whatever is in the way so we can refresh our sense of how rare it is to be alive at all. With nothing in the way, we can feel the strength of our kinship—that we are more together than alone.

So, while our caregivers are constantly in need of masks to protect themselves as they care for us, we are being called—inwardly and personally—to put down our masks, so we can stay current and real and have access to our heart. So we can meet the outer world with our inner life. This is what we can do inwardly to help strengthen humanity.

And though I wish this siege of disease were behind us, I am reluctantly grateful. For this has been a forced time of root dwelling and a renewal of all we know to be true. In the daily quiet, I'm rediscovering that silence is the aura that lets the simplest things shine: the morning light cascading slowly across my wife's face as she sleeps, the stretch of our dog between us, the slight quiver of the bare branches south of the house, the deep-throated gurgle of the coffee perking.

I'm coming to see that when afraid, we take more than we need. When we accept that love is the sea we move through, we give freely. For no fish owns the water it swims through, though it can't live without it. And no bird owns the sky it glides through, though it can't fly without it. And none of us own the care that builds within us. If we keep it to ourselves, we drown. It only brings us alive when we give it away.

The Recurring Tide

In the ocean of history, things build and then are worn away to what is most essential. This is an irrevocable and recurring tide of time. And while the storms and diseases and disasters, whatever their form, first push us away, it is only by coming together that we endure and emerge even stronger, clearer, and more loving. This seems to be where we are now. And the practice, so simple and so difficult, is how to move through the days with caution and care, without feeding our panic. For the other virus that keeps spreading is fear. We all feel it, calling us with its hypnotic frenzy. But one thing I've learned from almost dying from cancer is that fear is to be moved through and not obeyed. And we need each other in order to see clearly so we can right-size what is before us—day after day.

Just as you can only see stars at night, it is during times like this that our inherent light and kinship are most visible. And while the pandemic and its variants keep traveling across the globe, we must remember and reach for the miracle of life, which is still everywhere. This is not just stubborn optimism but a declaration of our need to stay available to the undeniable resources of life. It is those resources that remind us of the truth that we continue to affect each other and need each other. When one of us does something or doesn't, it affects all of us. As Dr. Sanjay Gupta has wisely put it, "When you care for yourself, you care for everyone." So when you wash your hands, you are keeping everyone you meet healthy. At the deepest level, caring for yourself is caring for others and caring for others is caring for yourself.

In later life, the German philosopher Friedrich Nietzsche said, "I want to learn more and more to see as beautiful what is necessary in things, then I shall be one of those who makes things beautiful." I invoke this as the anthem of our day. If we can meet the uncertainty with a covenant of care, perhaps we can make what is necessary beautiful. Perhaps the washing of hands can become a modern sacrament, a holy ritual by which we hold ourselves and our global family in the deepest regard. Perhaps a slight bow of love and respect can replace the handshake as a holy ritual that will lessen our fear while sharing our love, so that we can bear the uncertainty together.

As we practice caution and social distancing, let us not distance each other in our hearts. As we are forced to slow down and stop our busyness, let us feed more than our fear. Let us strengthen our inner resolve, both physically and spiritually, so we can meet the necessities of the day in hopes of making things more beautiful. For we are each being called to outlast the siren of fear until we can touch upon the reliable truths that reside beneath all fear. Like a strong net that softens the carriage of weight, the strength of our connections, even while physically apart, will soften the sharpness of uncertainty inherent in times like this.

In the Chinese language, the ideogram for *crisis* also means *opportunity*. And I believe that if we can share our fears and help each other not obey them, we will take the first step to making what is necessary beautiful. By practicing being all of who we are, we can strengthen the net of connection that is the human family. Like the rest of us, I can only try to navigate between caution and fear while maintaining our deeper connection. And in my own struggle to be more than my fear, I will affirm our strength of heart and commit to staying connected in our care. When larger than our fear, the kinship of being we all share endures.

This is a hard-to-grasp lesson—that light must move as quickly as dark, that care must move as quickly as disease, that give must move as quickly as take.

Questions to Walk With

- In your journal, explore one way you can grow in place. That is, what effort can you devote yourself to that will help you deepen your roots and widen your trunk so you can better endure the storms of our time?

- In conversation with a friend or loved one, describe how life changed for you while you were sheltering in place. Describe your daily path now between fear and insight, between love and suffering. What question is leading you these days?

The Truth and Grip of Our Feelings

Once awake, an essential path of learning is the art of being sensitive. No one quite knows how to do this. Once open to the infinite sensations and enlivening encounters that experience brings, we are often overwhelmed by such aliveness. It is a common malady for the sensitive to become whatever they encounter. Yet though we are enlivened by our feelings, we are not our feelings, just as a tree brought alive by the wind is not the wind.

Inevitably, we all struggle in discerning the truth of the feelings we must follow from the grip of the feelings that oppress us and rule us. I have experienced the truth of feelings when I can face what is mine to face and have been held in the grip of feelings when I avoid, deny, or run from them.

When faced with a deep feeling, especially a difficult or

challenging one, we often meet the initial surface of that feeling, but never open the door of that feeling. For feelings are doorways to the depth of life. They are asking us to be in conversation and journey with them. When we refuse, they circle back in louder, harsher ways. When I open the door of the feeling that is calling, I enter the depth of life and the feeling becomes a teacher. When I knock on the door and run, I am suddenly in the grip of that feeling.

Fear is a good example. When I knock and run, fear only chases me down. When I open the door of my fear and walk through, it always right-sizes to a deeper question or quandary that I am facing in my life. When in the throes of my cancer journey, I was faced with having yet another bone marrow sampling. These were terrifying for me. No matter how I tried, I couldn't seem to face them.

Of course, the more I resisted, the more insurmountable each passage became. Then, when exhausted of being afraid and scheduled to have another such test, I opened the door of my fear around this just a crack. It allowed me to look more directly at exactly what I was fearing. I kept looking in my mind at the tip of the instrument that would extract another sampling of bone from my hip. And the fear intensified but rather than destroy me, it opened like a blossom.

In its center, I could see for the first time that the needle was the size of a needle and that the procedure I couldn't see my way through would actually last about twenty seconds. This gave me a way to make it through. For the first time, I could see that there would be life on the other side of those twenty seconds, horrible as they might be. Opening the door of that fear allowed for the fear, unraveled, to show me how to move through it. Later, I came to understand that the fear of some needle puncturing all of life was a Cinderella form of thinking that, unfaced, had plagued me. Fear had me believing that with the puncture of a needle, my life would collapse darkly and I would turn into a pumpkin.

Another compelling example of opening the door of our feelings is found in Wendell Berry's poem "I Go Among Trees":

> *I go among trees and sit still.*
> *All my stirring becomes quiet*
> *around me like circles on water.*
> *My tasks lie in their places*
> *where I left them, asleep like cattle.*
>
> *Then what is afraid of me comes*
> *and lives a while in my sight.*
> *What it fears in me leaves me,*
> *and the fear of me leaves it.*
> *It sings, and I hear its song.*
>
> *Then what I am afraid of comes.*
> *I live for a while in its sight.*
> *What I fear in it leaves it,*
> *and the fear of it leaves me.*
> *It sings, and I hear its song.*

After days of labor,
mute in my consternations,
I hear my song at last,
and I sing it. As we sing,
the day turns, the trees move.

Berry displays the quiet courage necessary to outwait the noise and clouds that block us from the truth of what is. It always begins with our need to "go among the trees," to walk beyond the life of our tasks and expectations and disappointments to where life lives regardless of what we do or do not do. Then, in the silence that waits just beyond our exhaustion, what we fear and what is afraid of us can come to terms and join, if only for a brief, eternal moment.

Their meeting releases a song that has been ringing long before we came into consciousness and which will continue to ring long after we are gone. For the doorway of feelings, once opened and entered, leads us back to the Ultimate Reality that is our home—the bareness of being that holds us all—which waits beneath the turmoil of any circumstance. This foundation of being is not a place to take refuge in but a place that will uphold us as we make our way through any given circumstance.

Hard as it is, we must open the door of our feelings and enter, listening to the truth they point to. So we can unravel the noise and tension that living on Earth tangles us in and find the deeper current that will carry us and help us live.

Though we are enlivened by our feelings, we are not our feelings, just as a tree brought alive by the wind is not the wind.

Questions to Walk With

- In your journal, describe a feeling that is calling you, which you have avoided. Describe the doorway this feeling represents for you. What step can you take to open the door of that feeling?
- In conversation with a friend or loved one, discuss a feeling that has gripped you and a feeling that has led you to a deeper truth. Discuss the difference in how you come upon these feelings and how you react to them.

The Pull of Power

Everything that liberates our minds
without adding to our resources
of self-mastery is pernicious.

—Goethe

There is outer power and inner power, the power to conquer and the power to belong, the power to assert our uniqueness and the power to thread our commonness. The power that makes us want to gather and hoard and the power that makes us share what we have and serve. Everyone alive is tempted by these powers and how we negotiate their pulls determines whether we become cold and cutting or warm and kind.

Here are some stories about power. Near his house by the sea, the great Roman orator Cicero was murdered by a tribune he'd defended for parricide. It was Marc Antony's doing. They say Cicero, as an old man, opened his neck to the blade, demonstrating yet another kind of power.

Then, Antony had Cicero's head and hands cut off and

fastened to the speaker's platform in the Roman Forum—
those hands which had outpoured those elegant orations.
It was a spectacle that Plutarch claimed said more about
Antony than Cicero.

Centuries later, in the late 1800s, on a chilled October
night, at his aunt's home in Genoa, Italy, the French poet
Paul Valéry was lying on his bed, unable to sleep, when
a horrific storm pounded his very sense of the Universe,
battering him mysteriously until he gave up his quest
for fame.

So which powers trap us? Which tempt us in the distance like a palace with its doors open? And which call like
a soft lover we'd do anything to be near? And which powers strip us of everything extraneous like a terrible storm
in the night?

They say Sappho, in the sixth century BC, was small
and lighted, that she drew others to her, the way bread
lures gulls to the shore. Then she let those made fragile
by the world stay as long as they needed. Is this then
power, too, to console the loveless with everything soft
and personal?

Or consider the German poet Goethe who, as he aged,
was on the hunt for something irreducible and lasting. It
was then that he fell so madly in love with a nineteen-year-
old woman that it unexpectedly ate at his being. And in
1823, shortly before his seventy-fourth birthday, he pro-
posed to Ulrike Levetzow. When she rejected him, the
power of her beauty left him forlorn in a horse-drawn
coach, never to see her again, the horses clomping onward

through the snow, their white prints trailing him like pockets of emptiness he couldn't explain or get rid of.

Goethe might have loved Ulrike. But perhaps he was stirred by the power of her youth in an attempt to keep living beyond his allotted time on Earth. Perhaps his infatuation with her was prompted by his fear of death. And perhaps her rejection painfully left him with the bare power of being, forcing him to accept the one abundant life he had.

When driven by fear, we try to marshal power as a way to defy death and set ourselves apart. But when stirred by the depth of love, we are drawn to give ourselves over to the power of life, which can carry us, at times, the way a fish is carried by a swift and inexorable current.

Cicero wrote one poem in his youth about a fisherman who, after eating a magical herb, swam to the bottom of the sea to become a god of that element, the reward for such immersion. Yet, the sad and brilliant Virginia Woolf, so overcome by the prospect of another war, drowned herself in the River Ouse. What made that great heart sink and what god of what silent element has she become?

Perhaps it is our attendant spirit that releases our most enduring power, the animated life-force that drove a deaf Beethoven to jot his tonal thunder at his desk. Perhaps it is our attendant spirit that leads us to imitate the elements: opening our will like a waterfall, our mind like a tree in wind, and our heart like an inner sun compelled to shine on everything. Perhaps these are native powers.

They say that once learning to be eloquent, Cicero went to the Delphic Oracle, asking how he might rise to the greatest glory, and the Oracle told him to follow nature. But he was deafened by his own ambition and so he followed men.

We are each asked to resist the pull in our personalities that intoxicates us with illusions of greatness and power, so we can be obedient to the pull on our souls to enter the great, unseeable currents that surround us and sustain us. History has shown, far too often, that to wield outer power almost always leads to isolation and destruction, while to join with inner power almost always leads to a union with each other and the elements, evoking periods of wholeness and peace.

We constantly suffer the tension of these choices: to want power over others or to be a student of the elemental powers that inform life. Consider one of the fathers of Impressionism, Camille Pissarro. After fifteen years of painting every day, Pissarro had to flee the Prussians, who took over his farm. Sacking everything, the soldiers wore his paintings as aprons while they slaughtered his sheep.

The painter, bereft but steadfast, had no choice but to meet the outer power of the Prussians with the inner power of his soul. At forty-one, Pissarro began again. The best survive and thrive because they only believe in the power of beginning.

When stirred by the depth of love, we are drawn to give ourselves over to the power of life.

Questions to Walk With

- In your journal, tell the story of a time when you felt subject to the power of others. Then, tell the story of a time when you felt uplifted by the powers of life. What has each situation taught you about the nature of people and the nature of life?
- In conversation with a friend or loved one, explore which has the greater position in your life: the power to control or the power to belong. Describe the circumstances that lead you to want the power to control and the circumstances that lead you to want to experience the power of belonging. How do you understand the choice-point between the two?

I Can but Will I

The moon has watched us come forward and retreat forever. In its light, we rise and fall. In the pause between what has happened and what will be, it is our turn. And today, with all that is happening in our world, I am stopped by someone hesitating to speak the truth. If honest, I have been here, coiling in my own hesitation.

This tension between hesitating and coming forward works us the way a caterpillar recoils in order to move forward as it inches its way along the earth. In just this way, the humble recoil and surfacing of our soul in the lives we're given takes time—time to try and fail, time to hesitate and then move forward anyway, time to lie and then admit the lie, time to want what we think will save us, only to drop it when we discover that it won't. What frees us is the turn inward after chasing paradise, when we finally decide to live in the world.

I referred to the image of the caterpillar in the introduction to this book. It was first offered to us in the Hindu Upanishads as way to understand the rhythm of true growth, of how we fall down and get up, of how we take two steps forward then one step back. It is only when we are trapped by the fall or stuck in the one step back that we stall our growth.

So, it is not that we hesitate that is the problem. It is when we obey that hesitation that we give power to the dark. Then, we become agents of dissolution. In the tumble of situations that never stop coming, our resilience always constellates around the courage to take the step forward and tell the truth, initially to ourselves. This experience of truth arises from the courage to see things as they are. Then, of necessity, we are called to speak what is true to each other. But the first teaching of authenticity is to *listen* for what is true. This brings us into the flow of life-force where we can receive it.

To tremble with fear, tenderness, or excitement at what life puts in our path is a sign that we are coming alive. The tremble is to be consulted, not avoided. And whether it was the early cave person who carved the first flute from a mammoth bone, or the Ukrainian man kneeling before the barrel of a Russian tank, or the young girl who brought the bullied boy a glass of water, or the Lutheran tailor who hid sixteen Jews in Nazi-occupied France— acting on what we know to be true is the sinew that holds humanity together.

Each of us is part of this endless stepping forward and

going back. If we would only talk about how hard it is to keep going, it would help us keep going.

By the time you put this down, another crossroads will present itself in which you and I will have to decide, one more time, whether to hesitate or speak the truth. This is how life draws us out. And how we respond determines the strength of our care. The terror of being human is that we can allow cruelty to go on in a second. But the treasure of being human is that we can, in an instant, stand between the whip and whipped. And this gritty, noble gesture is the fulcrum on which history turns.

What frees us is the turn inward after chasing paradise, when we finally decide to live in the world.

Questions to Walk With

- In your journal, describe a time when you hesitated but then moved forward anyway. What made you hesitate and what made you summon the strength to move forward?
- In conversation with a friend or loved one, describe a time when you needed to stop running in the world and turn inward or a time when you needed to stop retreating into yourself and start living in the world. How did you become aware of your need to act and what did you do?

Stories About Learning

[People] can starve from a lack of self-realization as
much as . . . from a lack of bread.

—RICHARD WRIGHT

To Count and Compare

There is a story about two seekers who dreamt big and struggled hard to make their dreams come true. They both secretly wanted the whole world but falling, as we must, they found themselves each with one berry in their weaker hand. The more stubborn of the two could not let go of his dream, and the berry seemed so small compared to all he wanted. The gap made him bitter. The gentler of the two was shaken into wondering if the dream had led him to this berry and he was softened further to sense the whole world under its tiny skin.

Do you recognize this conversation? Do you recognize these voices? For there's always a part of us ready to complain, "Is this it? One stinking berry? After all I've done and how hard I've worked? Who do I file a grievance with?" And there's always a more humble, gentler voice in us, surprised and in awe, that says, "Oh my God! I had no idea! It's all right here!" And then, we're humbled to eat the one berry.

These two voices are always nearby, both the stubborn one and the gentle one, the one who sees what's missing in everything and the one who sees everything in what's before us. Central to the practice of being human is our ongoing conversation and relationship between these voices that live within us: between being wholehearted and halfhearted, between connection and isolation, between love and suffering, between wonder and fear.

One crucial thing I've learned throughout my life is that as soon as you count and compare, you can't be present. We're often kept from the truth of our experience by our urge to measure who we are and where we are. But as soon as we begin to count and measure, we are removed from the immeasurable aspects of life. You can't measure and be immersed at the same time.

Being human, we all tend to inflate or deflate ourselves and the situations we face, when the threshold to authentic living is to assume our full stature and to see things as they are—being all of who we are, not more or less.

Being present is always more restorative than our insistence on figuring out our trouble—no matter what it is. Often, the most reliable act we can engage in is to begin again. For no amount of counting or comparing can affirm our worth. Only presence can restore our direct connection with life.

No matter how oppressed or tangled we may feel, we can always put things down and begin again. This is what truth and friendship can do. They can help us put things down. Truth and friendship can make us stop counting. After all, raindrops don't count each other. They leap and join and disperse in a clarity that feeds the earth.

> *As soon as you count and compare,*
> *you can't be present.*

Questions to Walk With

- In your journal, begin a conversation between the voice in you that counts and compares and the voice in you that is fully immersed and present.
- In conversation with a friend or loved one, describe a current situation in which you find yourself entangled. Discuss what you can do that will help you drop what you are carrying.

Images that Educate
the Heart

*Art [is an attempt] to render the highest kind of justice
to the visible universe, by bringing to light the truth . . .
[that] is enduring and essential.*

—Joseph Conrad

The timeless role of art has always been to educate
the heart. The Greek word *pedagogue* means "to
walk beside, to accompany to learning." It originally referred to an adult walking a child to school. Since
the school is the world, we are asked to walk beside each
other as we learn from life. The Hindu word *upaguru*
means "the teacher that is next to you in this moment."
And so, images that educate the heart are *upagurus*. Once
discovered, these images become teachers who walk beside us.

There is an abundance of such images. Let me name
a few from literature: William Stafford's thread that we

hold on to no matter what, Carl Jung's view of the poet
as a lightning rod for the Unconscious, the Hindu notion
that we are called to keep lifting the veils of illusion, Oscar
Wilde's melting down of the sorrow that endures forever
so it can be transformed into the peace that abides in every
moment, and Ghalib's image that joy for the raindrop is
entering the lake. And here are a few images from nature:
the heart as our gill through which we extract what is essential, the self as the banks of a river that are shaped by
the water of Spirit it carries, the diamond of wisdom that is
compressed from the coal of experience, and the mind as
a tree in which thoughts come and go like colorful birds.

But where do we store these life-giving teachers? Often in books. This brings us to the practice of reading. In
our modern age, the art of reading has been truncated and
compromised. Today, a skilled reader is judged as someone who reads rapidly, who can scan the skeleton of any
piece of writing and abstract its silhouette of information.
This is like taking an X-ray of a person and thinking you
now have met the whole person.

The word *read* comes from the German *raten* which
originally meant "to guess." So reading is always a guess
at what matters, a leaning in to all that is beyond words, a
bow to all that gives rise to words.

I have always been a slow reader, not because I struggle with comprehending what I read, but because when
challenged or moved by what I read, I slow down in an
attempt to absorb what I'm taking in. Inherent in immers-

ing ourselves in books is the call to enter time and not just move through it. Understanding reading in this way, books become thresholds to living in moments beyond our own.

There is a story in the Talmud in which students notice that their rabbi has been quietly reading the same passage over and over for several days. Concerned, one of the students approaches his teacher to see if he is alright. The rabbi smiles and says, "When I come upon a small window into Eternity, why should I go anywhere else?"

The goal of reading is not to get anywhere, but to open where we are. The practice of reading is both simple and hard. In his journal, the great naturalist Henry David Thoreau said,

> To read true books, [with] a true spirit, is a noble exercise . . . one that will task the reader more than any exercise which the customs of the day esteem. It requires training such as athletes undergo. Books must be read as deliberately as they were written.

Moving too fast, we miss the thresholds that books offer. If we stay on the surface, even when reading studiously, books become placid, boring mirrors of our own speed and impatience.

The truth is that each book has its own way and feel, no one better than another. So, I encourage you to open a book where you will and read a paragraph or sentence and carry it with you. Don't worry about the sequence of reading a whole book in order. Just treat it as a friendly shore near a vast and unseeable ocean. Wander and pick up a shell here and there and hold it to your ear and see what happens.

A compelling and delightful practice I've developed over the years is to read many books at once. This way, they cross-pollinate and begin to speak to each other. I began working this way when I was stuck at a certain point in writing my book *Finding Inner Courage*. About two-thirds of the way through, I lost my way. So I made some coffee and, quite intuitively, began to pull books down from my shelves.

First there was Carl Jung's *Dreams, Memories, Reflections*. Then, I pulled down *Siddhartha* by Hermann Hesse. Then, Avicenna's medieval treatise *The Canon of Medicine*. One shelf down, I took out Galway Kinnell's *Mortal Acts, Mortal Words,* and Naomi Shihab Nye's *Words Under the Words*. I moved across the room and added a book by Einstein on the autobiography of his mind.

I laid them all out on the floor and began to open them one at a time, and randomly read a paragraph or a poem. Immediately, one seemed to be responding to the other. The books across cultures and time were in conversation. Then, I suddenly started writing my way between the voices and joined the conversation. The reverie of voices led me to the rest of my book. I have read this way ever since.

From time to time, my wife, Susan, and I do this with others. We hold a poetry evening. We invite friends over for dinner. And before everyone arrives, we set dozens of books in the living room, on the coffee table and the floor, piled at all angles on top of each other. Then, for dessert, we sit around and, one by one, each of us picks up a book we are drawn to, opens it, and, without thought, we each read whatever we find. After everyone has read a passage, we pause to discuss the conversation that has presented itself. Then, we go around again. And again. Until we know when the visitation of these authors has ended.

Reading requires us to slow down enough for our heart to fully receive the page before us. Then that page becomes a window we can step through. In this way, reading is a profound way for us to educate the heart. For it is better to read one word over and over until it opens its treasure, than to scan a thousand words in search of gold. Better to climb one mountain and stand on its summit until you are kissed by the sky, than to scale all the high peaks in search of the top of the world. Better to love one person so thoroughly that you drink from the well of all who have ever loved, than to love another and another in hopes of filling your emptiness.

The images that educate the heart are abundant, and need to be loved into view before they will spill their honey. When committed to reading, listening, and writing, we are worker bees intent on making that honey.

Inherent in immersing ourselves in books is the call
to enter time and not just move through it.

Questions to Walk With

- Experiment with your intuitive reading of many books at once. Pull at least five books from your shelves and place them about you. Begin by writing down a question that is working you. Now pick up one book at a time and read a paragraph or a poem. Write down the passages you have read. Then read them all in order. Now meditate on what this newly assembled set of voices is saying. In your journal, explore your reaction, your feelings, and your questions. Then, weave your reflections and the readings into one draft. Finally, read through the draft, journaling one more time from one passage to another. Put what you've written away for a day and then reread what you've written freshly. Respond to it one more time.

- Experiment with holding a poetry evening as described above. Gather some friends and place at least fifteen books in your living room. Then, one by one, have each person select a book and read a passage. After everyone has had a turn, discuss the terrain of stories and questions that have filled the room. Finally, have each of you share one image that has arisen to educate your heart.

Poetry and Education

Poetry and education are my twin loves. Without these deep and noble pursuits, I would be lost. But I remember hating poetry in high school. In retrospect, it wasn't the poetry I hated, but the feeling of being judged by someone peering down their glasses at me. Too often, school was where we were hit with something beautiful, and told how beautiful it truly was, while someone kept pointing out our inadequacies.

Later, I came to realize that the poetry itself was a friend, a tool, a resource waiting to affirm the joys and difficulties of living. It was an insecure, cynical teacher's use of poetry as a shield that pushed me away. Our teacher used her knowledge and expertise to maintain her authority and elevate her perch in the classroom. She was more committed to keeping herself at bay from her own sadness than to opening her students to the inner world of feeling.

Unfortunately, this is fairly common. Often, a teacher's inner struggle prevents the classroom from opening to the Mystery. Then, the rational tradition and pragmatic structure of our schools take over. When using poetry to learn about the mechanics of literature—its nomenclature, its classifications, its structure, and style—we are diverted from one of the great tools of meaningful living. For poetry is more than a means to understand the devices of literature. It is an instrument of self-knowledge, an instrument to foster an individual's unification with the world and the Universe that surround them. It is a powerful and muscular way to know the common aspects of the human experience. It is all these things, if we dare to let it enter the hearts and minds of those in the classroom.

The kind of poetry I'm describing is not limited to verses found in textbooks. Rather, it can be found in the glimmer of the smallest detail, whether it be an old, anonymous diary found in a ruined attic, or an overheard conversation of a grandmother weeping, or in the vibrant way a young man labors on the engine of his father's car, or in the sudden, unfiltered glimpse in the mirror that lets you see yourself as you truly are. Poetry, as I'm describing it, lives beyond any written and venerable word. Such poetry is found in any instant of truth that, for the moment, makes us whole.

Albert Schweitzer, the great humanitarian, said:

Bach was a poet; and this poet [before you] was at the same time a painter. This is not at all a paradox. We have the habit of classifying an artist according to the means he uses to interpret his inner life; a musician if he uses sounds, a painter if he uses colors, a poet if he uses words. But we must admit that these categories, established by external criteria, are very arbitrary. The soul of an artist is a complex whole, in which the variable gifts of the poet, the painter, and the musician mingle in infinite proportion.

The purpose of education, then, is to interpret the inner life, which holds a common ground for us all, no matter how it expresses itself. For each soul is a complex whole in which variable gifts mingle, if those gifts can be coaxed into the open. I urge you to center your classroom around this great fact: that each child must find their own means to interpret their inner life, to access their gifts, and thereby live more completely in the world.

In truth, we can't make anyone learn, not ourselves or children we don't know. But by having young minds live more closely to real knowledge, in themselves and in the world, they enlarge. As Irma Richter, who translated Leonardo da Vinci's notebooks, said:

To live close to great minds is the best education, and the happiest thing that can befall us.

We are not always near great minds, but we are all, by honest living, near great moments, and thereby, we are all artists who paint, write, and sing through our gifts.

The truth is that poetry is merely the window that makes clear the art of living. And teaching, at its unexpected best, is the joyful honing of the art of living which, as Walt Whitman reminded us, is always firsthand:

> Stop this day and night with me and you shall
>   possess the origin of all poems [. . .]
> You shall no longer take things at second or third
>   hand, nor look through the eyes of the dead,
>   nor feed on the spectres in books,
> You shall not look through my eyes either,
>   nor take things from me,
> You shall listen to all sides and filter them from
>   your self.

After all these years, I am finding that the line between poetry and teaching is disappearing. When we search together, inquiring into life, without presuming to know where we are going, we awake in the poem of life that is writing us.

> The purpose of education is to interpret the inner
> life, which holds a common ground for us all, no
> matter how it expresses itself.

Questions to Walk With

- In your journal, describe a moment of truth you experienced. What made it truthful? How did you enter this moment? How has it impacted who you are? Later, write a story about a character who is changed by a truthful moment that they enter.

- In conversation with a friend or loved one, discuss the most meaningful form of education you have experienced, whether in school or in life. How would you define a transformative education?

As We Go

Despite all our efforts to prepare, we can't plan who we will love, or who will be our most trustworthy friends. Nor can we plan who will be our teachers. You can't foresee who will have the most influence on your life. Nor can you foretell which books will change your life. If blessed, we are drawn below the words to the voices who brought these books into the world. It is their influence that stays with us as the presence of kindred spirits who affirm what it means to be alive. We discover these influences as we go. Certainly, we look for such voices, such teachers, even try to seek them out, only to trip and discover that the enduring teacher is underfoot.

I want to tell the story of my influences, the voices that transformed my mind so my heart could show itself completely. But first, let's unpack the word *influence*, which comes from the Latin *influere*, a combination of *in* ("into") and *fluere* ("to flow"). Influence, "to flow into." In ancient astrology, influence refers to "the flow that affects human destiny."

And it is the presence of unexpected teachers who flow into us that affects our destiny, the way sudden rain irrigates the roots of a willow that was two dry days from perishing. In just this way, a profoundly true story or pouring out of spirit across the ages can swell our roots and save us.

These are the influences that have saved me over the years. As you walk with me through their stories, I invite you to reflect on the voices, stories, and books that have flowed into you to save your life.

My Influences

Anthem by Ayn Rand

Before I'd written anything, I was captivated by the world of story as introduced to me by Miss Forshee, my eighth-grade English teacher. Her classroom felt like a wide cliff we would gather at, from which we could feel the wind from other times as we would gaze into the vastness of life. I couldn't wait to get there. I was blessed that she saw something in me. I'm not sure what. But one day, after class, she called me to her desk and we began to talk. After a month of such talks, I walked her home one afternoon. She lived nearby. She invited me in briefly to see her library, an entire wall in her living room covered with books. It seemed as if the books were alive, just waiting to

My influences

be held. She deliberately took a slim paperback off a shelf and gave it to me. She said, "I wonder what you will make of this story. Go on. Take it with you."

I was astonished at her kindness and belief in me. I went home and straight upstairs in our small house to my room, closed the door, and began reading *Anthem* by Ayn Rand. The futuristic story is told in the third-person plural, *we*. Toward the end, we learn that this is the story of a seeker who—in a world where the word *I* has been banished—discovers the singularity of his soul. When first writing from the *I* he affirms that "I need no warrant for being, and no word of sanction upon my being. I am the warrant and the sanction. It is my eyes which see, and the sight of my eyes grants beauty to the earth."

At such an impressionable age, Miss Forshee had led me to a story that affirmed the worth of my own being through our direct and common experience of the Mystery of Life. Though I learned in time—it is the Mystery of Life that grants my eyes the privilege of perceiving a beauty that already exists. And the surprise that the *we* of the story was, in fact, an *I* introduced me to the power of voice in a story. I felt these revelations at once though I had no language for them at the time.

Siddhartha by Hermann Hesse

Six years later, I was accepted to attend the State University of New York at Cortland. Part of my summer orientation was to read the novel *Siddhartha* by Hermann Hesse. For the first time, I traveled through a story as if it were a landscape painted by a magical artist. Each sentence, direct and clear, served as a window into a deeper reality. I couldn't see how this magic was performed but I was transported while reading this book, to places both familiar and new. The book made me grow while letting me feel more at home in my own life. This is something I have aspired to create ever since. The story also modeled deep forms of lasting relationship in how it depicts Siddhartha and his dear friends: one from his youth, Govinda, and one later in life, Vasudeva. This, too, gave me luminous models of how to journey through life with respect and care for each other, no matter the time or distance between us.

After the five-hour drive to Cortland that summer, I

sat in a circle with other freshmen to discuss the story and to explore how Siddhartha's journey—to discover himself, and through himself, his connection to a Living Universe— was indeed our own journey.

I have read this small magical novel at least six times throughout my life. Like viewing a mountain from different vantage points during the climb, it always serves as an inner reflector of where I am in life's journey. This, too, is something I have always aspired to in my own writing: to retrieve and craft a story or metaphor so truthfully that it can be returned to anew, again and again.

Livingdying by Cid Corman

During my freshman year in college, I went to my first poetry reading held at Corey Union on campus. There was a crowd of thirty to fifty of us. A kind, bearded professor walked in with the guest of the evening. He was a large, stocky man in his fifties, quiet except when he read his poems. He sat before us in a torn armchair with twelve to fifteen books, which were his own. I was sitting in front, on the floor, mouth open, my head in my hands, elbows on my knees—in awe of this sudden horizon of what I hoped to be. I hadn't come with that dream, but somehow knew upon hearing him speak that I belonged to this tribe of seekers and sayers.

The poet was Cid Corman and the book he read from most was his recent book of poems, *Livingdying*. He was part of the Beat movement and, like Gary Snyder, had spent transformative years in Japan, which helped to shape his sensibility. His poems introduced me to the quiet marvel and acceptance of things as they are. In the dedication to *Livingdying,* he says, from the start, "What more mountain than the one that is."

The Autobiography of William Carlos Williams

After my early years in college, I was certain that I wanted a life of expression, but unsure what that meant. It was then I was introduced to the work of William Carlos Williams, one of the steadfast innovators of twentieth-century poetry. At a time when his peers were fleeing America to work their creativity in the crucible of Europe, he finished medical school and rooted himself in Rutherford, New Jersey, where he was born. There, he practiced as a family doctor for more than fifty years. He had a typewriter bolted to a hinged desk, so he could leave mid-poem to deliver babies and return to the poem with a fresh sense of how life was always writing him.

Through his own story and unwavering poems, I felt and respected his vulnerability and honesty as gateways to deeper forms of truth. In his poem "The Last Words of My English Grandmother," I admired how he didn't polish his own image, but kept it as his grandmother saw him in her turmoil. I had found in him a model of how to be a truthful witness to all things.

Memories, Dreams, Reflections:
The Autobiography of Carl Jung

The last influence on me in college was anchoring and lasting. As a young mystic, I was overwhelmed by the kaleidoscope of Oneness I was sensing, both around me and across the ages. I had no reference point for this, other than the expansive moments of solitude when a child, which gave me a strength and clarity beyond my understanding. So, it was with great relief and excitement that I first read Carl Jung.

When wandering through the woods of the Unconscious in his writings, I stumbled on his essay about psychology and literature. The second part of that essay focuses on the poet. There, he says, clearly, that the poet is a lightning rod for the Unconscious. This sentence saved my life by giving me a way to understand how I was able to experience my own depth along with the depth of others. It wasn't madness. I was part of an eternal tribe of soothsayers and praise singers whose call is to record and affirm the history of Wholeness as it manifests through the living heart.

Ever since, I have been devoted to the understanding that every soul endures, when daring to live its life to the fullest. And through that enduring fullness, we become the lightning rod for the experience, suffering, and joy of others. The embodiment of this is what it means to be fully here. To record and honor what comes through such embodiment is the work of all art.

Pablo Neruda

I was teaching at SUNY Albany when my oldest friend, Robert, and I went for a walk in the fall along a colorful hillside on campus. We sat on the grass and Robert pulled out a book of poems by a Spanish-speaking poet I had never heard of, Pablo Neruda. A colleague of his had lent him the book because Robert said he had to show me this.

The first poem we read aloud was "There's No Forgetting." I had never heard a voice like his and felt an instant kinship. I certainly couldn't write like Neruda but felt that we drank from the same invisible Source. I felt such a joy of inner confirmation that I couldn't let the book out of my hands. I offered to buy his colleague another copy, which I did. That original copy is next to me as I write this. It is so worn that the binding is falling apart. The book, *Pablo Neruda: Selected Poems,* edited by Nathaniel Tarn, just falls open to the same poem we first read forty years ago.

Neruda's largess to all things modeled for me the vow to hold nothing back, to always lean into life, no matter what. A few years later, I came upon what in English is called Neruda's *Memoirs,* but which in Spanish he titled *I Confess That I Have Lived.* To read his autobiography is like taking a long walk with a human songbird.

There is one more story that comes from my lifelong love affair with Neruda. It centers on my copy of his book *Isla Negra.* I had recently purchased a first edition and was eager to dive in that weekend. I had it on an end table near my bed. That Friday night, I went to meet friends for dinner, leaving my six-month-old golden retriever, Saba, home alone for the first time.

When I came home, I found confetti all over the house. In her anxiety, she had tossed my books about and shredded a good part of my first edition of *Isla Negra*! I was beside myself. I yelled at her at which she cowered in the kitchen. Then, I simply held her till she calmed down. As I gathered all the shreds of Neruda's poems strewn around the house, I finally picked up the hardcover edition to find that Saba had eaten the front cover and shredded the first thirty-four pages.

The first intact remaining page was Neruda's poem "Shyness" which ends with this image: "my lament [was] buried deep like the whine of a hurt dog at the bottom of a well."

Gilgamesh
translated by Herbert Mason

In the early 1980s, I was teaching a reading poetry class at SUNY Albany when I came across Herbert Mason's translation of the anonymous Assyrian narrative *Gilgamesh*. More than 7000 years old, it was first carved on clay tablets. It is the story of a numb and enervated king who prompts war and conflict in order to stimulate his vacant life. In doing so, he loses his only friend, Enkidu. In his grief, he embarks on a journey to ask Utnapishtam, the Immortal One, to bring his friend back to life.

Having lost his father at a young age, Mason's own grief enabled him to access the timeless reservoir of all grief in rendering an immediate version of the story we all go through. Feeling the inescapable ordeal of loss in such an intimate and ancient way made me realize that the human experience is inextricably linked across the centuries. It made me realize that there is a prevailing kinship at the core of all stories and all poetry, if we can be honest enough to bear our humanity and share it.

After reading Mason's translation, I raced into my class, put aside whatever we were working on, and said, "We must read this together— Now!" I also embarked on an essay trying to unfold the timeless depths Mason's translation had unearthed. And through his publisher, I sent the essay with a note of tribute to Professor Mason at Boston University. To my surprise, he replied! This began a lengthy conversation, from which I continued to learn about the one heart we all give voice to.

The Madman: His Parables and Poems by Kahlil Gibran

Just before I fell into my journey with cancer in the late 1980s, I found this slim, hardcover volume by Kahlil Gibran, published after World War I in September 1918 with illustrations by Gibran himself. In the prologue, the poet tells us that he became a madman when thieves stole all his masks. For being seen naked, without any masks, people started to call him mad. But without his masks, he had a revelation and said, "For the first time the sun kissed my own naked face and my soul was inflamed with love

for the sun, and I wanted masks no more. And as if in a
trance, I cried, 'Blessed, blessed are the thieves who stole
my masks . . .' [For] I have found both freedom and safety
in my madness."

His being labeled mad by others immediately echoed
how William Blake called his sacred sayings "Proverbs
of Hell" because his true energy and vision were labeled
by his contemporaries as the work of the devil. Like Blake,
the inherent voice of truth in Gibran's post–World War I
book helped me understand more deeply the cost of being hidden and the cost of being seen, an archetype we
all must move through, if we are to live authentically with
truth as our arrow and love as our bow.

Rodin by Rainer Maria Rilke

On the other side of almost dying from cancer, I entered my
late thirties raw and thoroughly turned upside down and
inside out. It was then that I found Rainer Maria Rilke's
amazingly poetic tribute to the great sculptor Auguste
Rodin. Rarely do we get to see the creative force of one artist through the creative force of another. When twenty-six,
Rilke met Rodin who was sixty-one. Rodin hired Rilke as
his secretary and welcomed the young poet into his home
and studio for six months. During that time, the poet
wrote this monograph, which is a force of nature by itself.

This torrent of subject and voice helped me find my
own creative current in my new and fragile post-cancer
life. I knew, going forward, that like the truth of a string

resolutely plucked by a heart-broken cellist, no expression would be worthwhile unless struck like this in the chord of our being. And so, poetry and art became faceless teachers who revealed their lessons only through the hollowing of our joy and suffering, met and faced without shame or excuse. Both Rodin and Rilke have been stalwart guides confirming my belief in the human process, which, given voice to, becomes artistic. I have taken comfort in these lines from Rilke toward the end of his stay with Rodin: "I was walking lost in thought through that vast workshop, and I saw that everything was in the process of becoming and that nothing was in a hurry."

A Poet's Journal by George Seferis

Finding my way back into life, I stumbled through everything familiar until it revealed something essential. In this state, I resumed teaching and worked toward a more direct and penetrating manner of expression. It was then that I met the poems of the Greek poet George Seferis. The clear mind of this modern pilgrim seemed a wide-open window through which his very large heart recorded the world. His commitment to have his mind serve his heart was part of the covenant I had made with the ineffable once waking on the other side of being ill. This journal by Seferis covers the years 1945 to 1951 when his life, too, was being re-fired and reformed.

It was walking with Seferis in his journal that I discovered the Japanese master Basho's timeless instruction to

Kikakou in the 1600s: "We shouldn't abuse God's creatures. You must reverse your haiku. Not: a dragonfly; remove its wings—pepper tree. But: pepper tree; add wings
to it—dragonfly. The world depends on which way this
thought unfolds."

That Seferis kept turning inward for stories of joining
is proof that listening deeply is a restorative all by itself.
As he drifted across a postwar world rebuilding itself after immense destruction and atrocity, Seferis said, "Only
now are we beginning to discern things that could perhaps
come into the light . . . The point is . . . to write no matter
what happens, to keep alive whatever expresses my aliveness."

This has become an anthem by which I remember
the way.

Palm-of-the-Hand Stories by Yasunari Kawabata

It was in my early forties that I discovered the fiction of
Yasunari Kawabata who was committed to the literary cal-
isthenic of trying to write a novel in a page or two. Like the
Elizabethan poets who only wrote sonnets to hone their
skills, these exercises were never meant to be published.
Yet, thankfully, after his death in 1972, they appeared as
Palm-of-the-Hand Stories.

The first thing I felt when entering these potent tell-
ings was how we are swept into an already existent world,
thrown into its stream, and then cast out just as quickly. The

stories seem to penetrate depth-wise into the page and not sequentially page after page. One story in particular is imprinted on my being, "The Canaries." It is a letter from a recent widower to his former mistress, telling her that all he has left are the canaries she gifted him at the end of their affair. For years, without knowing where they came from, his wife now gone had cared for the canaries, keeping them (and the presence of the mistress) alive and well. In his painful letter, the widower can't return to either his wife or his past and asks his mistress if she will forgive him if he kills the birds. Then, we are swept out of that world back into our own.

For me, it isn't the moral situation that makes this story so remarkable, but the introduction of the canaries as a gift that is kept alive more than the marriage or the affair. It is the introduction of the canaries as a narrative device that is so instructive to me as a storyteller.

It makes me think of Jane Smiley's novel *A Thousand Acres.* In that story, there is the introduction of a detail that carries the story for a couple of hundred pages. The main character is so upset with her sister that she poisons a jar of sausages and leaves it in her sister's basement of canned goods. The story goes on and we are waiting in utter suspense to see if her sister cooks and eats the sausage. Eventually, the main character comes to deeper terms with herself and goes, just as quietly, and removes the poisoned jar. No one ever knows but her and the reader. And so, something incredibly true has happened silently, underneath all the events and dialogue entangled above it. That quiet detail is a compelling and powerful instrument of storytelling.

And if we can shed our familiarity with the skull of Yorick in Shakespeare's *Hamlet,* it is an extraordinary detail used to unfold the core of the plot. With his sense of life coming apart, with his pain and grief cracking his moral compass, Hamlet stumbles in his melancholy upon a grave being dug at the edge of the castle grounds. In his disoriented exploration of where life has led him, he jumps into the grave to discover that someone is already buried there. He picks up a skull. Then, he realizes that, of all people, it is the skull of Yorick, the court jester who made him laugh as a child. It is to Yorick's skull that Hamlet utters the eternally known soliloquy "To be or not to be?" It's as if Hamlet has descended into the dark gears of the Universe between life and death to ask, do we really exist and toward what end?

For all his brilliance with language, Shakespeare was an extraordinary imaginer of events. Sometimes, we get so focused on our use of language that we bypass the sheer magic of plotting, of introducing truthful and mythic events or objects that pry open the Mysteries, that dislodge our normal patterns of thinking.

And so, centuries later, Kawabata's canaries are a symbol for me of the magic always near in merging what is with the magic of what can be.

Dark Wood to White Rose by Helen Luke

I met the Jungian analyst Helen Luke in the spring of 1994 at her home in the Apple Farm Community, which she created in Three Rivers, Michigan, in the early 1960s. As an elder, she quickly became my mentor and guide, foreseeing my life as a spiritual teacher long before I had anything to say.

When staying at Apple Farm, she and I would meet mid-morning in her small day room, a table between us. Over a cup of tea, we would discuss dreams and the Unconscious and she would look at my writing with an eye to how much I was leading with intent or following what wanted to be said.

During one visit, I was struggling on my path and Helen, sensing this, asked, with her firm British voice, if I had read her book *Dark Wood to White Rose*. I was aware of it but shied away from the book because I mistakenly thought it was literary criticism, as it focuses on the journey of transformation in Dante's *Divine Comedy*. I sheepishly uttered, "Not yet, Helen." To which she simply gave me a sideways glance. Not out of ego, but out of a prescient clarity that what she had explored there would be apt medicine for me.

Two years later, Helen died at the age of ninety. A few years on, more deeply in my struggle, I finally picked up *Dark Wood to White Rose* and it changed my life. It turned out that I had read her book exactly at the right time in my journey and it was a comfort that, while reading it, I could hear her voice in the passages.

Helen's brilliant insight about Dante's *Divine Comedy* was to see it as a journey through consciousness in which Hell represents the cost of false living, Purgatory represents the struggle to be real, and Paradise represents the struggle to stay real. Notice we are never free of struggle and so, the implicit inner ethic is to love the process.

In *Dark Wood to White Rose,* there are literally dozens of metaphors through which Helen offers a waking soul an inner curriculum that serves the quest to live a joyous and meaningful life. Too many lessons and choice-points to speak to here. But above all, Helen declared that everyone needs a trusted other to bear witness to their journey. Without such loving, honest company, any effort to transform will remain sterile.

Helen's life and teaching helped me discern what truly glows from what distracts with its glitter. For all our dreams and schemes, the only path worth breaking is the one in which we struggle to be real and to stay real. Even if lost, the work of being real is healing and life-giving.

The Earth Is the Lord's by Abraham Heschel

Even as a child, I was certain of my ability to see, especially into the spaces between and under things. I never questioned my vision, only what it meant. After almost dying from cancer in my thirties, I never questioned my heart. And so, for decades, I have cleared my own path to discover a meaningful way of being, learning, and teaching. And though I have always felt a deep cultural tie to the Jewish heritage, I never practiced Judaism in conventional ways. Blessed to still be here, I became a student of all paths.

It was in my early fifties that my most recent mentor, Joel Elkes, came into my life. Joel was an extraordinary being: a child of the Holocaust, a groundbreaking physician, a metaphysical painter, a great listener, and a steadfast friend. We rowed through a river of deep conversation about everything from kindness to cruelty and from destiny to the exquisite randomness of the Universe. One day, Joel gave me Abraham Heschel's *The Earth Is the Lord's*. Without any context, he simply said, "Let me know how it speaks to you."

In this book, Heschel traces the source and lineage of the Eastern European Jewish mind, since so much of that splendid culture was decimated in the Holocaust. Heschel was born in Poland in 1907, the descendant of pre-eminent European rabbis. He moved to Germany to pursue his doctorate at the University of Berlin. In October 1938, while teaching in Frankfurt, he was arrested by the Gestapo and deported back to Poland. Six weeks before the German invasion of Poland, Heschel made his way to London and on to America in 1940, never to return to Poland or Germany. *The Earth Is the Lord's* was his first book, published in 1949.

In those pages, I was humbled to discover that my mind works with an Ashkenazi way of seeing and listening, that my mind is indeed Talmudic in how I understand everything through the life of questions. For I have always believed that there is never one answer but rather a constellation of openings that lead us into a field of Oneness.

After reading *The Earth Is the Lord's,* I realized that through my own authentic wandering, I found my way home. And what better way to find that you belong than by uncovering your own way. Leaving the tribe, I wandered over decades to assume my place in the tribe.

This is a humbling aspect of individuation, by which we struggle to go our own way, only to arrive, in time, as an authentic member of a larger tradition. Sometimes, the unexpected labyrinth of self-realization, if entered truthfully, becomes the path by which we humbly arrive—belonging to the deeper human tribe.

A few years after reading *The Earth Is the Lord's,* I discovered that a central tenet of the Kabbalah, the Jewish mystical tradition, is a belief in the inherent radiance of all things, the constant emanation of Spirit creating and remaking the world.

As a poet, philosopher, and long-term cancer survivor, I have believed fervently—my whole life—in the emanation of Spirit and light into the world. I was never taught this or about the Kabbalah. This affirms, in yet another way, how I have set out to find my own agreement with the basic nature of life, only to land in my tradition's deep center without the press or indoctrination of that tradition.

I think this is an archetypal unfolding, the journey we

each uncover when facing the truth of our lives. Becoming who we are will lead us to becoming everyone else. Perhaps the greatest truth T. S. Eliot ever uncovered was his deep insight in "Four Quartets": "We shall not cease from exploration, and the end of all our exploring will be to arrive where we started and know the place for the first time."

After seventy years of seeking and learning, I look back on these authentic teachers who shaped my mind and heart, thankful to have been shaped. I hold what each has shown me, not as an answer, but as a vow to inhabit while living a life. In particular, each voice has taught me:

- To affirm the worth of my own being through our direct and common experience of the Mystery of Life.
- To practice authenticity so that at the juncture of our realness we can discover the Web of the Living Universe.
- To look for peace in the marvel and acceptance of things as they are.
- To trust that vulnerability and honesty are gateways to deeper forms of truth.
- To trust that living life to the fullest will make our heart a conduit for all human experience.
- To hold nothing back, to always lean into life, no matter what, as an inner form of breathing.

- To be honest enough to bear our humanity and share it, so we can inhabit the prevailing kinship that waits at the core of all stories and all poetry.
- To outlive the cost of being hidden and endure the cost of being seen, so we can live without masks.
- To find meaningful resonance with others through the struck chord of our being.
- To have our heart serve our mind and, by so doing, become a vessel for care and kindness.
- To stay devoted to the magic inherent in all things.
- To love the struggle that living always brings, to treat struggle as a teacher.
- To be a lifelong servant of questions, always seeking viewpoints beyond our own.

I wonder what voice, what story, what book will be our next teacher? What flow will enter us, bringing more of us forward than we thought possible? Isn't this how flowers bloom, always opening a little further until all their colors are revealed?

These books and the voices that brought them into the world are old sages turned friends. They sit tattered on my shelf as quiet and reliable oracles. Like stones in the river, they release deep, mysterious songs, just by standing firm in the current of life. Perhaps this is their greatest lesson, that just by standing true, we help to shape the world. I would be much less, had I not tripped into them.

*Living life to the fullest will make our heart a
conduit for all human experience.*

Questions to Walk With

- In your journal, describe the books that have
  saved you and what each has taught you.
- In conversation with a friend or loved one, tell
  each other the story of your influences and how
  they came into your life.

The Arts of Liberation

The Artist is no other than he who unlearns what he
has learned, in order to know himself.

—E. E. Cummings

Everyone lives within the tension of writing our own
story or finding our part in the story of life. When
we can listen for the larger story we are in, the one
that keeps shaping who we are, we disentangle the smaller
story we insist on telling to compensate for where life has
taken us. The more we see the truth in things as they are,
the more we enter the magic of liberty. It is from the foundational ground of things as they are that the sweep of our
imagination opens.

When I was young, freedom seemed the distance I
could travel without having to slow down inside. But now,
after many sojourns behind the curtain of noise, after many
glimpses of what holds us up, after many elusive sightings
of God in the unthinking faces of animals and stones, freedom has given way to liberty, which seems now the depths

to which I can go within without having to move at all.
And there, I have learned that great thinking and feeling
bring us to the secret of being, the way great music brings
us to the secret of silence.

As a jazz musician must learn his scales and chords so
he can freely improvise, we must train our powers of expression by describing the details of nature and relationship, so we can freely convey all that matters which can't
be seen. This brings to mind Rodin's first drawing teacher,
Horace Lecoq de Boisbaudran, who believed, as art editor
Rachel Corbett tells us, "that keen observation [is] the in-
dispensable secret all great artists [possess]. He believed
young artists ought to master the fundamentals of form
only so they might one day break them."

Though the way is hard, we each make the world anew
by seeing it, loving it, and expressing it. Recently, I spoke
in the philosophy department at Hope College in Holland, Michigan, on the subject: What is Liberal Arts? In
essence, I shared that after all these years, after the many
ways experience has worn the excuses from my tongue, I
remain steadfast in my belief in the arts of liberation. For
me, underneath all attempts at education is the question:
How do we live together in our time on Earth? And what
does it mean to be alive? And what are the deeper skills—
the ways of seeing, being, holding, knowing, feeling, and
perceiving—that help us through the miraculous and dangerous corridor it is to live a life on Earth?

At dinner, afterward, one of the professors asked with

pain and sincerity, "How can I open the minds and hearts of young people when, honestly, I'm unsure if they can go into all that is opened?" He paused a long time, then said, "I'm concerned about leading people into places that will undo them."

But this is the crux of it, the wonder of it, the pain of it: to be alive, in every way, is both astonishing and full of peril. It can be abundant and collapsing. And nothing else matters but gathering the resources to make it through these paradoxical and poignant straits. We must be honest about this. Seeking what matters is an adventure that will inevitably undo us. And I believe every discipline—be it dance, botany, math, or psychology—every path of knowing has something to offer to the journey of being alive and being undone.

We talked further into the night through dinner and a bottle of red wine. At last, we stumbled into the deeper notions of faith: that when we are thrust so fully into life, our experience liberates unexpected resources that can help us negotiate the dark. So, though the prospect of pure being—of seeing the extraordinary in the ordinary—can take your breath away, it will show you Eternity. Though loving everything will make your heart feel like it might burst at the sight of rain, loving everything will cleanse you of all that is false. Though watching a mother dog lick her stillborn pup will make you cry out in silence, "I can't take anymore!"—it will steam away all pettiness. Though the passages are not always fun, there is a bedrock of calm that they return us to.

I am more concerned when we don't open enough. Then, we are caught in a living purgatory, neither in the world of relationship nor in the world of introspection. We just peer out from our isolation, alongside of life, though not living it. Opening enough is the razor's edge between loving and suffering the world.

Just what, then, is the charge of a responsible teacher? If you squeeze a drop of iodine into a glass of water, it will color the entire glass. So, let's not talk about teaching only to the mind. Whatever we carefully place in the mind will stir through the entire being before us. And what are we to do with that? How are we to hold them? How near is appropriate? How far away is criminal?

True education is messy, never clear, and the lessons shift and the boundaries change. So much of what we're called to do for each other is to simply listen and tend: to be a mirror of what the other is thinking, and to echo back with clarity and compassion what the other is saying.

The call of a noble teacher or loving friend is to guide someone so thoroughly to their own center that they, in hard-earned innocence, become their own teacher. Inevitably, the life of expression helps us endure being undone and helps us keep each other company as we suffer and love the world.

Shortly after this conversation, I had a dream about a school devoted to the practice of inner liberty. It was being constructed on several acres in the midst of an open landscape. I walked through the half-built site and came upon a central dome, its beams nailed into place. It was like the apse of a church, but its center point opened to the sky like the Pantheon in Rome. The open courtyard seemed to be a communal meeting place. Surrounding the central dome were terraces on plateaus, each at a different elevation, rising eventually to the height of the dome. Each of these terraces had benches from which to take in the world.

Finally, I stood inside the skeletal dome with blueprints in my hand. My oldest students were busy at work. I realized we were building a school whose physical layout was an extension of our deepest beliefs. I was so excited, as if I'd uncovered the purpose of my remaining years.

I then went to what everyone seemed to know was my favorite landing, as if I'd done this over and over. Once there, I looked out onto a small mountain with a cascading waterfall. Everyone seemed to know that watching this waterfall was what made this landing my favorite. In fact, some were remarking that the site for the school was chosen precisely to face this waterfall.

As I leaned over the makeshift rail, the sounds of construction surrounded me. I peered steadily into the mist of the waterfall. And there, near the top, where the stream of water cut through the peak, was the image of two figures, one male and one female, kneeling, each drinking from the falling water. Once seeing them, I knew that this is how we learn, helping each other drink from the river of our days, the truth always there, streaming before us. I felt complete on this landing, and woke believing that schools should be built in view of such mysteries.

The call of a noble teacher or loving friend is
to guide someone so thoroughly to their own center
that they, in hard-earned innocence,
become their own teacher.

Questions to Walk With

- In your journal, describe a time when you had to unlearn something in order to become more truly yourself. Later, write a poem or story about someone freeing themselves from an inheritance that was someone else's dream.
- In conversation with a friend or loved one, imagine the school of your dreams in great detail.

Vessels of Learning

The purpose of tradition is to show us that the gifts of
the Universe are greater than the boundaries of the ego.

—Joseph Campbell

For me, the deepest moments of learning have been those sudden bursts of insight that at once confirm what I didn't know I knew while introducing me to something completely new. We can't plan or manufacture these moments. We can only stay curious about everything so we can be ready for them.

Such a moment came to me years ago while studying Pablo Neruda's use of image and metaphor. At the time, I had just read the French Surrealists and their wild juxtapositions for the sake of sheer boldness. An example is the image conjured by Robert Desnos, "a parabola was bored in its cage." In contrast, Neruda applied his compelling images to the human condition. This was what I was interested in.

Earlier, I told the story of how I was introduced to the poems of Pablo Neruda. In the first poem I ever read of his, "There's No Forgetting," there is an image that took my breath away: "the yellowing pigeon asleep in our forgetting." I kept going over it and taking it apart, so I could use its dynamics on my own. Neruda would take a detail of the natural world, like a pigeon, and pair it with an abstract, invisible force, like forgetting. Then, he'd add a color or texture, like yellowing. The combination was surreal but the impact was thoroughly human.

No matter how hard we try, the deepest learnings present themselves when we least expect it. Even the brooding Sigmund Freud confessed that "Everywhere I go, I find a poet has been there before me." I believe this is true because true poets are wild learners. And we each have a wild learner stirring within us.

Another moment of wild learning came to me when I was staying with friends on the edge of a canyon in Santa Fe, New Mexico. Early, before dawn, I was awakened by the howl of a coyote. It seemed piercing and close. Without turning on the light, I went to the window and peered through the blinds. In a blue cast of moonlight, there were two scraggly creatures about twenty feet from the house. The larger one was standing perfectly still, its head pointing skyward in a continual howl. The smaller one was calmly grazing behind it. Together they seemed complete.

I sat at my friend's desk in the dark and there, tacked to her wall, were two handwritten quotes I'd never noticed. Both spoke of how to proceed in the world. The first quote was by Buddha: "Act always as if the future of the Universe depends on what you do, while laughing at yourself for thinking that whatever you do makes any difference." The second quote I mentioned earlier. It was by Friedrich Nietzsche. This is where I came upon it: "I want to learn more and more to see as beautiful what is necessary in things, then I shall be one of those who makes things beautiful."

The larger coyote began to howl forcefully. I peered again through the blinds and, suddenly, it seemed as if these two scraggly angels were sent to wake me to these teachings. And there I was, in the desert night, in my underwear, reading and watching, over and over, until it seemed that the coyotes were voicing the quotes. It made me name them. Of course, the howling one was Nietzsche and the grazing one was Buddha. I watched and laughed at myself. How much it takes, sometimes, for me to wake. After a while, I fell back asleep. In the morning, they were gone. I have carried the coyote quotes as a koan ever since.

Yet, despite our best attempts, things get in the way. The Buddhist teacher Jamgön Kongtrül Rinpoche describes three pitfalls to learning:

> There are three errors to be avoided, which can be likened to three types of vessels. The first error is not paying attention; this is like an upside-down vessel, into which no liquid can be poured. The second error is not committing the meaning to memory; this is like a vessel with a hole in the bottom, which cannot retain the liquid poured into it. The third error is being distracted by conflicting emotions; this is like a vessel containing poison, which will contaminate the liquid.

These are recurring pitfalls that we can repair in any given moment—with presence, heart, and the reclaiming of wonder. For only our presence can repair our inattention. And we can learn by heart what we forget in the mind. And we can inoculate our conflicts and judgments with our next baptism into wonder. Always, the love of others will return us to ourselves, as the love of small things will reveal their connections to everything larger and sustaining. When we can be students of presence, heart, and wonder, we become like old, worn pots. Then, we are the vessels of learning ourselves, meant to be used, repaired, and passed on.

No matter how hard we try, the deepest learnings present themselves when we least expect it.

Questions to Walk With

- In your journal, take a poem or story that you admire and try to understand how it works, so you can use its dynamics in your own voice.
- In conversation with a friend or loved one, tell the story of a moment of great learning for you. Through what small piece of life did this great learning present itself?

Freeing the Ox

We must not be afraid of
what anyone might say:
Be Source, not result.

—Rumi

It had been three semesters since I stopped one day before class to speak with a surgeon, never to return that year. As I was being wheeled through hospital corridors, I kept wanting to say one more thing to my students who were waiting for me to arrive that day.

Now, it was spring again, a year and a half after cancer, and I was well. For sure, completely changed: more real, more fragile, less able to stay on any one topic, which always spilled now like water through my hands. I was back at the university, blessed to be teaching at all, let alone creative writing. And so, I walked eagerly to my class, naming flowers along the way.

I began, as usual, asking for issues, feelings, or questions to be brought to the circle before moving on. Mike, an introspective young man, said, "Yes . . . you know, the way you teach is different . . . the atmosphere and all . . . not like my other classes . . . I like it, but I was just wondering . . . why . . . why do you teach this way?"

I was slightly stunned and moved that he would ask. As I thought how to answer, my entire life as both a student and a teacher flashed before me. For most of my life as a student, I felt excluded, and, no doubt, that has much to do with why my classrooms are so inclusive. And I have always learned more as a teacher than a student.

I told him, "All true education is holistic. Yet look around. We're so specialized that the power and energy of the Whole is left hidden in the unexplored seams *between* all these disciplines." I recalled that my first image of Wholeness was the sea. Looking into the water, I was pulled by a fascination with the deep, with the vast immeasurable world so close, but always out of view. But I continued with my train of thought.

"For instance," I said, "where do I go to explore the feeling I get from nature? I could study landscape, but its majesty is more than just geology. I could study how others have felt in the presence of nature, but this overwhelming mystery is more than just nature writing." I thought about the flowers I saw on my way in and said, "I could study botany, but the gift is more than just naming plants."

Mike interrupted me, "So, to teach means letting everything in—"

I finished his sentence, "And *not* sifting things out. That's why the name of whatever class I find myself teaching is merely the entrance to a field of issues that inevitably extends beyond the small opening we enter."

I felt the energy gathering around us, but kept inwardly flashing on my experience with truth. So I went there: "I guess I've always felt most alive when exploring the truth, when that sudden utterance from within—be it a question or a feeling—rings true between us."

Mike and everyone else seemed a bit puzzled, as if I'd changed course without bringing them along. I looked around the circle and admitted, "As a teacher, I do you great disrespect if I do not honor all of you when you walk through that door. For we are so much more than our minds."

I wasn't sure if I was making sense. It seemed that what I was feeling was losing focus as I was trying to share it. But I fumbled on, "Though we sit in separate seats, we are drifting in this room, as in a clear but turbulent sea. One person's struggle ripples into everyone else. It is my responsibility as your teacher and your responsibility as a student to watch for anyone going under."

Mike was intent, climbing with me, though it wasn't clear where I was going. But Caitlin had lost interest, while Kelly was silently going over the story she was about to read to us. I tried to be less abstract: "All of it—what we look at, who we are, how we relate—all of it is connected. I can't inquire into how you think without also inquiring into how you feel. And if you feel one thing, I must, in time, find out how others feel about what's happening to you, as well as sharing my own reactions."

Kelly stopped reading for a moment. I kept on a bit, "In order to do this, I must put all of me before you, which can be a scary thing. But hiding is like tying your wings." I got a little fired up: "Honestly, most teachers use their subject matter as fences. And I've had teachers play pinball with the facts of their discipline, bouncing information off young minds, assessing their own success by the number of hits that bounce back."

The class was interested, but restless, and I was ready to move on but Mike kept pressing me, "I understand what you're saying, but when we get out of here, we have to make it in the real world. How is any of this going to help?"

I thought of my harangues with my father when I came home from college and declared in our kitchen, "I'm a poet." How he bristled. I didn't share that story with Mike. Instead, I conveyed my deep belief that, "Unless we tend to who we are, we will defer all real living in attempts to safeguard our position in the systems we move through. Afraid we won't get the grade, the promotion, the tenure, the love, we seldom risk our honest opinion. Seldom being who we truly are. Always postponing the moment of living which is unrepeatable."

Of course, Mike still had questions. And so did I. But something alive and raw and not fully dealt with had been opened. We began looking at each other's work. Amazingly, the pieces we shared touched deeply on these issues.

Kelly read her story, *Aponoia,* which I later learned comes from the Greek meaning "despair." The story, drawn from her own life, is about a fifth-grade class run by a very disciplined teacher. The children are giving reports on the planets. The story opens with Jenny, a very good girl, completing her report on Venus. The teacher approves heartily and Jenny sits down. Eric is next. Eric, it seems, is very precocious, a hidden genius of sorts who is plagued by endless questions and who hides his loneliness of mind by being a wise aleck.

With disdain in her voice, the teacher calls on Eric, who tries to dodge giving any report. The teacher believes he is just lazy and unprepared. She refuses all his excuses. Eric, seemingly against his better judgment, blurts out, "I didn't do the report because I'm not sure Pluto exists." He then proceeds to show his concerns, all deeply felt. For nothing he has read offers any proof that there are any planets. Mere blotches through telescopes are what scientists base all this on. How can he be sure? How can any of us be sure?

The teacher ignores Eric's questions and humiliates him in front of the others by demanding a parent conference. School ends and, astonishingly, Jenny impulsively rides her bike to the nearby shore, staring into the waves, terrified that nothing really exists. She cycles home, locks herself in her room, and cries herself to sleep.

Kelly had answered Mike's first question about teaching, without even knowing what that question would be. We must acknowledge all parts of ourselves in the classroom, because what is not welcomed grows agitated. And like all agitations, it enlarges, like a welt or swollen knee, beyond its normal size. Young minds swell when agitated with their questions of existence and, unwelcomed, they affect the life next to them mercilessly.

I asked the group who was responsible for Jenny's terror. Alicia said Eric. Michelle said Jenny herself. Mike said the teacher. Brett thought that, in part, each of them was responsible. To me, the weight of it falls to the teacher for not truly welcoming all of Eric, even though it was more than she or her lesson plan had bargained for. We must remember that Eric and Jenny are only in fifth grade. To blame Eric for not being aware of how his questioning might affect others seems unfair. And, though we could expect someone older to share their terror as a means to alleviate it, Jenny is a small girl. To my mind, the teacher is solely responsible.

I suggested that a teacher open to questions would have discarded the plan for the day and entered a discussion about the nature of belief. This was an unpredictable moment in a classroom that an open-minded teacher would treasure and pursue. This teacher was poorly suited to be with young minds because she not only refused to see Eric's questioning as genuine, but refused to see how deeply it was affecting him. And she was oblivious to the impact of Eric's questions on Jenny and the others. Teaching is listening. It requires never forgetting that everything in the classroom is delicately alive and interconnected.

When I stopped to listen, I realized that Kelly's story had expressed my feelings more clearly than I had. For this brief time, Kelly, unknowingly, had become the teacher.

Caitlin went next, reading her poem "Feeling the Now," which bravely shared her vast experience at manipulating men in order to survive; how as a destitute adolescent she would manipulate men into buying her meals. The poem goes on to share how she has learned that such manipulation is essential to survival. But the wisdom of the poem manifests a deeper knowing in its culminating lines: "I have learned well. Learned in the wild. Learned to lie. Especially to myself."

Now Caitlin became the teacher, answering Mike's second question about surviving in the real world, without knowing that this question would be asked. While it was necessary as a poor child to manipulate others for food, the cost as an adult, that Caitlin was struggling with, was the cost of not finding her own congruence, of not being able to be who she is, where she is. Similar to the fate of the liar who, more than not being believed, doesn't know who to believe, Caitlin raised the corollary fate of the manipulator who, more than not being trusted, doesn't know who to trust, including herself.

All of this brought home the fact that while there is a pragmatism necessary to survive in the world, there is a cost for surviving by *not* being who we are. Whatever we do falsely, we do in some insidious fashion to ourselves. Each of us must meet the challenges of living without corrupting the inner reservoirs we are trying to protect in the first place.

I remembered how many times I had not listened to the truth of my soul, silencing my inner teacher so as not to displease others. How many times I had bridled my own heart to avoid conflict or tension.

I felt compelled to share what I had been reading just that morning. It was a passage from Chuang Tzu, the great Taoist sage from 300 BC:

> *Horses and oxen have four feet—this is what I mean by [who we are]. Putting a halter on the horse's head, piercing the ox's nose—this is what I mean by [what we do]. So I say: do not let [what we do] wipe out [who we are].*

I repeated it several times, after which we all said nothing. It was a treasured moment for me; the kind of sudden numinous opening that keeps returning me to the classroom; the kind of intangible reward that makes me thankful for the climb each day to a plateau from which we leave the assignments behind and enter the questions of real living; moments that can't be prepared for. And yet, I feel my whole life's experience has been bringing me here.

I left feeling touched and invigorated. That night, I walked my golden retriever and listened to her pads in the grass as I watched the stars flicker. Something in the silence made me think of Martin Buber's story of being a boy in a small academic gymnasium in Austria. Each day, they would file into a worn room that had five rows of six benches each, two boys to a bench. He recounts how at recess two boys began a pantomime, gesturing in strong emotional postures to each other, ignoring everyone else, their faces expressionless. Everyone gathered and watched. Recess ended and things returned to normal. Each day at recess, this inner dance of deep expression continued, gaining in intensity till, as Buber says, "The faces of the two looked . . . as souls in the pains of hell."

Every day, everyone would gather and then disperse and neither the boys nor any of their classmates ever would mention it. But weeks later, the headmaster brought young Martin in and interrogated him about the activities of his classmates. Young Martin found this more frightening than the pantomime he had witnessed. The headmaster badgered him, "You are a good child, you will help us." The young Buber wanted to reply, "Help you do what?" But instead, he burst into tears. He was kept home for several days and when he came back, the boys at the third bench in the middle row were gone, never to return.

I walked my dog underneath the quietly steady stars. How different was young Martin Buber from young Jenny who cried herself to sleep, both sent into terror by the elimination of all question and expression? How different were the young mimes from Eric, letting their confusions surface unexpectedly? How different was the headmaster from the fifth-grade teacher in Kelly's story? Didn't both behave as the police of the norm? Didn't both darkly snuff the life-force of their students? Didn't both pierce the ox's nose?

It seems to me that whatever deep force made those young boys give gesture to the pain of centuries is what the classroom is for. What ancient and timeless voice was begging to be the teacher that day? And where did it burrow back to, once slapped down?

My dog, in the spring air, under the stars, leaned into my leg. Her warmth made me think of Bronson Alcott, who in the early 1800s had his license to teach revoked because he had two radical ideas. He thought that every child should have their own desk, and that the schoolroom should have windows, so that when the children became bored, they could refresh themselves by looking at the trees.

What if those young boys had had Alcott as a teacher? What if they had had a window—both inside and out? From where living has taken me, what's real is what surfaces from the core we all share. What's real is the courage to let it out, to put it there between us, to break it apart and caress it for its meaning. What's real is the amazing wisdom that comes from the young lives who dare to make use of the free sanctuary we provide. Like water from a holy spring, the perennial dynamic of the classroom is how we are all healed for drinking of each other.

Teaching is listening. It requires never forgetting that everything in the classroom is delicately alive and interconnected.

Questions to Walk With

- In your journal, tell the story of someone who is shunned or exiled for being who they are and how they survive not being seen and heard.

- In conversation with a friend or loved one, tell the story of someone who welcomed all your questions and how that affected you. Then tell the story of someone who shut down your questions and how that affected you. What can you do to receive the questions of others more fully?

Waking Close to the Bone

Not too far . . . down this road of delusion,
I can see [that] yesterday I was wrong . . .
At the window my presumptions
drift away south.

—TAO CH'IEN

Under Our Stories

We arrive in this world with nothing between us and this life—no preconceptions, no experience, no history, no expectations. But very quickly, our immediate experience creates echoes of what has passed and dreams and fears of what will come to be, and these thoughts and feelings begin to form an invisible shell around us. This reflexive sheath of thoughts and feelings attempts to protect us from the unpredictable nature of life. Yet, as with all protections, a barrier is created between us and life itself. What at once protects us also keeps us from the direct experience of living. And we struggle, as long as we are here, with the tension between what is and what has been and what might be.

Inevitably, we also struggle with the stories we are given or forced to take on and the ones we create in reaction to these initial stories. We aren't here very long before a story envelopes us. From the moment our mother lifts us and our father kisses our head, we are held and shaped by the stories they carry. Very often, we are swaddled in great expectation that we will continue the dream of those who came before us or complete the dream that those before us couldn't manage to complete.

And so, the process of individuation becomes the inner, developmental journey by which we distinguish ourselves from the story we've inherited in order to create our own story of life. We may have been told that we're not worthy and so have a drive to prove ourself. Or we may have felt suffocated growing up. Or abandoned. And from these initial positions, we may develop and extend our own story as a victim or a hero. We may wind up seeking to be the golden child or running from being cast as the black sheep of the family.

Sometimes, we are thrust into the role of Atlas keeping the world of relationships as we know them on our shoulders and out of harm's way. And sometimes, our pain and trauma cause us to create a different story of life that we hope will protect us from being hurt again. At times, when scared or hurt enough, we desperately and secretly make bargains with the Universe in an attempt to advance our story. If my father will only respect me, I'll stop pretending to be other than I am. If I can just stop feeling lonely, I'll stop drinking.

At other times, we force our protective story of life on all we see. In an effort to protect ourselves, we keep reframing life—like a castle we keep building thicker and higher around us—until we cover life rather than reveal it. When I was a boy, I had a fear of dogs that grew from being bitten as a toddler. As a little boy, I also become afraid of dentists because of how blunt and hazardous our family dentist was. Somehow, I used these two fears as receptacles for all my fears.

Unconsciously, even as a boy, I bartered with the Universe, secretly asking, "If I put all my fears into dogs and dentists, will you let me live more freely, so I can take more risks everywhere else?" While this may have helped me get through adolescence, it exacerbated my real fears of dogs and dentists into phobias, which required great work to right-size later on.

My initial understanding of love is a good example of playing out an inherited story until suffering broke me from its spell. My mother was always behind the wall of her darkness and anger. I always thought she was on fire. So much so that I thought love meant trying to throw water on her. But there was never enough water. Then I thought that to love meant to live with darkness and anger and fire. I thought that to be a good partner or friend was to be a fireman.

In contrast, I came to learn that my father's mother was a strong matriarch, kind and benevolent. But I can see now, after they are all gone, that my father thought his mother was oppressive. And so, he went about creating his own story by loving my mother whom he found free and thrilling. Instead, he simply married the dark queen instead of the kind matriarch. And now, it's clear to me that in my first marriage, I married my mother. When leaving her, I thought I was creating my own story, though in my second marriage I wound up marrying my grandmother. It wasn't until I was on the other side of my cancer journey that I dropped below both stories and truly sought an equal partner. This led to my marriage with Susan.

I've learned over time that eventually, after we've struggled to endure and outlast the story we've inherited, the process of spiritual maturity has us put down even the story we've created, so we can inhabit our place in the greater, existing story of life. Putting down our story may happen when it proves false, or inadequate, or too brittle. Putting down our story may happen because of great love or great suffering, or because what we've imagined will no longer help us live.

This does not mean that we can skip over any of these phases. Being a Spirit in a body in time on Earth requires us to inherit a story at birth, to replace it with our own created story, and in time to put down our created story in order to enter a life-giving relationship with life on life's terms. This lifting up and putting down of stories is an inwardly developmental process that returns us on the other side of suffering to that original condition we inhabit at birth—with no preconceptions, no experience, no history, or expectations. We are returned to our direct experience of living.

But along the way, we need to understand what it's like to lose a story or to find that it has turned false. Just how do we know when a story no longer works and when it is keeping us from life rather than bringing us alive? This is the work of self-awareness: to discern between what is life-giving and what is life-draining. And whether we are under the weight of an inherited story or in the exhilaration of our own created story, it is all part of our journey to a deep acceptance of life through authenticity. Ultimately, a good life leads to a good death by eventually surrendering the stories we've inherited and constructed about life so we can accept our place in the mysterious timeless story of what is.

The process of spiritual maturity has us put down even the story we've created, so we can inhabit our place in the greater, existing story of life.

Questions to Walk With

- Describe the story of life you inherited.
- Describe the story of life you have created.
- Underneath these inherited and created stories, describe your sense of life as it is and your part in it.
- Finally, in a conversation with a friend or loved one, describe your evolution through these different phases of relating to life.

Falling In and Loving Through

My wife, Susan, and I have been together for twenty-nine years. We love each other dearly and know each other intimately. Like those who have lived within the rhythm of decades-long relationships, we understand that we inevitably move through periods of uneventful dailyness accented by illumined moments of remembering who we are to each other, marveling at how we've arrived here at all.

We were recently in New York City when I fell into such a moment. It led to this poem:

FINDING EACH OTHER

We're so desperate
to find someone, so we can
build a raft against the horrible

sea. And yet, through loving you,
I've learned to love the world.

Who would have guessed
that intimacy is a prism,
not a cave.

In caring for you, I've learned
how to care. And holding you,
I've learned how to hold. And
listening to your pain, I've
learned how to hear the
pain of the world.

So loving you has been
a threshold more than
a nest.

Who would have guessed
that caring enough to
lift each other, we begin
to lift the world.

It is astonishing but if we love long enough, we begin
to learn that "intimacy is a prism, not a cave." What often
starts as a refuge against a harsh world can, in time, become the lens through which we see the power and shimmer of all life.

When falling in love, we often make what we love our

entire world, and that enclosure, once enameled, can limit us and suffocate those we love. Yet, sometimes, if broken by suffering or blossomed by care, we can break through all our designs and protections to discover the whole world is carried in the tender truth of those we love.

When I examine my own flawed history of loving, it seems that I have often had to lose myself in order to find myself. That is, the cocoon, no matter how carefully woven, needs to be torn open to let our magnificent wings emerge.

But let's back up and reflect on our common struggle to love and not give ourselves away. Often, in learning how to care for others, we either remain guarded and self-centered or go the other way and lose who we are in the loving. When self-centered, our boundaries become too thick and hard. From the grip of this position, we half-love and life barely reaches us in what we think are muted tones.

Yet, when tumbling the other way, we can give too much of ourselves, until, like sand along the shore, we have no foundation. Then, loving becomes synonymous with self-sacrifice. Without any boundaries, loving another seems to always be life-draining and we begin to feel the pain and confusion of being inwardly bereft. In learning how to love, we struggle between these extremes.

We all know the myth of Midas where everything he touched turned to gold. Of course, while this made him rich, he could not eat or drink or be held by anyone he loved. In just this way, we start to make everything an extension of us when too guarded and too walled in. This is the Midas touch of narcissism—everything we touch becomes us.

The opposite is the reward for empathy and compassion. When letting the truth of others in, we start to become everything we touch. At best, we are informed and empowered by how we mix with other life.

Still, I think we all stumble through some developmental form of both: being self-centered for a time and being self-sacrificing for a time. Eventually, if we keep growing, the journey between having too many boundaries and having no boundaries becomes an apprenticeship in finding the health of true relationship, if we don't get stuck in either state.

In time, we are asked to establish porous boundaries through which we maintain who we are without shutting others out and without losing ourselves in the act of loving. If faithful to this unfolding path, we can discover the true authority of being that connects our soul to the timeless reservoir of all Spirit.

There are essential learnings that come from being drawn out of our extremely guarded, self-centered ways into serving the needs of others. But defining our worth by what we sacrifice for others is the other extreme. And with no direct sense of innate worth, we can fall into a personal darkness in which we become desperate for the love and approval of others. This only compels us to give away more of ourselves.

The truth is that being self-centered or self-sacrificing is debilitating, as both are equally unhealthy. But when led to the bottom of our experience, the ruin of all our schemes lands us in the tender bareness of being. Then, being broken of a self-contained sense of self or a self-sacrificing sense of self lets us receive the world freshly and nakedly, like Adam or Eve. Then, we start to discover that, rather than being our whole world, loving one person in particular is the practice ground for loving the entire world.

Shortly after our trip to New York City, I went to Pine Manor Retreat Center in Lake Elsinore, California, where I return to teach every year. It is an oasis of relationship. After dinner that first night, I entered a long conversation with my dear friends Gail and Rachelle about our apprenticeship in the lifelong practice of love.

It was a night of deep listening, as we spoke about times when we had given ourselves away and times when we had found ourselves because of the kindness of others. I woke the next morning with this poem:

INTRINSIC BRIGHTNESS

You can lose yourself in love
or find yourself. What we love can
become everything in which case we
spin endlessly, thirsting for someone
else's light to soften our darkness.

Or what we love can become the
veil we part to see and know what
holds the world together.

I know this because
I have done both.

And while making what I love
everything has kept me from my soul,
loving everything open, the way the
constancy of the sun opens flowers,
has allowed me to know the shimmer
where who I am is joined to
everything that ever lived.

Like it or not, it seems that *falling in* must come be-fore *loving through*. Falling into what? Our humanness. Until we love our way through. Loving through what? Our stubbornness and self-centeredness. Until we love our way into the surrender and acceptance that we need each other.

Much as we don't want to be sidetracked or derailed, it is the detours in life that reveal our teachers. All this to say, there is no shortcut to Wholeness, no skipping over the mess and magnificence of being human.

Repeatedly, the line between falling in and loving through is very fine. This is another way to describe the pull between addiction and wonder. When we fall into what we love as the solution to our loneliness, desperate for it to de-fine us or save us, we can become obsessed with what we love, dream, want, work at, build, use, eat, or consume—and whatever we hold on to will never be enough. Because nothing but our direct experience and acceptance of what lives within us and around us can be fulfilling. In this way, relying on the light and verve of other life while dismissing our own can lead us into the chaos of addiction.

Wonder, on the other hand, somehow makes us a conduit for the exchange of life-force as it moves from us into the world or from the world into us. And our ability to love is the gate that swings open to let life-force through.

Ultimately, the heart of relationship that we aspire to is always twofold. When wholehearted and authentic, our receptivity makes us clear as a still lake. In this way, we can mirror the other person completely and accurately, letting them know themselves in the reflection of our love. At the same time, our authenticity makes us transparent and see-through. With nothing in the way, our loved one can see all the way to our core and on into the essence of things. When both people are transparent and have nothing in the way, our very foundations of being can touch. Our relational work, then, is to be receptive and transparent. We stay receptive by listening to others. We stay authentic by listening to ourselves. We do the work of intimacy when listening to ourselves and others in a way that allows us to both reflect and be transparent.

Ready or not, we are called every day to enter the world, being neither completely self-defined nor completely other-defined. Every day, we are called to return to our simple, direct experience of life, loving whatever is before us until it opens, so it in turn can open us.

*Loving one person in particular is the practice
ground for loving the entire world.*

Questions to Walk With

- In your journal, describe where your boundaries
  are too thick and hard, keeping you from being
  fully alive. Then, describe where your boundaries are too thin, keeping you from maintaining
  your sense of self. How can you balance the two?
- In conversation with a friend or loved one, describe a time when you began to learn how to
  love the world through the healthy commitment
  of loving another. How does this experience differ from the experience of giving yourself away?
  What are the signs of loving healthfully and of
  giving yourself away? How can you nourish the
  healthy signs and change course when sensing
  the unhealthy signs?

When Faced with a Problem

The last thing I need when struggling is more of me.

—MN

When faced with a problem, I often zero in like a mechanic to look at the gears of the situation, to see what's caught or stuck or broken. Once looking that closely, I'm always surprised that the problem tends to feel bigger and more urgent than it is. I've often wondered why this magnification of trouble happens. The other day, it happened again. I had a difficult interaction with a friend and was looking at the gears of our relationship to see what was stuck or broken. As I kept going over the incident, more and more closely, it loomed so large that I couldn't think of anything else.

On the way to our kitchen, I began to wonder again why this keeps happening. Then, while reaching for a plate in the cabinet, I noticed that when you reach with your hand, your shoulder moves forward along with it. In that moment, it occurred to me that when our mind leans forward in discernment, it brings our heart along with it. And when the mind focuses and narrows its lens like a microscope, it pulls the heart into that narrow field of focus.

Once the heart is dragged into the narrowed field of focus, part of our practice is to give time and space and attention so the field of our heart can enlarge, so we don't stay small. Otherwise, decisions, problems, and situations narrow until they seem larger than they are, and our way in the world is colored with a sense of false urgency.

Over time, we are asked to develop a practice of focusing the mind while enlarging our heart. This way, we can see clearly what is before us and what needs our attention, while acting on the situation from a larger context of life.

Once we've seen a situation clearly and precisely, we have to find ways to let our heart regain the perspective of a unified view of life. The practice here is twofold. First, to recognize when our mental focus has dragged our heart along, making things too big and our heart too small. And secondly, to enlist the means by which we can restore our largeness of heart and meet the situation at hand.

We might restore our largeness of heart by sitting in silence, or walking in nature, or listening to music, or reading a favorite poem, or telling a favorite story, or talking with a friend, or learning something new, or by planting a bed of flowers. Only you will know the practice by which you can restore the largeness of your heart. How we re-animate our gifts when bent over by trouble is part of our personal practice of return.

Central to all efforts of return is that when overwhelmed

or mired in confusion or complexity, we need to re-enter our heart. Often, when stuck in our mind, no amount of similar thinking will calm us. As Albert Einstein said, "You can't solve a problem with the thinking that created it."

Clearly, the gift of consciousness is that, unlike other creatures, we can discern patterns and gather insights and weave those insights into meaning. When blessed, we can weave those meanings into wisdom. However, the liability of consciousness is that, if not kept fresh, our thinking hardens into assumptions and conclusions. Then, like plaque that hardens in our arteries, our assumptions and conclusions keep us from clear and direct living.

Unattended, assumptions and conclusions harden further into bias and prejudice and even hatred. Like plaque in our arteries, assumptions and conclusions make the heart work harder. If not broken up and cleared out, assumptions and conclusions become dangerous to our health. I invite you to personalize this by asking yourself: What practices enable you, in your life, to break up and clear out your assumptions and conclusions, so you can restore direct experience?

When tangled mentally, over-thinking can just tangle us more. So, try giving attention to anything nearby and it will relax the tension in your mind. Express the truth of your situation and it will give pause to the judgments in your mind. Try giving to anyone when tangled and it will undo the knot in your mind.

These acts of thoroughness can cleanse our eyes and ears, giving us fresh perspectives with which to engage what's before us. These acts of wholeheartedness can re-store our presence and direct experience of life. They give us access to life's unitive resources, which always wait below the tangle.

Another mental habit that tangles the mind away from the heart is our adherence to preferences. The more encumbered we are with preferences, the more muffled our heart becomes, as too many preferences layer themselves between us and our immediate experience of life. The fewer preferences we have, the more wholehearted we are. We will have likes and dislikes because we are human, but to install these likes and dislikes as prerequisites to our participation in life is limiting and draining.

I don't need five reviews to take a chance on a movie or a new restaurant. Or endless criteria to say hello. After all, you don't interview ambulance drivers, you take the first one to come along. So, when feeling gray and lonely and covered by our web of choices, we can suspend our want for a guaranteed good outcome and simply hold nothing back and lean into life, welcoming all experience—one more time. Being willing to be touched by life and being grateful for the whole spectrum of experience restores our aliveness.

One of the aims of self-awareness is to assess when we are stuck in our own experience or too removed from life. Being human, we all get darkly entangled in the judgments of others or the impact of powerful emotion. At other times, we stay too removed and skim over our experience.

Not wanting to feel what is ours to feel, we don't stay vulnerable and, therefore, we remain out of reach.

The challenge for each of us is to return to living at the pace of what is real where we are neither too mired in our experience nor too removed from life. We want to be centered enough to lift ourselves from the dark tangle of any one experience, but present enough and vulnerable enough to be touched and animated by other life. This is the transformative pace of authenticity, which no one can master but which everyone must engage. Again, I ask you to personalize this by entering the question: What are the specific skills in your life that can help you return to the pace of what is real when you stray?

And yet, when faced with an impending difficulty—a chronic illness or the loss of a job or a sudden change of life—it is a challenge not to empower the worst-case scenarios. But while it is natural to try on what might come to pass, doom is not inevitable, only possible. Our inner task is to neither be a stubborn optimist nor a recalcitrant pessimist.

In every situation, all things are possible but none are true—yet. The practice of thorough awareness is to try on all possible futures and then to return to what is known in the moment at hand. This represents the swing of an inner pendulum by which we rehearse where life might take us, but return to the truth of where we are with all its unknowns.

When I was first diagnosed with cancer, I had to try

on the possibility of my death, as well as the possibility of my being disabled. But there were infinite unknown steps between where I was and all those possibilities. I had to return to the present to find my way, a step at a time, to the one future that was mine.

This shift of perspective—from trying on where life might take us to returning to the moment at hand—is a practice we can develop over time. The effort to see things as they are helps us keep the present more empowered than the future. After all, the sea is propelled to the shore and not pulled to it. Likewise, it is the present that propels us forward into life, not the prospect of the future that pulls us into it. Being present drives all life.

Ultimately, we live in the endless corridor between what is life-giving and what is life-draining, between what is broken and what is Whole, and between what is known and what is possible. We stumble and veer but find our way in that corridor where what we touch and what touches us brings us alive and keeps us alive.

So, when confused, when unsure how to proceed, when things seem too complex to unravel, I return to this one question: Is what's before me heartening or disheartening? If it's heartening and life-giving, then I will see it through, even if it's difficult. But if it's disheartening and life-draining, then what am I doing there?

The word *trust* means "to follow your heart." And so, I encourage you to give attention to those small moments that stir you to follow your heart. Let those small moments lead you to the Teacher-Soul in you, the place where you feel the deepest. No need to do anything when you feel this place but to enter it the way a fish lets the stream carry it.

In truth, the more we hide, the more hidden we are. In truth, we do not arrive, we course-correct. So, never underestimate the light that lives within you, even, if for the moment, you can't find it. For though all is repeated, nothing is wasted. It's how the Universe inhales us and sends us on our way. And living wholeheartedly allows us to be the mysterious drop that enters the water. What happens next is just the ripple of you being you as you join with the world.

Over time, we are asked to develop a practice of
focusing the mind while enlarging our heart.

Questions to Walk With

- In your journal, describe a time when thinking your way out of a problem didn't work. What other ways of being did you turn to? What helped?
- In conversation with a friend or loved one, discuss a situation in which your assumptions and conclusions are preventing you from seeing your way through a difficulty. How might you dismantle your assumptions and conclusions in order to meet life freshly again?

In the Awakened Flow

The bee of the heart stays deep inside the flower,
and cares for no other thing.

—Kabir

You can't tell when strange things
with meaning will happen.

—William Stafford

By virtue of being human, we are asked to neither deny our suffering nor let our pain define us. When we deny our pain, our heart stops flowing. This can lead to emotional blood clots. When we let our pain define us, we can't stop bleeding. This in turn can lead to emotional hemophilia. Both are life-threatening. Somehow we need to stay *in the awakened flow*—between these extremes—which affirms that we are alive in our vulnerability *and* part of a larger current that carries us. When in the awakened flow, we are each a vessel for Spirit—able to carry a delicate and vibrant portion of being into the world.

In my own evolution of awareness, I have denied my suffering and let my pain define me many times. I have also experienced both resignation and sadness along the way. When first tripping into the vastness of life, I was uplifted and in awe. Then, I felt how small and insignificant one speck of being, like you or me, really is. This is where the resignation and sadness crept in, when feeling the vastness of but not our connection to the living Web of Life.

As I began to feel the Web of Life, I started to know my proper place in the Living Universe. This was heartening and remains so. But when we are at that intermediate stage of grasping the vastness but not yet inhabiting our connection to it all, it can render us infirm. For without feeling the presence of our connection to everything, we live on the edge of a cliff with no way off, able to see the vastness but with no way to join it and with nowhere to go. So, while I can't readily specify a word in English for this intermediate state of awareness, I can offer a phrase, in the spirit of Native American naming, that might point to it: edge-of-the-cliff-thinking-with-nowhere-to-go.

The word *conduit* means "to bring together." When the inner life and the outer world can move through us without impediment, we are a conduit for wakefulness. This is why I love being real with others. To be in a room full of tender souls exploring life with our common heart is like standing before a waterfall that has been wearing away the jagged edge of its face for years.

When I look back, I can see that from an early age I learned to protect the inner life by keeping the world's

imposition and undue influence at a distance while I engaged the depth of being as best I could. Now, later in life,
I'm learning that to fully engage that depth of being means
staying in relationship to all that is around me. I'm being
asked to let life *get closer.*

This shift reveals another law of spiritual physics: that
the deeper we're grounded in the Center of All Life, the
less we need to separate from other life; the deeper our
connection to Source, the more we can welcome the vari-
ety and diversity of all life; the more we stand in that depth
of center, the closer we can let life come. Conversely, the
less grounded we are, the more distance we need in order
not to lose ourselves. The less centered we are, the farther
away we need to keep other life, in order to maintain a
semblance of predictable structure in our world. The less
connected to Source we are, the more intolerant we are of
anything different.

At its knotted core, stubbornness is a compensation
for not being grounded in the Center of All Life, for not
being in relationship with the underlying authority of
being that connects all life. The need to be rigid outside
grows because there is no sense of foundation inside, as
if making things rigid will hold us up. The less centered
we are, the more we push in an effort to control events.
When pushing, we appear certain and are often imposing. When tending, we are inquiring and living into the
unknown. When we push without tending, that's when
things break.

The questions arise: Are you tending or pushing your

way through life? Are you unwavering and imposing or open and inquiring? How can you move from pushing to tending, from being prematurely certain to being inquisitive? How can you restore your direct experience of life and shed the patterns that others have instilled in you?

It's important to remember—no one has ever been here who is you. No one can discover what it means to be alive for you, in your time, with your spirit, in your body, on Earth now. Therefore, it's imperative to discern what parts of what we inherit are authentic and what parts are not. Only our direct immersion in life can show us the way.

In the South Indian Hindu tradition, *alvar* means "those who dive deep, those who are immersed." Ancient examples are the Twelve Alvars, the Tamil poet saints who remained immersed and devoted to the unseen masters who spoke to them through the Many Faces of the Universe, to land in their poems. In particular, they were immersed in their devotion to Vishnu, the preserver and protector of the Universe, who returns to Earth in troubled times to restore a balance between good and evil. These twelve poet saints, who lived between the seventh and ninth centuries, retrieved and compiled four thousand Tamil verses that form the sacred *Divya Prabandham.*

In the daily life of the soul, we are ordinary descendants of the Alvars, each of us an honest breath away from being one who dives deep, from being one who is immersed. It is this immersion into the depth of life that awakens our soul and makes the connection between things knowable. This immersion is our daily practice in being fully here.

Being one who dives and one who is immersed is how we become a conduit for wakefulness. So, what commitments can you make to the art of living that will keep you in the awakened flow, not denying your suffering and not letting your pain define you?

When we can dive and stay immersed in the awakened flow of life, we become preservers and protectors of the Universe in our small way. Being immersed in the depth of life is what allows us to be balanced.

We must pause here to offer a word about balance. Balance and the middle way are often misunderstood as a muting of passion or exuberance, when a deeper sense of the middle way involves opening our heart thoroughly in the middle of all directions like an inlet, letting the fullness of experience flow through us and around us, in order to soften and strengthen us at the same time. In this way, staying in the middle or center of the stream of life and opening our heart in all directions is essential to finding our place.

Spiritual balance, then, is a way to let the forces of life merge and integrate, rather than trimming the highs and lows off of deep feeling until we land in a muffled temperament. Balance is not a leveling of the heart, not a regulation of how much or how little we feel and express, but an *opening* of the heart in the middle of everything, so it can receive *all* the dimensions of life and integrate them in a way that releases their aliveness. So balance is not muting the degree to which we live, but integrating the full presence of all our capacities.

Instead of sorting, prioritizing, and analyzing, the heart is called to open like the timeless basin that it is, so that the disparate things of the world can simply merge as they move through us. In this way, Spiritual balance is more like pouring three different streams of water into one bowl, letting them merge and integrate into one complete water.

Two timeless qualities that help us stay in the awakened flow are blessing and responsibility. These are two faces of Spirit that move through us into the world. Often, one leads to the other. Facing inwardly, we discover and experience blessing, the emanation of being in which we feel the awakened flow of life wash over us. Facing outwardly, we experience responsibility, our ability to respond to the movement of life in the world. Being fully alive requires us to constantly turn blessing into responsibility, by turning love into care and truth into justice. Through blessing and responsibility, we remain a conduit for the awakened flow.

Another term for the awakened flow is *grace,* which is always present like the all-encompassing movement of the wind though no one can see it. Or the sway of the oceans around the planet. Ultimately, grace reveals itself when we inhabit the Web of Kinship that animates the Living Universe. The way a fish feels all aspects of the river for swimming completely where it is. The way a bird feels all aspects of the sky for flying completely where it is. We access grace by being real. Though it is important to remember that grace remains ever-present, even when we are estranged from ourselves. The way the current of the river is still moving, even when a swimmer refuses to jump in and swim.

And we are always challenged to jump in and swim. For embodiment is the practice of authenticity. It is akin to saying I *love you* rather than thinking it. It is how the heart moves into the hands. It is how we open our heart in the middle of everything.

A few years ago, I was guiding a retreat in the majestic woods north of Victoria at Royal Roads University in British Columbia. That first night we could hear the wind come in off the sea and bend the trees. Out of that great silence, a woman named Lydia said, "We all have the capacity to let the wind through." This is a simple and great truth that has always been known and which is often forgotten. The unseen world in its mysterious totality is always waiting like a secret wind hiding in the open. Beneath the noise of the world, the trees sway in silence. And beneath our stubbornness, truth moves through us like the wind through those trees.

I confess that I have stumbled and hoisted myself back into the flow of life countless times. Through it all, I have learned, more than once, that while being hardened will help us get through life, being softened will let us experience life. No matter how many times we fall asleep or are stirred awake, our recurring challenge is to endure the path, wherever it leads, so we can experience what matters.

By virtue of being human, we are asked to neither deny our suffering nor let our pain define us.

Questions to Walk With

- In your journal, describe one way you are pushing events in your life. Then, describe one way you are tending events in your life. What is leading you in each direction and what are you learning about pushing and tending?
- In conversation with a friend or loved one, describe a moment of blessing you have experienced in which you have felt the awakened flow of life wash over you. Then, describe a moment of responsibility you have experienced in which you have felt compelled to turn your love into care.

Now You Must Choose

My dear friend Don is an eighty-six-year-old painter who sketches the air when he talks. Tonight, as we gather, he pulls out his three oldest brushes, which he bought in 1960. The brushes are over sixty years old. They are beautifully worn, like us, and the bristles are rounded after years of dabbing and stroking on canvas after canvas. In his floating memory, he remembers being a young art student in New York City: "All I wanted to know was, 'Why am I here?' And all I wanted to do was paint."

He recalls how one night he came home and decided that he would light a candle and stare into it until he understood the meaning of life. Eventually, he fell asleep and the candle set the nearby lampshade on fire. He quickly knocked it to the floor and put it out. On the floor, where the burnt lampshade lay smoking, were three volumes on

Zen Buddhism by D. T. Suzuki. Don had been laboring his way through these books, but he exclaims, "I just couldn't get it." Then, he pulls out the books, which are as old as his brushes, and holds them before us like ancient, indecipherable runes.

Though he never finished the books, they and his brushes have been with him ever since. All this reminds me of the Three Brushes of Ōbaku (Ōbaku no Sanpitsu). They were three revered Zen teachers who lived in Japan in the 1600s, each a master calligrapher, one seeming to have taught the other. Sokuhi (1616–1671) was the youngest and perhaps the most accomplished poet and calligrapher among them.

In 1650 at the age of thirty-four, Sokuhi was badly burned while fighting a forest fire and nearly died from asphyxiation. It is said that, in the midst of the fire, he was suddenly enlightened. As the temple was burning, master Yuan stood before Sokuhi, flames everywhere, the forest crackling. With the empty temple waiting to be saved, master Yuan stood calm as a lake before dawn. With the flames getting closer, he spoke softly, "Now you have to choose, Sokuhi." A burning limb fell behind them. The master stepped closer and said, "Will you bring in there out here? Or keep watching from the rim?"

This lesson from across the centuries has stayed with me. And I think of my dear friend Don, so in love with life, as the Fourth Brush of Ōbaku, mesmerized by the fire within that never goes out. With his sixty-year-old brushes, he has spent his life bringing in there out here. I think of my dearest friends, companions on this journey to bring what matters into the world. Like orchids and peonies that unfold their magnificent color by turning inside out, we are meant to bring what is in—out, repeatedly. Then, hold each other up.

For when I am stalled, which is inevitable, it is my friends who stand before me, like Yuan before Sokuhi, speaking softly as the flames rise around us, "Now you must choose, my friend. Will you bring in there out here? Or keep watching from the rim?"

After sixty years, the handles of Don's brushes have worn to fit his hand, the way our face fits our soul after a lifetime of trying to be honest and loving. It is the dive for truth and the reach for each other that let us know we are alive.

This is our charge: to discover why we are here by being completely who we are and holding nothing back. We are forever mesmerized by the fire within that never goes out, while staring into candles that refuse to share their secrets. Yet when the temple bursts into flames, we are called, one more time, to show the strength of our care or watch the world burn.

It is the dive for truth and the reach for each other
that let us know we are alive.

Questions to Walk With

- In your journal, tell the story of a time when you were watching life from the rim of your inwardness. Then, tell the story of a time when you stepped into life, bringing what lives within you out into the world. Describe the difference between these two experiences.

- In conversation with a friend or loved one, tell the story of a tool or instrument or special book—like Don's brushes and books—that you have carried with you for a long time. Why have you carried these things for so long? What do they mean to you and how do they sustain you?

PART 2

The Deeper Teachers

Heroes didn't leap tall buildings or stop bullets with an outstretched hand; they didn't wear boots and capes. They bled, and they bruised, and their superpowers were as simple as listening, or loving. Heroes were ordinary people who knew that even if their own lives were impossibly knotted, they could untangle someone else's.

—Jodi Picoult

• • •

Like it or not, fear, pain, and grief offer us sacred ground on which to practice falling down and getting up. What we learn here is crucial to how we survive and thrive. For facing fear, pain, and grief only brings the art of living into sharp relief. The truth is we all have to endure the extreme experiences in being alive, every day. And the art of living requires us to stay present to all that happens while leaning into all that has yet to happen, not making a refuge of either, but letting the forces of love and suffering merge within us.

In this part of the book, we will explore these

deeper teachers—fear, pain, and grief. As we listen for their truths, let's admit that no one knows how to do this. Then, we can keep each other company. For fear, pain, and grief are, at once, heartbreaking and transformative, if we can face what is ours to face and hold each other up.

So be gentle with yourself as we make our way here together. Go at your own heart's pace. Enter the things you can now and bookmark the things that feel too difficult, so you can enter them later. There is no one way to do this. But do it we must.

The Life After Tears

Some things cannot be fixed. They can only be carried.

—Megan Devine

My dear friend Paul lost his wife, Linda. Their love was deep and he has fallen into a chasm of grief. Over thirty years ago, Paul helped save my life when I struggled with cancer. And so, it is an honor to walk this chasm with him. In doing so, he offers up wisdom after wisdom through his pain. He speaks of losing Linda as being forced to live with what is unacceptable.

A few months after Linda's death, Paul came to stay with us and we would get up early each morning and have coffee in my study. On the third morning, he talked about how his heart has been cracked open into the life after tears. We began to explore how tenderness and the truth of living inside out are only possible in the life after tears.

This notion of being permanently opened by life rang true for me. It echoed and affirmed my own experience on the other side of cancer. It is only after being broken of our will that we cooperate with life rather than try to control it.

We sipped our coffee and it was clear to me that Paul was more tender. He stared off and, through his tears, felt completely bereft that he would never be able to share this newfound tenderness with Linda, which was painfully brought into the open by losing Linda. Our hearts were breaking in ever new ways. This is what walking in the chasm of grief with another is like: stepping in the bottom of the ravine, winded, feeling their heart and yours break again and again until wonder and grief are indistinguishable. Until there is nothing left to say, only to walk, side by side, and to sit together, when we can no longer walk.

Ever since that morning, the notion of the life after tears has become part of our spiritual vocabulary, signifying a transformative threshold that everyone will have the chance to cross into a more ordinary and luminous existence. Before crossing this threshold, we bounce about like coconuts with our sweetness trapped inside our hardened shell. But in the life after tears, the sweet milk flows beyond our control, in the open for others to drink. This is the miracle of how we can become a sweetness that spills everywhere.

In truth, when we deny the breaking of our shell, we only dream of sweetness and never taste it. This is an ancient truth, referred to in the Gnostic Gospels, the fifty-two texts discovered in Nag Hammadi, Egypt, that include poems and myths attributed to the followers of Jesus, which are quite different from the New Testament:

If you bring out what is inside of you,
What is inside you will save you.
If you fail to bring out what is inside you,
What is inside you will destroy you.

It is in the life after tears that we are blessed to help each other bring out what is inside of us. We cannot plan such an opening. We can only encourage each other to bring out what we find once opened. As if our life depends on it. Because it does.

As if this rite of passage by which we become fully alive isn't difficult enough, there is the resistance of those who fear such open living. As Paul crosses his chasm of loss, some of those around him are uncomfortable with the rawness and duration of his grief. One old friend blurted out, "You gotta move on!"

Painfully, rather than admit his own fear of the depths where life can take us, this old friend pathologized Paul's grief. Rather than admit his own discomfort with pain, loss, and grief, he tried to make it about Paul. He could have said, "I'm afraid of the depth of your grief, but I am here. Teach me about grief." He could have said, "I don't know what to say or do, but I will walk with you." That life opens its chasms before us in inevitable. The true test of friendship is whether we walk through those chasms together, not knowing how to do so.

I have experienced such cold distancing as well, losing friendships when fear outsized love. The truth is it's next to impossible to live this tender life alone. We need the loving truth of others to cross the chasms of pain and grief. Inevitably, some come with us and are forever changed while others watch as we struggle. It's the power of love that enables those who come along, where a language of experience is unearthed that can't be translated to those who stay behind.

As I mentioned in the beginning of this book, eventually, everyone will be dropped into the depth of life. The perennial questions remain: Will we meet that depth and will we help each other cross into that depth?

In the very center of his epic journey in *The Divine Comedy,* Dante comes upon a wall of fire. He is afraid to go any farther. At this crucial moment, his spirit guide, Virgil, appears, declaring, "It is the fire that will burn, but will not consume. You must go through it." Dante is stunned but still afraid. At this, Virgil hovers closer and repeats, more firmly, "It is the fire that will burn, but will not consume. You must go through it." Seeing Dante's fear grow, Virgil adds, "I will meet you on the other side." Then, he vanishes.

With this assurance, Dante summons his courage and dives through the wall of fire. And what Virgil said was true. Though he is nicked and even burned, Dante has more than survived. He is now whole. But he never sees Virgil again. Because by moving through the fire of transformation, Dante has become his own guide.

Being dropped into the depth of life is meeting the wall of fire, no matter how it appears. And life on the other side of the wall of fire is humble, tender, and forever vulnerable. Life on the other side of the wall of fire is the life after tears. And while we can be like Virgil for each other, no one can go through the fire of transformation for us. We can only walk in friendship through the chasms of grief and loss together.

After Paul went home, I sat in my study and stared at the rocker in which he sat, where we came upon the phrase *the life after tears*. It led me to this poem:

THE LIFE AFTER TEARS

In the life before tears,
there are endless plans
and we avoid the difficult
feelings at all cost, as if grief,
pain, and loss are canyons we'll
never be able to climb out of.

But, then, one day, while
not looking, someone dear
dies, or a dream breaks like
a plate, and our world, as
we've known it, is blown
apart.

Then, we discover that
falling in the canyon is
our initiation, and
the river at the bottom
is the only water that
will keep us alive.

I wish it were different.
But the reward for being
hollowed out is that the
song then sings us.

Perhaps you recognize this tender clearing. Perhaps you recognize the fire that will burn but not consume. Perhaps you are hesitant to have your heart broken open. It is not ours to choose when this will all transpire, but only to love each other deeply enough that we find the strength to meet that depth together.

It is in the life after tears that we are blessed to help
each other bring out what is inside of us.

Questions to Walk With

- In your journal, tell the story of someone you have become close with for sharing either their grief or yours. How did this experience bring you closer?
- In conversation with a friend or loved one, describe a wall of fire you are facing. Explore what is calling you to cross this and what is holding you back. How are you being asked to grow?

Inside Fear

*Courage is not the absence of fear, but rather
the judgment that something else is
more important than fear.*

—Ambrose Redmoon

I know a great deal about fear because, like so many of us, I have spent a lot of time in my life being afraid. I've come to understand it is not the appearance of fear that is crippling but the added weight we give it, how we let fear permeate everything in our attempt to be rid of it.

The legitimate role of fear is, of course, to alert us to real danger. But we, in our humanness, exaggerate the sense of danger, hoping that more caution will protect us. When I burn myself on a stove, I note how much distance I need from the flame to be safe. Being afraid, though, I take the actual distance needed to be safe and add a few inches, just to be extra careful.

The problem arises when I believe that the added distance is what is necessary to be safe. Now, though what is dangerous is farther away, the circle of isolation necessary to feel safe is larger. However, this added distance doesn't always make me *feel* safe. So, I add more distance to what I think is necessary in order to alleviate my fear. And my circle of isolation grows even more. This inflation of fear goes on until I am both afraid and lonely.

There is an important distinction between the actual ring of safety between us and danger and the ring of fear we keep inflating in order to *feel* safe. How, then, do we stop inflating our fear without being careless? We are challenged to see things as they are. This is the art of return, the practice of right-sizing what frightens us.

During the early days of my cancer journey, I was terrified of everything. I had been through very little up until then, and so, everything was alarming. Eventually, I exhausted my heart. I couldn't keep up with the extreme alarm. I finally had to learn how to see what was before me more accurately, so I could meet it with the appropriate amount of energy. This also gave me space to let other resources in, such as light, beauty, and the generosity of others. All of which began to heal me. This journey of integration awaits everyone. Letting life in right-sizes danger.

In very precise ways, as we have noted, fear gains its power from not looking. Consider the proverbial boogeyman in the closet. The longer we don't look, the bigger the boogeyman gets. Until some kind grandfather or aunt takes us by the hand, saying, "Well, why don't we take a look in there, together?"

Once the door is open, the closet appears dark but,

with the comfort of another, we begin to see that the closet is empty. In time, the very dark of the closet begins to lighten. Now, the quality of light in the closet hasn't changed. Rather, our eyes have become accustomed to the dark. Once accustomed to the dark, more is visible.

A crucial skill in meeting fear resides in this simple story. For a steadfast way to right-size our fear is to out-wait the potency of our not looking. Once accustomed to the weight and darkness of our fear, the situation lightens and more is visible. So much depends on our courage to look and wait.

Fear also gets its power from the future and the past. The moment we are in, even if painful, is known, and so is hard to distort. When I fear that a painful moment will not end, then the future expands my fear into a sense of terror, in which I dread being trapped in this difficult moment forever. Or a moment of pain or difficulty can be unbridled by a fear of the past repeating itself. When I was younger, I had the nerve of a tooth go bad. It was extremely painful. And while I have never had a tooth behave quite like that again, any time I have a toothache, my fear of that early experience repeating itself takes over, filling me with unfounded fear.

All this to say that, as natural as it might be to exaggerate any moment we are in, we need to return to the circumstance at hand, in its precise integrity, so we can let the moment be exactly what is—no more.

When I can let things unfold as they are, I can see that fear has its normal rhythm as one of the many forces of life that open and close. Just as we inhale and exhale, as our eyes open and close, as the valves in our heart open and close, our sense of safety and danger opens and closes. We suffer greatly when we don't let this normal rhythm progress.

We cannot eliminate fear, only let it normalize by running its course. In my heightened moments of fear, I try to remember that fear is to be moved through and not obeyed. Two great lessons I have learned from fear come from my cancer journey, one from the beginning and one near the end.

When thrust into a gauntlet of tests and biopsies, I was overwhelmed with fear. I had never been through anything life-threatening and was sorely unable to cope. Everything made me jumpy. I was at a loss how to continue. It was then that Tu Fu, the great Chinese poet of the Tang Dynasty, visited me in a dream.

He was sitting cross-legged on a shore, drawing in the sand with a broken branch. I rushed up to him and asked intensely, "How do I block the fear?" He ignored me. It made me angry. I went closer and demanded, "How do I block the fear?!" Without looking at me, he waved the branch above him and said, "How does a tree block the wind?" And with that, he disappeared.

And I woke up, startled by the truth that a tree doesn't block the wind. It lets it through. Ever since, I have tried to accept that we can't block fear. We can only let it through.

The second lesson came about six years after the heat

of my cancer journey. I was taking a shower when I felt a bump in the scar on my head. For a cancer survivor, a pimple escalates into a tumor in a heartbeat. I felt my adrenaline rush as I pressed the tiny bump where the tumor had been. With the lightning speed of terror, I had lived into the worst. What if this was a recurrence? I didn't need a wakeup call. I was already awake. What if I needed another surgery? I began to sweat. My heart kept pounding. What if I needed chemo again and it didn't work? What if, this time, I was to die? In thirty seconds, my fear had raced through an improbable but entirely possible future.

I felt the water running on my head. I remember thinking, "If this is it, what will I do?" I felt love and gratitude sweep through my heart. And in that illumined moment, I thought, "If all of this is true . . . I will finish my shower." My fear had played itself out into acceptance. For there is nowhere more holy than where we are. This is the strongest antidote to fear—to live our life to the fullest in the moment we are in.

Fear gains its power from not looking.

Questions to Walk With

- In your journal, describe one fear that has your attention. Where does this fear reside in you? Describe the place nearest you that is free of fear. Begin a conversation between the place in

you that is afraid and the place near you that is
free of fear.

- In conversation with a friend or loved one, describe your history with fear. What has been the
greatest lesson fear has taught you? And what has
been the greatest challenge fear has given you?

Right-Sizing Our Pain

Stop hiding. It only prolongs the pain.

—from the movie *Shang-Chi and the Legend of the Ten Rings*

Pain is knowledge rushing in to fill a gap.

—Jerry Seinfeld

No one wants pain but it is inevitable, like gravity. And so, we need to work with it. At once, pain humbles us and reminds us that no one can do it alone. The truth is that suffering is to humans what erosion is to nature. In time, life wears away all that is not essential until we are reduced to joy. Through my own suffering, I've learned that, if we can stay true to our experience and to each other, and face the spirit that experience and love carry, we will eventually be reduced to joy. Like cliffs worn to their beauty by the pounding of the sea, if we can hold each other up, all that will be left will be wonder and joy.

Like it or not, fear, pain, and grief are agents of this erosion. They are, at once, constant obstacles and constant teachers. Resist or not, we tumble into existence, trying to sustain the wonder of first arriving, trying to ride the angel of life when in time we have to accept that the angel of life rides us.

Each of us is gifted and desperate and the great battle is to dive through our desperation into our gift. This is the journey of the native self: to pass by the dragon and, most of all, to stop being the dragon. No matter how we twist or dream, the indifference of all this beauty says, "You are not little gods, but many chambered gates. If you stay open, I will flood you with all you need."

All things join in the flow of life. In this regard, turbulence and peace are inseparable, as are pain and ease. As far back as 2500 BC in Mesopotamia, humans have expressed the want to set aside our difficult teachers, such as fear, pain, and grief. Our very human frailty has always pined for the ease of conflict-free days. However, the resources of life are of a Whole, only restorative in their unity.

Consider the mystery of water. It is comprised of hydrogen and oxygen (H_2O). And yet, were I to ask for a glass of hydrogen, it would no longer be water and no longer be quenching or life-sustaining. It is the unified mix of hydrogen and oxygen that creates the element we know as water. Likewise, even though we would like to drink of life without its difficult teachers, this would prove impossible. Even if we could, the waters of life would no longer be whole and no longer be life-sustaining.

It is not by accident that the root of the word *suffer* means "to feel keenly." And the lessons of life show us quickly that to know love and beauty, you must also feel keenly. Ultimately, it is our depth of sensitivity that allows us to access the Unitive Whole of Life. This unending depth is what is life-sustaining. So, as the great poet of the interior Rainer Maria Rilke said, "Let everything happen, beauty and terror. No one feeling is final. Keep going."

How Does It Taste?

But how do we negotiate the deeper teachers when they are so difficult? I'm reminded of an ancient, anonymous teaching story from India. An aging Hindu master grew tired of his apprentice complaining, and so, one morning, sent him for some salt. When the apprentice returned, the master instructed the unhappy young man to put a handful of salt in a glass of water, and then to drink it.

"How does it taste?" the master asked. "Bitter," spit the apprentice. The master chuckled and then asked the young man to take the same handful of salt and follow him. The two walked in silence to a nearby lake, and once the apprentice swirled his handful of salt in the water, the old man said, "Now drink from the lake." As the water dripped down the young man's chin, the master asked, "How does it taste?" "Fresh," remarked the apprentice. The master looked at his apprentice and firmly said, "Stop being a glass! Become a lake!"

I recall telling this story to residents at Indiana University Medical School, when a young Hindu woman said, "My grandfather told me that story when I was a little girl." What this passed-on piece of wisdom suggests is that the pain of life is our handful of salt. Everyone gets their handful of salt. But the amount of bitterness we taste depends on the container we put the pain in. So when in pain, the only thing we can do is to enlarge your sense of things. Become a lake.

You may hear this story and think, well, being a glass isn't good. I won't do that again. But we all will, because this is how pain says hello, by constricting and making our aperture to life small. An essential part of being human is learning how to become a lake.

What, then, do you do when pain makes you small? What is in your toolbox that can help you enlarge your sense of things? Do you befriend silence and meditate? Do you talk to a loved one? Do you listen to that piece of music that touches your heart? Do you write or draw or paint or dance or go outside and garden? Do you read that favorite passage that reminds you what it means to be alive? What can you learn that will enlarge your sense of things?

The other response to pain, that is so understandable and all too human, is becoming stubborn and intransigent when we resist what comes our way. In the Buddhist view, such resistance only doubles our pain. Imagine an ant trying to stop the Earth from rotating on its axis. This is how overmatched we are by the turn of the Wheel of Life. As Oprah Winfrey says, "All pain is the same. We just choose different ways to release it."

When I was being wheeled into surgery during my cancer journey, I had a vision while looking up at the fluorescent lights in the hall of the hospital. At first, I saw a winter scene in which an old tree fell into a frozen river and both the tree and the river shattered. Then, I saw the same scene in springtime. But when the same tree fell into the flowing river, neither the tree nor the water shattered. The water flowed around the fallen tree.

As I was lifted from the wheeling bed to the pre-operating table, I realized that to resist the pain was to be a frozen river. I would only shatter. Ever since, I have tried to be like water when meeting pain.

These deeper stances—to enlarge our sense of things, to be like water, to move with the Wheel of Life—help us to right-size pain when we meet it. How, then, can you personalize these deeper stances?

In the Native American tradition, shamans and healers would ask four diagnostic questions when meeting with someone who was ill and in pain. They would ask: When was the last time you sang? When was the last time you danced? When was the last time you told your story? And when was the last time you listened to the stories of others? These are timeless ways to enlarge your sense of things.

Bad Needles

As difficult as it is to face pain, we also have to be aware of when we bring needless suffering to ourselves. I had a profound teaching moment in this regard during one of my medical procedures.

I was on an examination table with an IV needle in my left arm. It was nothing serious, but my wife, Susan, was concerned. Some test was being done. Someone was next to me, also having blood drawn. The nurse was busy with this other person. My arm was sore from the needle and my bicep was beginning to swell. Susan noticed the swelling and said, "Something's wrong. Why don't you tell the nurse?" I said, "No. It's nothing serious. They just didn't do a good job of putting the needle in. It's alright." The nurse, without looking up, jiggled the tube collecting my blood, while treating the other patient. I said, "Thank you." She said, again without looking up, half sarcastically, and half in admiration, "We treat him like hell and he thanks us." Part of me took it as a compliment. But Susan was furious.

Now, all these years later, I realize that, for much of my life, I have accepted bad needles and said it is alright. I'm almost polite, accepting ill treatment in order to be seen as good and kind. I feel, all too often, that if I say the needle has been put in badly, I'm causing trouble or being ungrateful or complaining. Worse, there have been times I've pretended that there isn't even a needle stuck in me, so as not to hurt the one poking. For the first time, I see how I've colluded in my suffering. Like a fish who dreams the hook will save him.

Living is hard enough without vanishing from the journey, without apologizing for feeling keenly along the way. Loving your self requires not accepting bad needles. Loving life means voicing the truth of our experience. There are no shortcuts. You have to live through the dark to wake in the light. You have to swim across the sea of *no* to land on the shore of *yes*. You have to break all certainty to find the pearl encased in your tenderness. Shells are meant to incubate, not last forever. Like dreams or wounds or beliefs. These are shells too. Not meant to live in but to shed like cocoons. If not, the soul will earthquake through the walls we cling to.

There is another deep metaphor at work in being human. The only way to speak of it is to recall how original flutes were carved in prehistoric times from mammoth bones. A bone would be hollowed out with holes carved into the hollow. No two carved flutes would be the same. And so, no two flutes would release the same song. Every soul on Earth is such an original flute. And like it or not, experience carves holes in us, so that the breath of life can release our unique song through the holes. This is a deep and enduring purpose of suffering, which no one has to seek and which no one can avoid. We can only hold each other up while experience carves its holes in us and rejoice in hearing each other's song.

Pain remains a deep and unwanted teacher, one we must not resist or collude with. Along the way, people we love fall from the tightrope of life and vanish and we wonder, why not me? Then, there is a pandemic and thousands cough and die with no warning. Or we simply grow old and the view widens as the path narrows. As if we're dancing on the edge of a cliff. But it has always been this way. We are only now aware of it. This is what the ancients were honoring when they painted their faces and danced around the fire. As if pain is the bark and joy is the sap.

What other dance is there?

*In time, life wears away all that is not essential
until we are reduced to joy.*

Questions to Walk With

- In your journal, surface and give voice to the most pressing question you have for each of these deeper teachers: fear, pain, and grief. What is it you need to know about each?
- In conversation with a friend or loved one, describe a bad needle you are accepting. Describe how you are colluding in your own suffering.

The Heart of Grief

You don't need to know people in order to grieve with them.
You grieve with them in order to know them.

—Valarie Kaur

The heart of grief is not repairable. When we lose someone or something dear, the old world is gone. The landscape as we've known has blown up. Therefore, our old maps, no matter how dear, are no longer useful, because they are no longer accurate. And so, just when we can't bear to meet the world, we are forced back into the world in order to make new maps. But the depth of loss tears open a ravine in us and life seems uncrossable. Yet somehow, we have to try to map the ravine.

To be sure, grief can be engendered by any form of death: the death of a loved one, the death of a marriage, the death of a family, the death of a way of life, the death of a dream, the death of a self, or the death of a friendship. In the last fifty years, the understanding of grief has evolved to include more ambiguous losses, such as a loss of place, a loss of time, a loss of opportunity, or a loss from being disenfranchised.

Being thrust into the realm of loss and grief causes us to live in between worlds. The world as we've known it is nowhere to be found and we're not yet in the new world. My old friend Gail Warner speaks of this in-between time as the pull on the living into the netherworld. When Hades, the Greek god of the Underworld, would take a soul with him, all those connected to that person would feel a pull into the Underworld. This pull was known as grief.

Imagine Hades pulling the roots of a giant tree further underground. All the boughs and branches can't help but be drawn deeper into the earth. Likewise, when a soul is lost and brought into the netherworld, those who love that person can't help but be drawn deeper and closer to death themselves. In this way, grief can be understood as the struggle to mourn those we lose while still staying committed to life. For the time of grief, which can know no end, we are caught living between worlds—feeling pulled in both directions—with one foot in the netherworld and one foot in the days to come.

Still, as the old cliché holds, it is better to have loved and lost, than to never have loved at all. This is achingly true. If you love, you will know loss. And if you don't love, what's the point in being here? Yet how do we go on living when who or what we love has died? For all the myths and stories that have been told for centuries, no one really knows. In truth, no one quite knows how to navigate the in-between world or how to return to life fully.

Those we love and lose become an indelible presence in our lives like shadows cast by trees on the brightest of days; there for a long moment and, then, seemingly gone when clouds appear. I carry the wavering shadow of so many in this way: my father and his love of wood; my Grandma Minnie who was sturdy as a redwood; Susan's mother, Eleanor, whose voice was gentle as a feather; my mentor and friend Joel whose love of light survived the Holocaust; and our beloved dog Mira; and even my contained and angry mother who I could never quite understand. And there is my great-grandmother Bella, who set foot in America at the age of sixty-five. And now, Paul's wife, Linda.

The initial ripping away of someone we love is like having part of our heart amputated, like having an arm or leg removed that we still feel but can't find. And just as amputees still reach for what is missing, we reach for those now gone. How can they be gone when we still feel them so near?

During my cancer journey, I had a rib removed from my back. When first waking after surgery, it felt like a corset was tightening around my chest every time I took a breath. I couldn't imagine living this way. In the months that followed, I found that when I focused on it, it would become more acute. But, after a few years, the tightness began to merge with my breathing. After a decade, I came to understand the pain of my missing rib as a form of grief that never went away. It only diminished in its intensity as the years went by. I have come to experience my grief for people in a similar way. It's been thirty-five years since I had that rib removed and, all these years later, I can't recall what breathing before the loss felt like. I only know that the tightness when breathing has been subsumed by this new feeling of breathing that has become my new normal. I think, over time, grief thins like this.

I also recall, when healing from my surgeries, looking in the backyard where I lived. There was an old twin oak. And strangely, there was a piece of barbed wire knit into the trunk of the tree. At one time, that piece of wire was loose. But over the years, the twin tree had grown around it, subsuming the wire. Seeing this made me realize that the wire of loss lives inside the tree of our heart. As we heal, as we learn how to go on, the wire of loss is knit into the very tissue of our heart.

All this to say that we don't overcome grief but grow our lives more completely in a way that incorporates the loss into our sense of living. Somehow, we are challenged not to get past our grief, but to love life enough that our life-force becomes large enough to encompass and integrate our loss. As time goes by, the one lost is knit more into us. It's forty-five years since my beloved Grandma Minnie died. With each year, I feel closer to her. And with each year, it is harder to conjure her physical features. Though I am ever more intimate with the scent and flavor of her soul.

In truth, mourning those I've lost has brought into view another paradox about heartache and grief. It seems the tears caused by our heartbreak water what's exposed in the break, helping to grow what has never seen the light in us. This is another law of spiritual physics that no one can avoid or plan—an inner form of gravity. If we don't run from what has been opened.

The Underlying Absence

Grief and resilience live together.

—Michelle Obama

When facing the enormity of having lost someone dear, the underlying absence is unrelenting and everywhere: in the closet, in the bathroom, in the favorite glass sitting in the kitchen cabinet, in all the trips taken, and in all the trips never taken.

Even months later, the acute depth of grief can come on like a tooth whose nerve has gone bad. Without notice, a deep shot of absence can course through our entire being. It is alarming and the after ache and throb can take a good long while to subside. No one can predict when that nerve will act up and bring us to our knees. Grief can rise up like this. And the acuteness of the grief is in direct proportion to the depth of the love that is lost.

So, when walking through the chasm of our grief, letting in other life becomes essential in order to mitigate the unbearable truth of loss, which is never far from the surface. When living with our grief, engaging in tasks, conversations, and events as life goes on is not a distraction but a commitment to letting other life in. For it is the inevitable mixing of other life with our grief that recasts the world in a way that lets us slowly move into tomorrow.

However, if we refuse to face the enormity of our grief, then diversion becomes outright denial, which simply buries the truth of what life has opened in us. Denial only makes the potency of our grief worse and prolongs the time needed to re-enter life. Other life is only a distraction when running from our loss.

When facing our grief, we somehow grow closer to those who loved the one we lost. When a link is removed from a chain, the chain falls apart. But paradoxically, when the remaining links are rejoined, the chain is closer and stronger. This speaks to the web of relationship among those who share the loss of someone dear. Once that beloved one is gone, the chain of relationship falls apart. However, if the truth-work of facing loss and grief is done together, the chain can be reconnected in a new way that is strangely closer and stronger, because it is built on the shared grief of the one who connected everyone in the first place. The web of relationship will never be the same, but it can be remade by honoring the love of the one who is lost.

Yet whether alone or with others, the painful journey of grief seems to grow ever more subtle. About our awakening, Ram Dass said, "You may have expected that enlightenment would come like *zap*! Instantaneous and permanent. This is unlikely. After the first 'aha,' it can be thought of as the thinning of a layer of clouds."

I think that the ongoing journey of grief mirrors this

notion but in the opposite direction. In time, our grief doesn't disappear but thins like a layer of dark clouds that colors our sense of reality.

What Is Next?

In the depth of grief, these questions are inevitable: How can I ever move forward? What kind of life awaits? Will I ever know joy again? But these are questions that have no answers. Rather, they open us to a deeper relationship with the unknown, where we're challenged to give up finding an answer and to accept each unexpected step as our teacher.

Once thrust into the life after tears, joy as we have known it seems to be redefined. More than a peak mood of contentment or happiness, joy becomes more like the ocean of being that holds all the waves of feeling.

Once on the other side of loss, emotions never seem to be singular again. It's like pouring a cup of blood into the ocean. The sea and all its waves will forever have a tint of red. And so, loss colors the Ocean of Being and the thousand waves that we call feelings. Likewise, once we experience all-encompassing joy, it, too, will color our days. But this is like pouring a cup of light into the Ocean of Being. The sea and all its waves then have a tint of luminescence. In just this way, joy and sorrow color our very being, allowing all feelings to merge, bringing us ever closer to life.

In this raw and integrated realm, we tend to experience more than one feeling at a time. We can feel sadness while also feeling beauty. We can feel deep contentment while being agitated. We can even feel clear and confused at the same time. Ultimately, being broken open broadens and deepens the range of what the heart perceives and feels. While this is unfamiliar ground, it is not problematic but growthful. Before experience deepens us, we use only half of what the heart is capable of.

In this newfound depth, the heart is asked to feel, hold, and embrace the many aspects of life all at once. In this way, grief and wonder cause the heart to grow in its mystic dimensions as we become more and more versed in a deeper logic of the heart that is released by experiential wholeness.

This is the world of paradox, where we no longer live in one aspect of reality. Now, we are challenged to no longer waste energy trying to move from one feeling to another, such as running from sadness to happiness. Rather, we are called to be present to many feelings and thoughts at once until Wholeness is our teacher.

Once thrust into the grip of loss, nothing is the same. Beyond the rawness of having our heart ripped open by the absence of someone we love who we will never see again, there is no going back to what was and no normal to return to.

Instead, the days ebb and flow as grief keeps mixing with life, coloring everything around us. Until a new whole—composed of grief and life—is stirred in our consciousness. In the same way that the line of shore forever shifts as the tide comes in and out, grief and life erode and remake the line between worlds. What once was submerged is now visible and what once was visible is now submerged. This is how life goes on. There is no resolving grief, no climbing over it. But more, life is reconstituted against our will.

Ultimately, grief recasts how we see and experience life. And when time has its way with us, we somehow let other life in. Until the abundance of life, even when unwanted, begins to absorb our grief and loss. So we can go on, as best we can.

Punctured by a Holiness

I had just had my first chemo treatment at Columbia Presbyterian Hospital in New York City. We then stayed overnight in a Holiday Inn, where I became very sick, vomiting every twenty minutes. Finally, just before dawn, in the heart of my pain and fear, I was suddenly aware that other life was going on. Somewhere nearby, a baby was being born. And somewhere nearby, a couple was making love for the first time. And elsewhere, a father and son were reconciling after years of not talking to each other. In my exhaustion, I realized that to be broken is no reason to see all things as broken.

It is the same with grief. Though we can never be free of the loss, life goes on. And though I may be in constant grief, there is laughter and conversation and someone is mowing their lawn while someone else is wrapping a gift. We have no choice but to honor those who are gone while letting life continue. Not trying to sort or prioritize the two, but letting them merge. Inevitably, the sea right-sizes the wave. The sky right-sizes the storm. And life right-sizes our grief.

During my cancer journey, I fell in love with a dear soul, Nur, who struggled through many recurrences and surgeries. She outlived so many death calls that we magically thought she was somehow immortal. When she died, I was stunned and totally bereft. I had seen her the day before. As I put down the phone, I realized how beautiful the day was. I didn't want it to be so. But the light was mercilessly beautiful, as if to say, "Do whatever you have to do, traverse whatever darkness you find yourself in, but I will be here no matter what." This was my first initiation into the remedy of Wholeness.

Yet, I still can't delete the phone numbers of those I've lost. And my father's tools—his calipers and T-square and awl—sit on my desk as I write this. And in the corner on my bookcase is the small glass Ganesh that the folks at Apple Farm gave me after Helen Luke died. It was on her dresser.

And when I was in Prague, in the Jewish quarter, unable to comprehend the enormity of grief metastasized by the Holocaust, I stood in the Pinkas Synagogue, the only synagogue with an empty ark, built as a living memorial to the eighty thousand Czech Jews killed in the camps. The walls were lined with all their names. Too large a grief to hold. And I leaned against a wall, compelled to focus on one name, any name. Tillie Fischlova, thirty-eight, transported April 4, 1943. I couldn't stop staring at her name. Was she married? Alone? What foods did she like? Did she have a sweet voice? What barracks was she in? Hundreds of children drew art in the camps, made dolls and toys, sang and danced. Did Tillie have a child? What did her child draw?

Earlier, I mentioned that the oldest narrative we have— the story of Gilgamesh, told five thousand years ago, and carved in clay tablets in ancient Assyria—speaks of the never-ending impact of grief. If you recall, when King Gilgamesh loses his only friend, Enkidu, to a war the stubborn king created, he seeks to have his friend resurrected by the Immortal One, Utnapishtim. And the enervated, grief-stricken king is led on a long, arduous journey to meet with the Immortal One. When finally before Utnapishtim, Gilgamesh pleads his case, demanding to be free of his grief. And Utnapishtim chides him, saying, "How dare you? You are human. You will want to remember and forget. But I am immortal. I can never forget. I can never be free of this thing you call grief."

And so it goes for each of us. The human in us struggles to remember while the immortal one in us struggles to forget. And we live in between, never the same.

In the heart of our grief, we are left with these challenges, day by day: not to drown in our grief and not to run from the pain or memory of our loss, not to define life by lack and loss, and not to create a false sense of happiness that always has us casting a net of denial over our grief, and not to run from the hardships that living opens, and not to sink into the quicksand of hardship at every turn.

As we struggle, in the very center, under it all, what we

have that no one can take away and all that we've lost face each other. It is there that we drift, feeling punctured by a holiness that exists inside everything. This is where grief leads us: onto a relentless precipice where we stand rawly in the open, more in pain and more awake than we thought possible, and closer to both life and death, ripped open to both unthinkable loss and unexpected tenderness. It would be impossible to imagine, if it weren't so readily true.

> *Those we love and lose become an indelible*
> *presence in our lives like shadows cast by trees*
> *on the brightest of days.*

Questions to Walk With

- In your journal, identify someone you have lost in your life and identify someone important to you now who didn't know them or didn't know them well. Write a letter to the person you have lost describing your living friend to them. Then, write a letter to the living person in your life about the person you have lost. Later, meet with your living friend and read both letters aloud.

- In conversation with a friend or loved one, describe your history with grief and what kind of teacher it has been for you. What has grief taught you and what is it trying to teach you now?

PART 3

The Journey to Where We Are

*To learn from all we've been through is the work of
awareness. And to dive through the hours like Adam
or Eve is the blessed work. Yet we can't give up the
struggle. We secretly want what the wave does to the
shell as we scamper from the sea.*

—MN

. . .

The inescapable truth is that we don't travel from
here to there, but from in to out. The great
Hindu sage Ramana Maharshi said, "You are already
that which you seek." Humbly, we search and search
until we become what we are searching for.

In time, without knowing, our want for more is
worn like the crags of a cliff effaced by the sea. Eventually, suffering wears us down, while love brings
us to the surface and we meet at the flashpoint of all
that is real, no longer able to hide. Now, everything
is irreducible. Though we look for it everywhere, we

enter the treasure more than find it, winded to land right where we are.

Nature affirms this as well. There is a minute form of sea life, an underwater plant known as a squirt. It migrates till it roots in one place for life, then eats its brain. Once rooted in the deep, it no longer has a need for its incessant seeking. Once having found its place, it absorbs and internalizes its searching mind in favor of a life of being.

Eventually, we, too, give up our endless searching in favor of a life of being. Along the way, we mistakenly think that doing things more than once is a sign of failure, when the timeless art of living opens us to the transforming truth that we always need to learn it all again. We are always on the precipice of growth. And the work of integrity is to stay faithful to the journey which never ends.

In the final part of this book, we will explore the imperative work of bringing what lives within us out into the world. From the cavern of our soul, we can give everything we have. And by staying clear and authentic, we can discover that all things are true. Within this paradox, we can, in time, inhabit the work of flourishing and impart bliss. It is humbling to accept that our dreams seldom come true. But in devoting ourselves to their journey, sometimes we come true, which is more important.

All Things Are True

All paths lead to the same goal: to convey to others what
we are. And we must pass through solitude and difficulty,
isolation and silence in order to reach forth to the enchanted
place where we can dance our clumsy dance and sing our
sorrowful song—but in this dance or in this song [we fulfill]
the most ancient rites of our conscience in the awareness
of being human and of believing in a common destiny.

—PABLO NERUDA

Our Conversation
with Death

*Death is the conductor of an infinite orchestra
that advises us through its many instruments how
to cherish the melody of life.*

—MN

Everyone who lives is called to be in conversation with Life and Death. Our conversation with Life is inescapable because we wake to it, day in and day out, the way fish wake to the river they must swim in. And while no one wants to accept that our time is limited, that we will perish, running from this fact, or denying it, only exaggerates our fear.

Running from this bittersweet truth makes the smallest disruptions urgent, while staying in conversation with the great forces of Life and Death makes our time here more precious. When Death is not faced, its presence and our need to face it don't go away, but simply aggregate into the

smallest trouble we encounter, which then becomes the repository of all our fears.

In this way, a fear of spiders, or the dentist, or a relentless worry of sudden storms can grow intensely out of
proportion. Then, we urgently run to the hardware store,
imagining that if we can just install one more lock on top
of the two we already have—then we might feel safe. But
as long as we don't face our eventual death—that we won't
be here forever—a mistrust of life will grow until fear will
find its way into every irritation we stumble through.

In this regard, compassion, to ourselves and others, is
not the well-intentioned want to quiet each other's fears.
Rather, the true work of intimacy is to keep each other
company in the midst of our heightened fears and worries, while supporting each other in the difficult journey to
right-size what we encounter in the world.

How? By inhabiting our ongoing conversation with
Life and Death, which no one can do for us. The gift of
staying in this conversation, hard as it is, is that we begin
to feel how unrepeatable and life-giving every moment is.
And this, and this alone, enables us to take the unending
risk to live completely— Now!

One of my great teachers about staying in conversation
with Death is my dear friend Don who is eighty-six. He is
the eldest in our men's group, which has been meeting for
fifteen years. We joke that he is our scout. Though he is in
good health, Don is being talked to by Death. He recently
said, "It's in my face." He's calm and clear and honest

enough and kind enough to share his innermost thoughts. The last time we met, he said, "It showed up in these new boots. My old boots lasted twenty years. I just bought these new ones and thought, these will be my last pair of boots. They stare at me from the closet now."

Just after this, I traveled to teach at a retreat center where the founder is also in her eighties. It was good to see her again. When we met, I asked how she was. She stared at me with urgency and said, "It's a tough time, but we'll get through it. Our mission is too important." I immediately felt her fear of death tightening her grip and squeezing her need to do one more thing before she goes.

That night, I dreamt of my father, who is gone. I came into his shop and he was falling asleep while guiding a piece of wood through his band saw. I rushed over and pushed him quickly away from the saw, shouting, "Dad, you're falling asleep!" He was startled awake and wanted to return to cutting the piece of wood. I could tell by his urgency that he feared he wouldn't be able to use his tools anymore. He was frightened that he would lose access to what he loved. I turned the saw off and said, "Dad, it doesn't mean you can't use your tools. Just that you have to be more careful." He began to cry. Then I woke.

Whether awake or asleep, whether in the grip of our days or the drift of our dreams, the harmonics of Life and Death are always near. We are still in the grip of a world-wide pandemic and death is everywhere. Our conversation with Death is there when we wake and there when we sleep. And under the drone of fear, life is ever more precious.

It's made me understand how Life and Death are the arms of God nudging us awake. It's made me see that the weight of time on our body diminishes how far we can reach and how long we can last, while the light waiting to escape from the body makes everything infinite. Each day, we diminish a little more to become a little more infinite. Each day, we let light out as we let light in. Such wakefulness is the opposite of an eclipse. It is a moment when everything gets out of the way. In that recurring moment of surprise, we are brought alive—again. The work of faith is to stay enlivened by the light of the infinite and not buried by the weight of diminishment. The work of love is to care for each other as time breaks us down and as light emanates through us to inform the world.

My conversation with Death became irrevocably real thirty-nine years ago when I almost died from a rare form of lymphoma. And Death, in harmony with Life, have been my guides ever since. But we need to have this conversation together, out in the open. It is not morbid, but elemental. When we refuse the Whole of Life, we create darkness wherever we turn away.

As we speak, souls are dying while others are being born. For those dying, I pray that we, just waking to how precious life is, will be conduits for the essence you are leaving. May we, in the gasp of our hearts, scatter the dust of your wisdom on the eyes of those about to be born. So

the lineage of kindness can keep weaving its threads beyond what any one person can do.

This long journey from Life to Death is such a paradox:
sweet and harsh, raw and covered over. And our endless
call is to see through the layers when we're covered and to
soothe the soul's body when we are raw. I pray that when
my time comes, I will lean into the gift and not grip it.

The weight of time on our body diminishes how far
we can reach and how long we can last, while the
light waiting to escape from the body makes
everything infinite.

Questions to Walk With

- In your journal, describe your first encounter
  with Death and what it said to you about Life.
- In conversation with a friend or loved one, describe how Life and Death have most recently
  been speaking to you.

The Cemetery, the Market,
and the School

Unused pathways are covered with weeds.

—Mencius

Mencius (372–289 BC) was a Chinese sage considered second only to Confucius himself. While Confucius focused completely on the relational aspects of community, Mencius spoke directly about the goodness of human nature and the generative place of the human heart. However, this inborn goodness is not enough to ensure goodness in the world. Like a seed that needs to be watered, we need to cultivate these gifts and create environments in which our goodness can flourish. And so, Mencius believed that education must awaken the innate abilities we carry within us.

We have two profound images from the teachings of Mencius. First, he offered that human beings are innately good. The way that water, allowed its true nature, will always flow downhill and join other water, so will human beings. Though we can be manipulated or even manipulate ourselves to be distrusting and even cruel, allowed our true nature, human beings will always flow to each other in kindness and join.

The second image came from the sage's attempt to convey what the Chinese ethic *ren* means. Often translated as *benevolence* or *kindness,* Mencius characterized this trait as the impulse in us that will rush, without thinking, to save a child about to fall into a well.

His inexorable belief in our capacity for goodness sets Mencius apart from others in the Confucian tradition. In many ways, Confucius himself avoided the life of the Spirit, focusing on how to steer communities toward the cultivation of a moral life. However, the early Taoists believed that we don't need to be steered toward goodness at all. We only need to inhabit our goodness by shedding falseness and staying true to our nature. And so, Mencius was uniquely able to thread the heart of Taoism with the mind of Confucianism.

For Mencius, the noble quest of all education is the cultivation, release, and practice of benevolence or ren. Still, there are those who reject any notion of innate goodness. A younger contemporary of Mencius, Xunzi (310–219 BC), precedes Machiavelli in his insistence on the innate evil of human beings as evidenced by the insufferable appearance, again and again, of our greed and self-interest.

These ancient positions on the human journey are relevant today and beg for us to personalize them. I am compelled to ask: Do you believe that we, as human beings, are innately good or evil? Do you believe that we are unable to surmount our greed and self-interest? More to the point, how do you view your own true nature? How are you struggling today between your self-interest and benevolence? How can you reclaim and resurrect your goodness? Is our impulse to help each other teachable? If so, how? The kindness or cruelty of our age depends on how we enter these questions in very particular and immediate ways.

The story goes that when Mencius's father died, his mother, Zhang, raised the young boy alone. Being poor, they first lived near a cemetery. But when Zhang found her son imitating the paid mourners, she was determined to move. This led them to live near a marketplace. But then, she found her son imitating the deceptive ways of merchants. And so, she was determined to move again. This time, she settled in a small house near a school. Finally, her son began to imitate the true ways of learning.

So, where we grow who we are matters. What, then, were your early influences? How much of your way in the world comes from imitating the dead or the living? How much of your attitude toward others comes from imitating the give or take of life? Do you look for an advantage when meeting others or for ways to help each other on our way? What would you say to a child about the nature of people and the nature of living? Who taught you about the true ways of learning? This is a conversation we need to stay engaged in.

Mencius is buried in Yasheng Lin, about twelve miles

north of Zoucheng. On his grave is a stone monument that rests on the back of a giant stone turtle. And the monument itself is flanked by a dragon on either side.

These ancient symbols serve as totems to guide us. For our goodness lives between the inner and outer worlds. And our ordinary destiny is to draw on the depth of all life and translate that depth into the care that carries the world. To live this way, we must rely on that in us which, like a sea turtle, carries us to and from the deep. And it is, then, incumbent on us to feed that eternal knowledge into the goodwill of our dragons who can breathe benevolence into the world.

Allowed our true nature, human beings will always flow to each other in kindness and join.

Questions to Walk With

- In your journal, describe the turtle in you, that aspect of depth that connects you to all depth. Then, describe the dragon in you, that aspect of goodwill that brings that depth into the life around you. What role does your heart play in being a conduit between these two forces?
- In conversation with a friend or loved one, discuss your experience of your own goodness. How did you first experience your goodness? How is it your teacher now?

Four Sages Find the Garden

Four seekers meet in the journey of their seeking, having loved and lost a great many things. Sensing there is more than their tumble through existence, they travel together in search of the radiance inherent in all things.

But the first distrusts whatever he finds, while the second is afraid he'll offend others by living out his quest. The third always feels bereft and is ever ready to run off with the goodness dropped by others. And the fourth isn't sure what to believe. She just loves the search and the company of others. They travel this way through the landscape of their fears until others call them sages, which the first three are happy to believe. But the fourth refuses another's name for the truth of her journey.

After many years, they come upon a garden, so abundant in its stillness, it stops them with its beauty. For it seems there is nowhere else to go. The first thinks it an illusion, sent to tempt him from the needs of the world. He won't enter, saying, "I can't drink of this peace while so many are suffering." The second thinks it a rich man's estate. He won't enter, saying, "I will not trespass another's kingdom unless I am invited." The third goes straightaway to steal some fruit, thinking, "No one will punish a frail, aging sage."

But the last one thinks it is Heaven opened before them. And so, she kneels before the pond in the center of the garden, thankful to see—through her thinning reflection—Heaven in all things.

This parable is loosely based on a story in the Talmud about four famous sages who enter a garden looking for lasting knowledge. But only one finds peace because the others have built their stance in the world on the assumption that they don't belong.

The assumption of existence for the first three seekers is one of being in exile from life itself. The first distrusts whatever he finds. His fundamental perception is one of a skeptical outsider. He doesn't feel at home anywhere. He seeks the radiance in all things as a sedative to his pain of exile. The second seeker is afraid his truest steps will offend those around him. He cannot sanction or affirm his own direct experience of truth. The third seeker is always living from a condition of lack. And so, seeing no goodness in himself, he acts like a beggar or thief of worth, eager to seize the goodness dropped by others.

The fourth seeker alone is truly at home in the search

and longs only for the company of other true seekers. For her, the emanation of her soul in the world remains possible. In this version of the story, I have made the fourth seeker a woman. For it is the receptive, feminine nature that keeps all things connected.

When they are considered sages for their long faithful seeking, the first three accept this station readily without ever corroborating it with their inner nature. This gives them a false sense of belonging. But the fourth seeker refuses to be defined by others.

At last, coming upon a ground of stillness where beauty quietly grows, the first three, who have been denying their inherent nature, can't accept the beauty of the garden for what it is, because they can't recognize where this beauty resides in themselves.

The first sage thinks it must be an illusion. How could such a peaceful place be true? Rather than trying to inhabit the still beauty of the garden, he insists it isn't real. Then, he justifies dismissing it by reframing the garden as a trick to keep him from the needs of the suffering. Yet by not letting the garden be his teacher, he precludes the spiritual fact that we, in our authenticity, become conduits, able to bring stillness and beauty *to* those who are suffering.

The second sage thinks the garden is a rich man's estate and assumes he is trespassing. He won't accept that the kingdom of the garden is everyone's. In life, he is always trespassing and plagued by the weariness that the recurring position of exile creates.

Feeling always less than, the third sage is quick to steal

some fruit, scheming that his pose as a sage will be his protection if caught. The tragic irony here is that the fruit in the garden of stillness belongs to everyone. And so, he is only stealing from himself.

The fourth sage is the only seeker to recognize that the still beauty of the garden has been revealed to them as an earned manifestation, if they can accept that they belong here in life with all its sufferings and obstacles. In our struggle for lasting worth, we are asked to accept our full humanness. In time, after much experience, the inner garden of worth emanates through all our trouble. Then, from the experience of our own radiance, we can recognize the radiance of Heaven on Earth when we come upon it.

The truth is that we all carry these debilitating voices in our quest to find the garden—the voice of skepticism, the voice of fear telling us that we will offend, and the voice of lack. At times, we are so full of distrust that we feel the world is a crime about to happen. At other times, we feel so out of place that we fear being who we are is somehow a crime. Still, at other times, we feel so bereft that we steal from ourselves. And all the while, it is the receptive, feminine quality of worth in each of us that, given the chance, will recognize our kinship with everything. In time, worth recognizes worth, light recognizes light, and truth recognizes truth.

If we live long enough, we can outlast the moods of feeling foreign, so we can receive the radiance in all things. To do this, we must love the exiled parts of our life and care for the garden within, so we can recognize the garden of stillness and beauty as our home.

We, in our authenticity, become conduits, able to bring stillness and beauty to those who are suffering.

Questions to Walk With

- In your journal, describe a time when you were seeking some quality outside of you to fill yourself. What did trying to fill yourself feel like? Did this complete you? Then, describe a time when you recognized a quality of life outside of you, because you could recognize that quality within you as well. What did it feel like to find what lives within you in the world? Did this complete you?
- In conversation with a friend or loved one, describe the four seeking voices—distrust, a fear of offending, a sense of lack, and the receptive sense of worth—as they live in you. Which one has most of your attention? Which one needs more of your attention?

Resilience and Prayer

Somehow, when I face what is mine to face and empty myself of all that is agitating me, I go clear like a lake after a storm. It is then that I can see through to the bottom of what is me, only to see that I share that bottom with all other beings. When I face my heartache and reach its bottom, there is the bottom of all heartache which is both comforting and renewing.

When we can be completely authentic, resilience is the flow of strength that comes to us from everything that is not us. Because when being ourselves to the bottom of our personality, we trip into the well of all personality. When giving all our care to what is before us, we trip into the well of all love. When diving into the depth of our soul, we also swim in the depth of all being. Once opened that deeply, summoning and marshalling what is dormant in us to face the situation at hand empowers our fortitude.

The deeper reward for inhabiting our full humanity is that the Universal Life-Force floods us with enlivened capacity. Just as you must plug in a lamp to access electricity, our presence and full humanity are required as a way to "plug in" to the Universal Life-Force that flows through all things. When holding nothing back and being true, we are lifted by the healing forces of life and illuminated. In just this way, resilience fills us with strength from everything that is not us, when we can be thoroughly who we are.

Like it or not, we are challenged to cooperate with the forces of life as they shape us. One way we do this is to speak from our heart. Because speaking from our heart makes us strong enough to endure the erosion of suffering. Speaking from our heart keeps us strong by clearing the inlet we call soul of unprocessed experience. This thoroughness of being and congruence of relationship between us and other life opens us to a deeper, more enduring form of resilience, through which the core of our being opens to the core of all being, making us for the moment stronger than we are.

The other way we are challenged to cooperate with the forces of life is to listen with our heart. To be still and listen, beyond all urgency and intent, opens us to the true nature of prayer. When in trouble, we often pray, the way we might scheme—desperate for a way out. When overcome with fear, the prayer can sound more like a demand of someone or something or some force to rescue us.

But the deeper sense of prayer has always been to still ourselves enough to listen and receive, to ask for nothing. When we can empty ourselves of schemes and demands, when we can let the fear settle and open ourselves without intent, this quiet bravery lets us be renewed by the forces of Wholeness. As an inlet, when clear, channels the larger body of water into streams of water that can irrigate the fields, this is how true prayer welcomes life to sustain us.

Both speaking from our heart and listening with our heart enable the soul to breathe. It is this rhythm that saves us from going numb. It is this rhythm of heart that makes pain and grief bearable. It is this rhythm, which no one can enliven but you, that enables us to endure the pressure of life by which experience is compressed into the jewels we call wisdom and joy.

So, what is your history and experience of speaking from your heart and listening with your heart? How do these deep ways of being and feeling inform each other? How can you deepen your practice of each? This is work worthy of your commitment. It will help you both survive and thrive. For listening with your heart will deepen your roots and speaking from your heart will help you break ground.

When I can see through to the bottom of
what is me, I can see that I share that bottom
with all other beings.

Questions to Walk With

- In your journal, describe a situation that is calling for you to speak from your heart. Practice doing so in this reflection. Notice and detail how speaking from your heart, even in practice, affects you.

- In conversation with a friend or loved one, describe a time when you listened deeply with your heart. What caused you to stop and open this deeply? How did listening with your heart affect you? Describe a situation that is calling you to listen this deeply now. What is keeping you from listening in this way?

Fidelity to the Journey

*Perhaps we'll find what eluded us in the places
we once called home.*

—Wes Anderson

When faced with the pain and suffering of others, we are constantly challenged to feel what others are going through as thoroughly as possible without losing who we are.

Keeping our heart open to the suffering of others while renewing our own direct connection to life marks the steadfast practice of compassion. At the same time, keeping our heart open to our own suffering while accessing the flow of life that exists under our own turbulence marks the steadfast practice of integrity.

How we practice compassion between us and integrity within us is the ongoing journey of the inner self. Like atoms that make up all forms of matter, the essence of who we are exists independently of all we encounter. Yet, like the molecules that contain atoms, the self that contains our essence is never in isolation from other life. Our worth is innate, affirmed and renewed by our direct experience of being, while the evolution of a life is completely dependent on the web of relationships we create and care for in the world.

So, how do we stay open to others and not lose who we are? What does this look like? Being human, we fall into the extremes and make our way back to center, time and time again. Loving you, I feel your pain, your fear, your heartache, your worry. Loving you, I can easily over-identify with you. In such cases, I become your pain, your fear, your heartache, your worry. This can be overwhelming and even debilitating.

When weighed down by our identification with the feelings of loved ones, we can surface like a swimmer who was suddenly and frightfully tossed under. With our heart pounding, we can rebound the other way and say, "If this is how it's going to be, I want none of it." Then, we can find ourselves putting up a wall to protect us from this over-identification. Sometimes, almost drowning in the feelings of another can be so alarming that we cut off ties altogether. But we must beware when protecting ourselves, for we always wall in as much as we wall out.

I know these extremes because I have lived them. Eventually, when outliving the extremes of over-identification and isolation, we come to the true learning ground of intimacy whereby we keep our heart open to feeling the experience of others, while sustaining our own center of living from which we experience our own life of feeling. Then, we venture into a poignant and enduring dance between two beings living their lives.

In Dante's epic *The Divine Comedy,* we chance upon two lovers, Francesca and Paolo, in a ring of Hell where they are spinning in endless identification with each other for Eternity. As the journey of transformation for Dante continues through Purgatory into Paradise, he chances upon the same two lovers, still spinning in orbit of each other. But now, they each have a center. Profoundly, one of the crucial differences between experiencing Hell or Paradise is whether we can maintain our center while in love.

The never-ending work of love challenges us to keep our heart open to the pain and suffering of others without becoming their pain and suffering. I have a friend who struggles with depression and I am committed to be on that journey with her. Yet, it is imperative that I remember that I am not depressed. I have my own trials and weights to bear, but depression isn't one of them, at least so far. And so, loving my friend means feeling as best I can what she feels and then affirming my own direct experience of life. Often, I do this by walking and feeling the sun on my face with nothing between me and the Universe. Then, I can return from my own center of being to let in her pain.

When facing our own pain and suffering, we tend to inflate or minimize what we're going through. Under the weight of our own experience, we make the world a projection of what we are going through. If we are in pain, the world's a painful place. If we are afraid, the world is a fearful place. If we are confused and dark, the world is dark and foreboding. But if we glimpse life beyond our particular struggle, we tend to go the other way, minimizing what we're going through. In the face of all life, what I am experiencing must be insignificant.

But all things are true. And when exhausted beyond our projections and judgments, we can feel the press and urgency of what we're going through *and* the enduring ease of life continuing around us. When we can feel both, the Wholeness of Life is affirming, not diminishing. As a struggling fish is swept along by a sudden lift of current, we can be lifted and held by life beyond our trouble.

Just as I must renew my direct experience of life while opening my heart to the suffering of others, I must also drink from the wellspring of being that is always flowing beneath the turbulence and disturbance of my own attempts to live. For the thousand moods of being human are the many waves that rise and fall on the surface of time, while it is the ocean of being that holds all the waves. We must remember that it is all one water—the wave and the deep. You can't tell where a wave ends and the deep begins. Likewise, you can't tell where our psychology ends and our depth of spirit begins.

It is helpful to note psychologist Michael Mahoney's definition of *self-confidence.* He traces *confidence* to the Latin *confidere,* fidelity, and so, he frames self-confidence as a fidelity to the true self, staying faithful and devoted to the journey of our evolving inner self. Indeed, it is only a devotion to that sacred bottom beneath our endless moods that brings us back in accord with the center of the heart, which shares the same living center with all beings. This is what the Hindu tradition calls *Atman,* the shared immortal self.

Confidence is not the swagger or certainty with which we convey what we know. It is the fidelity with which we listen to and relate to the irreducible foundation of all life. For there is a difference between how we carry what we know and how we know what we know.

León Felipe was a Spanish poet and friend of the great Chilean poet Pablo Neruda. Their personalities couldn't have been more different. Pablo was outgoing and uninhibited, exuding his curiosity and care into everything. León was more introspective and hesitant around others. While the shy poet admired the soaring presence of his friend, he knew he could never approach life that way.

In Felipe's poem "The Great Diver," dedicated to Neruda, he softly declares, and I paraphrase, "I am not the great diver that you are. I tremble at the light on the spider's web and don't know what to say." Both are confident, that is, faithful, to the foundational reality they each experience. Both are beautiful and true. Each is a different instrument playing the music they know in their soul.

There are infinite ways to be thorough and clear. And, as there are many instruments to convey music—from a two-string erhu played in a field in ancient China to a brass trombone played in a marching band at a county fair—there are a thousand moods by which to convey the fundamental truth of life. Our confidence comes from our direct experience of this fundamental truth, not the mood of how we convey it. So, don't doubt what you know to be true because you stammer or go quiet. A quivering reed knows the rain as fully as a stone. And *fail* is not a word in the language of Source.

The work of self-confidence, then, is staying committed to both the work of compassion and the work of integrity: honoring the real experience of others and ourselves while also honoring the continuous flow of life that exists beneath our experience. This is how a bird pumps its wings while being carried by the wind, and how a fish flaps its fins while being carried by the current, and how a heart pumps and flaps its way through the days while being lifted by the Mystery of life.

> *Our worth is innate, affirmed and renewed by our*
> *direct experience of being, while the evolution of a*
> *life is completely dependent on the web of relation-*
> *ships we create and care for in the world.*

Questions to Walk With

- In your journal, describe a time when you over-identified with another's feeling. Did you lose yourself in your feeling for another? How did this affect you? How did you return to yourself?
- In conversation with a friend or loved one, describe a turbulence you are currently experiencing. It might be a disturbance of pain, fear, heartache, or worry. Then, try to describe the

flow of life that exists beneath your current mood of disturbance. Without valuing one more than the other, describe the relationship between your experience of turbulence and the flow of life beneath it.

Breathing Spell

*Faith is the willingness to give ourselves over, at times,
to things we do not fully understand . . . the full engagement
with this strange and shimmering world.*

—Alan Lightman

I was having an overnight sleep study done in a lab. Turns out I have sleep apnea. The technician Ed was helping me accept the mask that jettisons air into your lungs. We got talking in the middle of the night. He's done this for sixteen years. He was caring and thorough. He has two grown kids and still wants to learn everything.

Between measurements, I shared that I'm a poet, a philosopher, and a cancer survivor. Ed went silent, then said, "So, you're an optimist, a pessimist, and a realist—all in one."

I chuckled. "I guess so."

Then, the kind one who helps people breathe in the night offered, "That must give you some peace."

Ed had surfaced a thread of wisdom in our brief exchange: that peace comes from accepting that all things are true. It is partiality that is painful and diminishing. When we can listen to all sides of life, we begin to integrate and weave what is with what can be. Then, the myriad ways we can bridge the gap become visible. Letting all things in does offer us some peace because the Mystery of Life in its diverse magnitude grounds us, no matter how difficult the situation we find ourselves in.

What does it mean, then, to be an optimist, a pessimist, and a realist—all at once? It means we balance the voice in us that sees what is possible with the voice in us that sees what is not. Then, having listened to both, we consult the voice in us that walks the days. For all these possibilities are true. We can live. We can die. We can be stuck in between. How, then, do we let these voices enliven each other? For, too often, we let them war against each other.

I told Ed that it is the poet in me that sees, and the philosopher in me that tries to understand what I see, but it is the cancer survivor in me that tries to make use of it all. We tend, as humans, to get lost in the big picture or in the details, when peace comes from holding the big and the small at once. It is letting everything in that keeps us from dispersing into abstraction or from drowning in the grit of every step along the way.

We each have a part of us that sees, a part of us that tries to understand, and a part of us that tries to make good use of what we see and understand. These qualities are not reserved for artists. Rather, they come alive as the living arts we each carry within us.

And so, I encourage you to become more familiar with

these inner allies. I encourage you to treat them, not as codes to live by, but as individual instruments we must learn how to play.

The truth is that no matter what anyone tells you, order cannot bring you peace. Believe me, I've tried. Yes, order can bring a certain ease to living. But it is only a facsimile of peace. Peace comes from opening our heart and mind and letting the sluiceway of life find its common depth within us. It is the unification of life within us that settles into peace.

At first, we try to define our sense of self by separating what makes us an individual from others. We individuate by contrast. Part of this is natural and part of it is emphasized by our culture of exceptionalism and specialness. The exaggeration of specialness has us, in time, put other life down in order to lift our sense of worth up. This becomes a troubling and false distinction.

If blessed to endure the scouring of love and suffering, we start to find vitality in what we have in common with other life. We start to define our sense of self by the fully inhabited moments in which we join with other life.

Earlier, I mentioned this remarkable image offered by the Sufi poet Ghalib: "For the raindrop, joy is entering the lake." At first glance, this compelling image seems to suggest that the raindrop surrenders its individuality to join the Whole. But looking more closely, the raindrop doesn't lose any of its self. It actually adds its individuality to the lake. In that joining, the felt distinction between *self* and *other* is healthfully blurred.

We know this sensation as those moments when we are at one with what we experience. We are listening so deeply, we are at one with the music. We are feeling so deeply, we are at one with those we çare for. We are so at home in nature, we are at one with the wind through the creaking trees.

When wholehearted and holding nothing back, we, like the raindrop entering the lake, do not lose who we are but expand and deepen who we are by letting all of life in. Paradoxically, such a felt sense of Oneness is only possible if we have a firm and steadfast center. Growing that center until it welcomes all of life is being who we are—everywhere.

This is what Ed and I were exploring in our brief exchange in the middle of the night as I was relearning how to breathe. In truth, we all keep relearning how to breathe—in the deepest ways. And becoming intimate and skilled at seeing what is possible, and what is not, and how we can find our way in between leads us to a peaceful experience of Oneness—one opened and lived each moment at a time.

Peace comes from accepting that all things are true.
It is partiality that is painful and diminishing.

Questions to Walk With

- In your journal, describe the history of your inner allies: the part of you that sees, the part of you that tries to understand, and the part of you that tries to make good use of what you see and understand. Which are you strongest at? Which needs more of your attention?

- In conversation with a friend or loved one, discuss your struggle to let all things in. Share a moment in which you experienced that all things are true.

The Work of Integrity

This is true alchemy—the transformation of fear into love.
It's available to all of us. It can save the world.

—SPARROW

The Timeless Art

You and I are just swinging doors.

—Shunryu Suzuki

At a fundamental level, Spirituality is the timeless art of how the living part relates to the Living Universe. All the traditions have different names for this, but essentially when a fish swims with the current, it is being spiritual. When a bird glides on the wind, it is being spiritual. When the stem of a flower breaks ground and blossoms, it is being spiritual. And when we grow into our being and find our place in the world, we are being spiritual.

In Chinese medicine, the term *spiritual* describes anything that is life-giving. In Japanese, the word *inochi* means "the life-essence that is in everything." And in English, the word *spirit* comes from the Latin *spiritus* meaning "breath." So, Spirit reveals itself in anything that is life-giving. Spirit is the life-essence that knits us together, that keeps us together. Spirit is in every breath.

When we inhale, we bring air from the sky into our

lungs. When we exhale, the air from our lungs mixes with the sky. This exchange—from inner to outer that keeps us alive—is spiritual. It applies as well to the exchange of our thoughts and feelings. When exchanging what we see and feel, we are more together than alone. In this deep regard, Spirit is anything that joins the inner with the outer.

Being human, we are destined to live within this paradox: that while we are always imbued with life-essence, while we are always filled with what is life-giving, while we are always breathing in what matters, we continue to drift from what matters. And so, when we are disconnected from the life around us, we are ill. When connected, we are well.

The first practice of self-awareness, then, is to discern when and where we are disconnected from the life around us. And the ongoing resource of Spirit is how it reconnects us with the life around us. Being human, we will always fall off or down. But being spiritual, we are always close to our repair.

Living in the Open

Let me share a recent poem that offered me a lesson about being spiritual. It's called:

NOTICE

Imagine a lantern in an open boat,
the light flickering as the boat drifts
in the night lake.

Now imagine it rains and look closely
at how the drops plop in the lake
and thud in the boat and bead on
the sides of the lantern.

Notice how the flame doesn't
go out.

I was surprised by this poem, which came to me in a dream. For me, it evokes an extended image of how the courage to live in the open works. The image—of a lantern, in an open boat, in open waters—is an instruction in how we can inhabit the courage to carry the light of our soul, in the lantern of our heart, in the boat of our life, across the sea of life.

In daily terms, we are each challenged to discover:

- How do we tend the light within us?
- How do we care for the lantern that is our heart?
- How do we care for the boat that is our life?
- How do we live in the open with courage?

To live out these questions, we each need to personalize and inhabit:

- The courage to be who we are, by seeing and accepting the truth of our unique life.
- The courage to face each other, by seeing and accepting the truth of others.

- The courage to stay in relationship, by listening and holding without judgment.
- The courage to be kind and useful: by being real and staying real, by holding nothing back and not hiding, by giving more than taking, and by asking more than telling.

What, then, is your next step in each of these practices: in being who you are, in facing each other, in staying in relationship, and in being kind and useful?

When inhabiting these practices, we experience faith.

Faith

Faith is an act of ultimate concern.

—Paul Tillich

By faith, I don't mean obedience to any principle or doctrine or person, but more, a faith in life. Faith is our covenant with life no matter what befalls us. It is our belief that we are part of something larger than us. It is our commitment to let all that is larger than us be our teacher. What light is for plants and flowers, faith is for human souls. It is that which causes us to grow and that toward which we grow. Imagine a seed growing underground toward a light it can't yet see. In just this way, love and suffering cause us to break ground and flower. We break ground by following our heart, by being real, by being kind. This stirring, this breaking ground, this flowering is our transformation. When faithful—when full of our belief in life—we reveal the force that joins us. There are many names for this force. Some call it God. Some call it Allah. Some call it the Holy Ghost. Some call it Yahweh. Some call it the Collective Unconscious. Some call it Atman. Some call it Oneness. Some call it the Great Spirit. Some call it Nature. Some just call it life-force. I welcome it by any name. It has saved my life.

When we grow into our being and find our place in the world, we are being spiritual.

Questions to Walk With

- In your journal, describe one way that you are disconnected from the life around you. What does this look like? What does this feel like? Then, describe one way you can begin to reconnect to this aspect of life. How will you start?
- In conversation with a friend or loved one, discuss how each of you is tending the light that flickers in the lantern that is your heart.

Learning It All Again

With everything and nothing to lose,
I love, so my soul can dance closer to home.

—MN

Each of us is born with a complete sense of Oneness and an inherent knowing of all the connections in the living Universe. When we first
arrive, there is nothing between us and all other forms
of life. Then, as we develop the many things we need to
live in a world full of diverse tugs and pulls, we develop
an identity.

Now there's a self and an object. Now there's inside
and outside. Now there's weather. Now there's gravity.
Now we hold something and drop it. There are a million
distinctions and distractions. With each one, we're challenged to trust or distrust the spirit we arrive with or the
world we are born into. The Wholeness of Life starts to
feel fragmented as we go about our human journey of dis-

covering and learning and embodying our way into that Oneness all over again.

Plato agreed with this notion, believing that we are born all-knowing, arriving with everything we need. He further believed that the moment we take in air and cry, we forget all we know in a conscious way. And the journey of being human is relearning piece by piece all that we were born with. Until, at the end of our life, our conscious knowing and unconscious knowing are one again.

It seems the heart's journey over a lifetime is to inhabit the inner sense of Oneness we are born with. Many traditions speak of this journey as bringing what we know inwardly into the world through a life of relationship. In Swahili, *mkeka* means "the foundation of all knowledge and understanding that living together returns us to." In medieval Turkey, Symeon the New Theologian (949–1022) was a Greek Orthodox abbot and poet whose relational teachings led to an abiding awareness of God's original presence within each of us.

And all traditions confirm that learning of the deepest order takes time. Ralph Waldo Emerson said, "Respect the *naturalangsamkeit* [German for 'the slowness of natural development'] which hardens the ruby in a million years, and works in [a] duration, in which [the] Alps and Andes come and go as rainbows."

Another example is Kukai (774–835), one of the first Japanese abbots and scholars to teach that we are all innately enlightened. He put forth that, regardless of status or education, we all have the capacity to awaken to that enlightenment through experience. Kukai implied that moments of Oneness come upon us with the all-knowing mood of birth. He said, "The first word, *Ah,* blossoms into all others. Each of them is true."

So, in a world that condemns repetition as failure, stay open to learning it all again. When we circle, we are just beginning to go deeper. And when we resist, we are often knocked down in order to look more closely at what we ran by. Some birds fly thousands of miles in migration, over and over, year after year. We find this astounding and beautiful. We find their long, determined pump of wings, alone in the far reaches of the sky, quietly heroic. And we, as spirits in bodies in time on Earth, have our own human migration, between love and suffering, year after year. This, too, is quietly heroic. All so we can wake to what is true, one more time, and utter, "Ah, it's as I've always known, each thing is irreplaceable."

The journey of being human is relearning piece by piece all that we were born with.

Questions to Walk With

- In your journal, describe a time when you drifted away from what you know to be true. How do you account for losing track of what is true? And how did you reawaken to this truth?

- In conversation with a friend or loved one, discuss one thing about life that you understood conceptually that you now embody in a felt way. How do you describe this difference and what caused you to move from understanding to embodiment?

Grounded but Not Buried

I take my time, looking for what [lasts] . . .

—Tao Ch'ien

We are constantly challenged to marry what is with what can be. If we only bear witness to the trials of existence, we will be weighed down by the burdens of time. If we only pine after what is possible and ideal, we will become airy, romantic, and completely removed from the embodiment of life. So these questions of practice remain: What are the tools by which you stay grounded but not buried in the ground? And what are the tools by which you are lifted but not removed from all that is real? Staying grounded but not buried and lifted but not removed is how we repair, reimagine, and rebuild the world.

The translator David Ladinsky speaks about the enduring gift of poets in this regard when he says, "I believe the ultimate . . . success [of poems] is this: Does the text free the reader? Does it contribute to our physical and emotional health? Does it put 'golden tools' into our hands that can help excavate the Beloved whom we and society have buried so deep inside?"

These questions speak to the journey of all souls. And it is the enduring gift of poets and teachers to help us navigate life by entering these parallel questions: Does the experience at hand free your soul on its journey? Does the lesson at hand contribute to your health and resilience? And what tools can help restore your direct relationship to the Life-Force and Presence that informs and renews everything?

The poet that lives in each of us is the part of our soul that brings the water of life to our lips. The teacher that lives in each of us scoops the water of life and brings it to each other. The word *translate,* which comes from Latin, means "to carry or bring across." And the deeper vow of all poets and teachers is to bring themselves and others across the divides of ignorance and isolation, back into our kinship with all things.

In 1897, the American painter and stained glass artist John La Farge wrote to his dear friend and mentor Okakura Kakuzō, "Your influence is [like] a stream run[ning] through grass—hidden, perhaps, but always there." This is the lasting effect of every true teacher—to always be there, though seldom seen, helping others grow.

In truth, this is the enduring work of every friend and loved one. For there is no substitute for what we discover by being loving and truthful in each other's presence. And presence, love, and truth are eternal medicines always available to us when we dare to listen with an open heart. By being who we are, we become an oasis for each other.

During times of adversity, the choices we face become more acute and obvious and necessary. This is why we must learn from those who suffer, because they are pioneering the practices of being that we all face in the ease of ordinary days. And since we all suffer, we are all, at times, great teachers of how to be in the world. So, tell me, when you can, some of what you are learning from all you are going through. For I believe that every small gesture of truth affects the turn of the Earth.

When I speak of a small gesture, I mean an authentic action that has great consequence, the way a stone thrown in a lake causes a ripple to build into a wave on the far shore. Or a kindness that like that ripple builds into an ethic of compassion that is taught in schools to the next generation. In this way, every act of true kindness opens the hands of a child yet to be born.

We engage in these questions of practice in order to participate in a living Universe, not to manipulate or manage the world. In all we go through, we are a living part in a living Whole. Consider how a thousand shells are rounded by the sea. How a thousand flowers are drawn into blossom by the pull of light. And how a thousand theories of existence are offered as we burn ourselves and then expound on heat, projecting our inch of pain onto the world.

But though the whole of the ocean is in a drop of water, a drop is not the ocean. Though the Universe can be tasted in the bite of an apple, an apple is not the Universe.

And as the spirit of God can emanate from the core of a person, a person is not God. For though the trapeze artist spinning in midair would like to believe there is nothing in the world but he in his moment of spin, there was a hand that let him go, a rise that set him forth, and a hand waiting out of sight, which he will gladly grasp as he starts to fall.

In truth, if you feel complete in each step, life is touching you where you are. And so, we are challenged to treat each step along the way as a destination unto itself. Then, we can regard each place we land as home. In this regard, all that I have been through has been an apprenticeship for now. And I continue to struggle, as everyone before me, trying to stay grounded but not buried and lifted but not removed. I keep looking for the golden tools to add to my toolbox, not to survive alone, but to thrive together.

As Albert Schweitzer encouraged, "Open your eyes and look for [someone], or some work for the sake of [others], which needs a little time, a little friendship, a little sympathy, a little sociability, a little human toil . . . [It] is needed in every nook and corner. Therefore, search and see if there is not some place where you may invest your humanity."

And investing our humanity means meeting the challenges of being a spirit in the world, which include: marrying what is with what can be, finding that source of presence that keeps us alive, and treating each step along the way as a destination unto itself.

Being grounded without being weighed down helps us navigate the tug of war between our deeper angels and our frightened selves. And while each of us must enter these questions of practice alone, we can't help but explore them together, the way a flock of tai chi students practices the eternal set of 108 moves side by side, each refining their own dips and bows, together but alone. While no one can live your life for you, we can help each other cross the burdens of experience. The greatest blessing of love is being awake at the same time.

Staying grounded but not buried and lifted
but not removed is how we repair, reimagine,
and rebuild the world.

Questions to Walk With

- In your journal, describe your own balance in marrying what is with what can be. Are you too grounded in the trials of living, are you being buried? Or are you too lifted and removed in what can be, are you out of touch with life? How can you begin to marry what is with what can be in your own life? Choose one situation and practice there.

- In conversation with a friend or loved one, describe one small opening in the life around you where you can invest your humanity, one way you might water the seeds in a garden nearby. What small act of care might you offer in that direction to begin?

Staying Clear and Authentic

In Hindu mythology, the god of connection, Indra, has woven a mystical net around all of existence. At each point where a knot would appear in the mesh of the net, there is a jewel. If you look closely into the face of every jewel, you can see the reflection of all the other jewels and the entire net. For centuries, Indra's net has served as a metaphor for how the Living Universe can be seen in the soul of every human being and how we are intrinsically connected.

Each soul is a luminous jewel in the net of existence, in which we can see all the other souls and the entire Web of Life—when we are clear and authentic. When not clear or authentic, the jewel turns back to a knot. We're still holding everything together, but we can't see or reflect very much while a knot. Yet, underneath our trouble, we are still connected. When tossed about by our trouble, we go in and out of being aware of our inherent tie to everything. When feeling disconnected, we drift into believing that nothing relates to anything else. But we are only, for the moment, blind to the Web of Life, of which we are still a part.

There are three internal processes, akin to breathing, that are essential to the life of the soul by which we can restore our luminous place in the Web of Life. They are presence, meaning, and connection. Each of us must discover—in very personal and specific ways—how these processes work within us. For when enlivened, presence, meaning, and connection return us to the radiance in all things. They return us to the way under the way. They return us to the place of true meeting. And they return us to that moment where everything touches everything else.

To begin with, presence is the means by which we inhabit our direct experience of life. Through presence we restore our sense of how rare it is to be alive at all. This original sense of grace restores our ability to see, hear, feel, and think. Through these scoured lenses, we can make more sacred choices that will help us find our way and place in the Unity of Things.

But if all we have is our own experience, we can quickly become hardened by what is familiar and stop growing. Limited to our own experience, we can become stubborn and inflexible. Meaning, then, is how we gain access to the experience of others. Meaning is the conduit by which presence is informed by other presence. And connection is the process of relationship and flow that allows presence and meaning to inform each other, and to sustain each other.

These spiritual processes are animated by how each soul faces their journey. You can study them, as you might study respiration or circulation in the body. But it is the actual practice and experience of breathing and movement that enables us to live. This marks the difference between explanation and embodiment, and between the pursuit of why and the living out of how.

Presence, meaning, and connection appear in infinite forms that human beings can inhabit. Presence can come alive for each of us by immersing ourselves in whatever is before us, by listening, reading, birding, or walking in nature. Meaning can come alive for each of us by devoting our complete effort to whatever needs to be built or repaired, be that gardening, or creating a home, or evoking the stories of others. And connection is the electricity of authenticity that sparks between presence and meaning. Connection is the unformed energy of relationship, which is fluid and lasting.

Over a lifetime, we are each challenged to tend and balance the inner processes of presence, meaning, and connection, letting them integrate. Inhabiting these eternal processes is crucial to the practice of being human. Tending these processes is crucial to restoring our place as a clear jewel in the net of existence.

I invite you to explore the current state of your relationship to presence, meaning, and connection. Which is your greatest teacher? Which are you immersed in? Which needs more of your attention?

These spiritual processes require our attention because unless we see, the eyes go dark; unless we feel, the heart goes numb; and unless we breathe, the lungs stop working. As presence opens our heart, meaning opens our mind. And connection allows our heart and mind to enlarge each other. Connection allows our heart and mind to act as one. As presence enlivens our sense of being, meaning enlivens our capacity to understand. And sweet, resilient connection enlivens our birthright to love.

In those unavoidable moments when we are not clear or authentic, when we are half-hearted and blocked from the flow of life, we lose track of our connections and the world seems random and chaotic.

However, chaos often reflects a larger sense of order out of view and beyond our understanding. In our anxiety and discomfort, we often try to manage or restrict what feels chaotic in order to give ourselves the illusion of control. Like someone trying to divert a waterfall with their arms, this only adds to the chaos. But when still, long enough, we can often see the larger order at work around us and begin to relate to it. By larger order, I mean the natural and mystical currents of life that carry us, the way the strength of rivers carry fish.

In truth, all the various forms of spiritual practice, across the traditions, are aimed at staying clear and authentic, so we can embody our position as a jewel in Indra's net. The Japanese word *ikigai* means "the purpose that gets you out of bed in the morning." The word *enthusiasm* from the Greek means "at one with God." We could say that purpose and enthusiasm describe the rush of life-force that flows through us when the soul is clear and authentic.

Meaningful service, care, and compassion are the concentrated actions that come from the Web of Life moving through the jewel of our soul into the work of our hands in the world. Rabbi Harold Kushner speaks of the worth of meaning as found in the thought of Holocaust survivor Viktor Frankl:

> *Frankl saw three possible sources for meaning: in work (doing something significant), in love (caring for another person), and in courage during difficult times . . . [His] most enduring insight [is that] forces beyond your control can take away everything you possess except one thing, your freedom to choose how you will respond to the situation.*

Having the wherewithal to respond to any situation truthfully comes from having an open mind and a clear heart, which allow us to stand firmly on the Ground of All Being. When our life is on solid footing, we can reach in many directions. This is not a state to arrive at, but a continual process of living thoroughly, of taking in what is essential and discharging all that is extraneous.

The openings to the Ground of All Being are often particular and small. For it is the small questions that open the Mystery, the small gestures that puncture trouble, and the glimpses of unassailable truth that allow us to feel contentment and acceptance.

Finding an irrevocable still point from which to act in the world is a practice addressed in all the traditions. In Sanskrit, the word *Santosha* combines the word *sam* (which means "completely, altogether, and entirely") with the word *tosha* (which means "contentment, satisfaction, and acceptance"). Santosha implies an inner state of equanimity that comes from accepting the circumstances of reality completely without denying their impact. This inner state is an earned quality of being that does not try to flee the path of being human, while not being oppressed by the difficulties of being human.

When engaging life while in the spiritual mood of Santosha, we don't try to alter or stop the Wheel of Life, nor do we acquiesce to all that befalls us. We participate by holding nothing back while accepting that we are part of forces larger than us. This state of being alive in the world requires an inner skill that is difficult to inhabit but deeply worth pursuing.

The spiritual teacher Elesa Commerse describes Santosha as the inner state of durable happiness, which comes from seeing what is possible while accepting what is. In the anonymous Hindu text *Yoga Vasistha,* Santosha is described as part of our path to inner liberation:

There are four soldiers who guard the road to Moksha (liberation). They are Patience (Peace of Mind), Atma

(Inquiry through the Self), Santosha (Contentment
through Acceptance), and Association with the Wise.
If you can succeed in making one of these a friend,
then the others will be easy . . . one will introduce
you to the other three.

We can cultivate a readiness for clarity and authenticity by practicing patience, acceptance, inner inquiry,
and seeking out the wise. How can you begin a personal
practice in each of these paths? For try as we do to uplift and shape the lives of others, the only way to change
the world is to uplift and shape our own life. We cannot
force others to face the truth or to be loving. We can only
inhabit the truth so completely with love that they will
not be able to resist the appearance of love like light.

The key to staying clear and authentic centers on
our commitment to refind the Ground of All Being from
which we can know acceptance and contentment. Then,
we can reach from a solid foundation to act in the world.
For authenticity involves recovering from the fall into
what might have been and resisting the intoxication of
what might be, in devotion to the intimacy of what is.

Meaningful service, care, and compassion are the
concentrated actions that come from the Web of Life
moving through the jewel of our soul into the work
of our hands in the world.

Questions to Walk With

- In your journal, describe one step you can take to deepen your personal practices of patience, acceptance, inner inquiry, and seeking out the wise.
- In conversation with a friend or loved one, describe a recent experience of presence, meaning, and connection, sharing what you learned from each.

Ready, Set, Go

I want to explore the relationship between being prepared and being ready. Being prepared centers on
thinking ahead and gathering the tools necessary to
meet a situation. Being ready centers on the foundational
ground we stand on and the clarity of view we meet a situation with. We often mistake being prepared for being
ready, though the process of getting prepared can be the
exercise by which we ready ourselves inwardly to meet any
situation.

When Winston Churchill said, "Planning is essential
but plans are useless," I think he was speaking to the difference between inner readiness and outer preparation. For
the process of planning—of imagining different scenarios
and what each possible venture might require—is more
important in how it sharpens our perception and fortitude than any of the plans that we might conjure. Once in

the moment, which can't be foretold, any particular scenario can easily fall short of what will be required of us. Further, our insistence on what we have planned instead of meeting what is unforeseen can actually make matters worse.

In preparing to teach, I always think of the terrain I want to invite people into and create sessions around perennial questions, which I support with metaphors, stories, and poems. Then, I type up and print out all this material and put it in a folder. But once I'm with folks in real time, I hardly refer to my notes at all. I actually treat my notes more like a jazz musician's set list, choosing which tunes to play given the feel and needs of the people I'm with.

What I started to realize is that all that preparation is really to ready me inwardly to be thoroughly present with people once we're together. I still do all the work to imagine the themes and sessions as well as gathering all the support materials. Because I believe that the notes and plans are kindling for the fire of unrehearsed connection that we enter once together.

Another example of the difference between preparation and readiness comes from the legendary play of New York Yankee shortstop Derek Jeter, specifically the improbable and incredible fielding play executed by Jeter known as "the flip." In the 2001 American League play-off series with the Oakland Athletics, the Yankees had a 1–0 lead late in game one when a liner down the first-base line gave Oakland slugger Jason Giambi an almost certain chance to score from first.

The ball was thrown toward home from right field as Giambi was circling third, when out of nowhere Jeter crossed the field to scoop up the short relay and flip it another fifteen feet to catcher Jorge Posada who tagged Giambi out a few steps from home plate. What everyone had witnessed seemed unthinkable and exquisite.

What Jeter had done, with precise and fleeting reflex, was to field the relay as he would have any grounder hit to his position—though it was nowhere near his position. Then, he tossed the ball as he would have to second base to start a traditionally short double play—though the play was at home plate.

Like all infielders, Jeter had prepared for the unpredictable bounces of a live game by fielding thousands of ground balls in practice, day after day, year after year. This was his preparation. But his readiness enabled him to go where the play would unfold. There, he applied his practiced skills to the unforeseen situation as it happened in real time—across the field.

We can also hide behind preparation, as if enough plans will somehow prevent hurt and loss from finding us. The truth is that, no matter what we draw on, we can't avoid hurt or loss, only temper its harshness with the authority of our being and the clarity of our response. For hurt and loss are unavoidable passages in the human experience.

Life at its best is always fresh and unrepeatable. Often, in the face of the unknown, our fear of being caught off guard has us over-prepare for situations that can't be anticipated. When I was forced to return for another chemo treatment after my first was horribly botched, I sat with a counselor in the hospital, wanting to know how I could best prepare to go back in there. I was near frantic, overly focused on lists and resources, my anxiety and fear just below the surface. The kind counselor took my hand and said softly, "You can't prepare for this." The utter truth of his whisper stunned me. Then, he squeezed my hand and continued, "It will be what it will be, but if you're ready, it will be okay."

I didn't understand what he was saying, but knew that somewhere under my fear, it felt true. In life and love and in meeting our suffering, we need both—to be prepared and to be ready. To be prepared is to know *how* to step. To be ready is to see *where* to step. To be prepared is to know how to pick up what is broken. To be ready is to have some sense of how the pieces go back together. To be prepared is to make a schedule. To be ready is to lean into the day with an open heart when the schedule is lost in the rain.

Being ready centers on the foundational
ground we stand on and the clarity of view
we meet a situation with.

Questions to Walk With

- In your journal, describe a situation you are facing and how you can both prepare and ready yourself to meet it. How are these efforts different?

- In conversation with a friend or loved one, tell the story of a time when the process of planning served you though the plans you arrived at didn't work out.

Trying to Walk Gently

In my forties, after growing up with an angry mother, and after two marriages in which I kept missing what was true, Susan came along and held my face, fully and gently, as if I were a surprising flower. Till that moment, I hadn't realized that no one had ever held my face. My life was cracked open that day by her tenderness.

So, we can be broken open by love. It isn't just the accidents and avalanches that change us. The whisper of beauty holds a power unmatched in its capacity to open even the oldest shell. And the whisper of truth is just as transforming.

I was eight when my grandmother brought me to her on the steps of her basement in Brooklyn. She held me firmly, as if the world were teetering and her deep immigrant eyes said that she'd never let me go. It is a steadiness I have carried in my heart for seventy years.

What I'm trying to say, in yet another way, is that we each have to find that corridor of aliveness that can carry us through the turbulence of life on Earth. And it's the unexpected kindness and strength of those along the way who, with the slightest nudge, can save our lives. Of course, we seldom know if we've made such a difference. Though, in time, we are humbled to realize when someone has saved us in this way.

Perhaps the most insidious modern illness is the underside of self-reliance that has us believe that we can make it alone. The truth is that in resisting help, we often break things more quickly than we can put them together.

I remember falling hard on our yellow lab's foot when she was five. My heel splintered her toe. I felt awful as she limped over to lick my face. She had to have surgery, which gave her arthritis. I never forgave myself. How she hurt made me walk lightly. I think this was her gift to me. I still try to walk gently—even on leaves—so I might break as little as possible on my way.

It made me understand that everything is a teacher, if we let it in. The wind teaches the hole in the fence what it was made for. And experience teaches the hole in our heart what we are made for.

When I was a boy, a friend of my father caught an eel, killed it, and went to fry it in a pan. I was horrified to see it still twitch after it had died. But since, I've come to see that what lives in us refuses to die, no matter what is done to us. When allowed to surface, that pulse permeates everything as kindness and tenderness. It's how a fist becomes an open palm. How the dissipation of anger comes full circle to become a soft embrace. And how every flower is coaxed to blossom by the presence of light and warmth.

Under all the wreckage and ruin, the very pulse of life waits to spark and spread. At times, we're blessed to ride it like a comet of Spirit, which everyone feels, but which no one can see.

Everything is a teacher, if we let it in.

Questions to Walk With

- In your journal, describe something soft and tender that cracked you open to a deeper way of being. How did this person or moment come into your life?
- In conversation with a friend or loved one, describe how your insistence in a situation caused something to break. Were you able to repair it? How would you enter this situation differently? Is there anyone you need to make amends to?

The Endless Vows

There are four vows we can practice in any given moment that will return us to what matters, that will return us to ourselves and each other. They are simple and always in reach, though they require everything from us. They are the utterances: *help, thank you, I'm sorry,* and *I love you.*

These are the most reliable doorways to being fully here. Each requires courage and vulnerability. Once truly entering these vows, we are never the same. *Help* acknowledges that we can't make it alone, that life depends on the web of relationship. *Thank you* renews wonder through the lens of gratitude. It returns us to how rare it is to be here at all. *I'm sorry* accepts our humanness and makes all repair possible. And *I love you* is the synapse between all life.

No one can live without these avenues of authentic connection, though pride and fear keep us from them constantly.

As if admitting we need help is some kind of failure. As if saying *thank you* incurs some debt. As if saying *I'm sorry* exposes our flaws. As if saying *I love you* leaves us forever at the mercy of those we love.

In truth, we are strengthened and deepened for entering these vows. Repeatedly, each invites us more deeply into the human journey. Each utterance is a form of acceptance that invites us to put down our masks and not pretend. Each reveals how tenuous and vital being human is.

Help

As you grow older, you will discover that you have two hands,
one for helping yourself, the other for helping others.
—Audrey Hepburn

There are always two sides to the bridge we call *help*: the calling out and the lifting up. Sooner or later, everyone will know both sides of this bridge. Crossing the bridge of help is what lets us know we are not alone. As British actress Lily Collins says, "Asking for help is never a sign of weakness. It's one of the bravest things you can do. And it can save your life."

To ask for help, we have to admit that we need others, that we are more interdependent than independent. To offer help exercises the heart and lets generosity flow through our being. At the deepest level, to ask for help and to give it opens a timeless synapse for life-force to move between us.

From the Egyptian slave who helped his other up from

the mud, to those in the revolution bringing a chunk of bread to the fallen, to you holding me all those years ago when I was throwing up from chemo, to the out-of-work chef bringing the old painter meals on Sunday—such giving is the unbreakable synapse that keeps the Universe going. After falling down enough, we realize: this is our destiny, to charge with care across the gap between living things.

The act of help draws us further into living and, often, our innate kindness perceives the need before help is asked for. As we make our way in the world, we know when people are in need. When we let kindness be our guide, we show up with the lift of an arm or the opening of a door. Suddenly, we are beside someone who is broken, helping them pick up the pieces.

Yet to withhold help or to hesitate when it is needed is a passive form of cruelty. As Dante said, "He who sees a need and waits to be asked for help is as unkind as if he had refused it." Though we resist, our unspoken covenant in our time on Earth is to help. As Muhammad Ali said, "Service to others is the rent you pay for your room here on Earth."

My grandfather, Nehemiah, who came to America from Russia, was a gentle soul who became a letterpress printer in New York City, only to lose his job during the Great Depression. Even with little to eat, he'd bring strangers home for dinner. When Grandma would pull him aside with "We don't have enough," he'd kiss her cheek and say, "Break whatever we have in half. It will be enough."

This brief saying during times of need has become a

code to live by for me. When in doubt, give. When in pain, help. When unsure of your path, help by answering every need with care.

Thank You

Gratitude turns what we have into enough, and more. It turns denial into acceptance, chaos into order, confusion into clarity.
—Melody Beattie

To say *thank you* stops everything. To say *thank you* unravels the tangles in our mind. To say *thank you* gives air to the wounds we carry in our heart. It is a simple mystery, a small act of acceptance that lets us be buoyed by the presence of all life. Much the way a raft carrying you can be lifted by the sea, and in that lift, you can briefly see Eternity.

It is particularly challenging to say *thank you* in the midst of difficulty. And though it's hard to be grateful in the midst of suffering, I confess that, more often than not, I have been touched by gratitude later, once the suffering has passed. This is a deep reflex of faith: to be grateful for what might reveal itself later.

The Greek philosopher Epicurus said, "Do not spoil what you have by desiring what you have not." He suggested that there are three ingredients to happiness: friends, freedom, and the reflective life. He also believed that false beliefs create unnecessary pain.

Practicing gratitude allows us to find wealth in what we

have and saying *thank you* allows us to put down false beliefs. The Shawnee chief Tecumseh said, "When you arise in the morning, give thanks to the food and for the joy of living. If you see no reason for giving thanks, the fault lies only in yourself."

When we can't find it in us to give thanks, it is a sign that we are blocked from our reverence for life. Rather than judge ourselves, we are being called to identify the blockage, to part whatever veils have come between us and life, and to reconnect with life directly. The antidote to ingratitude is kneeling to drink from the river of life one more time.

I remember a dark passage in my cancer journey. There seemed no way out. I was teetering between life and death, in the hospital, in a room with three other tenuous souls. It was just before dawn. They were asleep. I was terrified of what might happen next. Would this be my last week, my last day, my last hour? The sun began to rise and slip through the metal blinds. A bright, irrepressible ray spilled across their faces and then, onto the chrome sidebar of my bed. I briefly saw myself in the illuminated chrome. The brightness of this day yet to happen gave my face an aura. I was given a glimpse of my quivering soul and knew it was with me always. I began to cry softly in gratitude. For in that moment, before the day began, before my other suffering angels would wake, I was quietly more alive than I had ever been. It was a good day to die, even a better day to live. I gave thanks. And the thanks was the golden thread I pulled that led me to tomorrow.

I'm Sorry

Sorry means you feel the pulse of other people's pain
as well as your own, and saying it means you take a
share of it. And so it binds us together.
—Craig Silvey

Step nine of the Alcoholics Anonymous program (AA) is to "Make direct amends to such people wherever possible, except when to do so would injure them or others." This is a profound instruction for everyone. For making amends acknowledges the truth of things. Once the truth of our actions is acknowledged, growth and repair are possible.

Looking back, it is clear that causing injury and making amends is one of the oldest forms of falling down and getting up. As long as we resist saying we are sorry, we stay down and never get up. Saying we are sorry and, thereby, owning our actions and taking responsibility for the things we break, is the psychological equivalent of the moment a broken bone begins to heal. Without making amends, nothing can heal.

A stark example of this in my life was my mother. In the sixty-four years I knew her, I never heard her apologize for anything. More than how this lack of amends strained our relationship, it kept her forever in the simmer of undousable anger. For her anger covered up her hurt. And so, she forever bubbled and simmered, no matter where she was. This made it impossible to get close to her without getting burned.

In my own journey, I have been called to say *I'm sorry* countless times. One of the most difficult apologies was to my former wife upon leaving that marriage. Having survived cancer with her enormous help, I had to leave to live the one life I was given. It's as if almost dying changed me into a sea creature and I couldn't live on land anymore.

Even more humbling is that it doesn't matter how long it takes for an apology to surface. The impact of making amends is always healing and restorative. Here are a few examples across history.

On January 25, 2011, the head of France's national railway company (SNCF) made the company's first formal public apology directly to Holocaust victims. The regrets came just a few months after survivors and their descendants threatened to block the company from signing contracts in the United States if it did not acknowledge its role in the shipping of thousands of Jews to Nazi death camps and make amends.

Therefore, Guillaume Pepy, the company's chairman, did as much during a ceremony at a railway station in Bobigny, a Paris suburb. He said, "In the name of SNCF, I bow down before the victims, the survivors, the children of those deported, and before the suffering that still lives." The company deeded the station to local authorities to create a memorial to the twenty thousand Jews shipped from there to Nazi camps from 1943 to 1944.

Even though the company was forced to make this public apology and even though it took sixty-eight years for the apology to come, the power of this acknowledgment was meaningful in repairing some of the deep wounds that scar Europe.

Another example. In October 1992, 359 years after the insidious Inquisition made Galileo recant his views, Pope John Paul II accepted that Galileo was right in his declaration that the sun was the center of the solar system and not the Earth.

In 1632, Galileo was put on trial because his theories and publications contradicted official Church doctrine. The Inquisition restricted Galileo from publishing his works and imprisoned him. The order was later changed to house arrest, which lasted eight years until his death in 1642 at the age of seventy-seven.

Centuries later, with a statement at the Pontifical Academy of Sciences, Vatican officials formally closed a thirteen-year investigation into the Church's condemnation of Galileo. Paul Cardinal Poupard, the head of the investigation, announced at the time, "We today know that Galileo was right in adopting the Copernican astronomical theory."

And though it took 359 years and a thirteen-year investigation into the obvious, such amends make a difference in the alignment of truth.

One more example. In 1998, six descendants of the Sahtu Got'ine tribe from the northwestern United States made a pilgrimage of reparation. In the 1940s, their fathers, desperate for work, had hauled heavy loads of ore from the mines near their village to barges on the coast. Long after their fathers died of cancer, the tribe learned that the ore they had hauled was radioactive uranium, used to make the bombs that were dropped on Hiroshima and Nagasaki.

Fifty-three years later, this small group of elders made amends to the Japanese people for their part in their pain. When the descendants of those who had unwittingly helped make the bombs crossed the Pacific Ocean to say they were sorry, some part of the dead was put to rest, and a dark, callous part of the heart of humanity was reclaimed. Making amends, even for things we're not aware of, can alleviate the suffering of what we are carrying.

The great twelfth-century rabbi and physician Maimonides held both parties responsible in the healing process of making amends. Maria Popova summarizes it this way:

> *Maimonides offers a very precise prescription: The wounder should make three earnest attempts at apology, showing both repentance and transformation—evidence that they are no longer the type of person who, in the same situation, would err in the same way; if after the third attempt they are still rebuffed by the wounded, then—and this is Maimonides's brutal twist—the sin now belongs to the wounded for withholding forgiveness.*

Like inhaling and exhaling, making amends requires both giving and receiving. Then, we can help each other up and move on.

I Love You

Being deeply loved by someone gives you strength,
while loving someone deeply gives you courage.
—Lao Tzu

No phrase is more binding and uplifting than *I love you.*
And no phrase is more inadequate, as it can only point to
a vast depth of feeling that exists beneath all words. Yet, to
say *I love you* and to hear *I love you* will stop us in our tracks
and touch the very core of our heart, changing us forever.

For admitting that we love someone betroths us to that
person. The word *betroth,* from the Middle English *troth,*
means "to bind oneself in loyalty to the truth." When making a vow of love, we are binding ourselves in loyalty to the
truth of our kinship to the soul of another. When making
a vow of love, we are saying that we and the other share a
foundational ounce of being, that we are made of the same
eternal stuff.

To say *I love you* and mean it—whether to a partner,
friend, or family member—is to cast a lifeline that either
of you can hold on to throughout your lives. When feeling
shaky after falling down, we can steady ourselves and hoist
ourselves up by taking hold of the lifeline of *I love you.*

Truly loving others over a lifetime creates a net of relationship that can't be broken. It is that net that keeps us
from oblivion. So, say *I love you* freely and mean it and you
will be weaving a net of care that will catch most things
that fall. And in wanting to hear *I love you* we can only

be who we are and wait, the way buds wait for light to open them after rain. Give and wait, the two great imperatives that we are born with, the heart's way of rooting and breaking ground.

Causing injury and making amends is one of the
oldest forms of falling down and getting up.
As long as we resist saying we are sorry,
we stay down and never get up.

Questions to Walk With

- In your journal, describe your most recent experience of the four endless vows. When did you last ask for help and what happened? When did you last say *thank you* and what happened? When did you last say *I'm sorry* and what happened? And when did you last say *I love you* and what happened?
- In conversation with a friend or loved one, discuss which of the four endless vows is most difficult for you to invoke and why. What can you do to be better at this?

On the Precipice of Growth

Bless what forces us to invent
goodness every morning, and what never frees
us from the cost of knowledge, which is
to act on what we know again and again.

—MARGE PIERCY

Mending Things

When their knots are untied,
hidden souls return to their Origin.

—Abraham Abulafia

As children, we play hide and seek. As adults, we play avoid and find. This painful game limits us to a narrow path of what's familiar beyond which we seldom dare to live, though we are prompted, time and again, into unrehearsed moments when things turn real and immediate. Despite our resistance, we are often stirred by kindness or pain to follow our heart into the unpredictable days.

We all live out this pattern, being drawn out of what's familiar, only to retreat there, until the next time we are challenged to step into what's real. This pull beyond what is comfortable requires us to keep shedding what is false and keep imagining what is possible. If we can't while in war imagine peace, can't while confused imagine confidence, can't while in fear imagine safety, can't while falling imagine rising; if we can't while desperate imagine God—we will lose all sense of hope, which, more than a wanted outcome, is the assurance that we are part of something essential, larger than any one person.

Sometimes, we surround ourselves with complications, as if they can protect us from the world. They might be complications of busyness, or complications of the past or the future. We might try to hide from life in our web of memory, good or bad. Or try to hide from death in our web of golden dreams. Sometimes, we hide in the complications that arise from becoming a devout follower of another's path, trying to escape the uncertainty of direct living.

Yet under the complications we create and uphold, there are moments of true living we can't avoid like when something we love breaks, or someone we love leaves or dies, or when we lose what matters like the keys to the house. The task is not to run from these moments but to be calm enough and clear enough to see our way through them. Like walking barefoot through a patch of briars, you just have to slow down and look very carefully before you step. And just keep going.

Refusing the moments of true living or urgently running from them can lead us into the narrowing tumble of addiction, where we try to hide in the feverish and endless pursuit of one thing. In the Tang Dynasty, the great Chinese poet Li Po died while drunk one spring night because, seeing the moon in the water, he tried to drink the moon in its entirety and, falling from his boat, he drowned. This tragic undoing holds a lesson for all of us.

When intoxicated—with anything—we can mistake the reflection for the Source. We can mistake the agitation of wanting for the energy of being. We can endanger ourselves and those around us when we try to drink what is undrinkable rather than accept and inhabit the life we are given. This quandary invokes a practice for each of us by which we try to discern, day by day: What is reflection and what is Source? What is agitation and what is the energy of being? And which efforts are consuming and which enliven us?

I have a friend whose horse was kept in her stall too long after having a miscarriage. Her horse began to bite a board repeatedly and inhale wildly. The rush from sucking the air stimulates endorphins and creates a high for the horse. Once feeling this, the horse keeps sucking the air as a way to self-medicate its own anxiety. Sadly, her horse became crippled by this behavior, a victim of *wind-suck addiction*. The habit is generally caused by boredom or trauma. Such boredom can be heightened by an inability for the horse to graze or roam. Some horses spend as much as sixteen hours a day in their stalls or paddock. The wind sucker is often underweight. Some, unable to break the addiction, die of malnutrition.

When confined to our narrow path of avoid and find, when confined to our stall of complication or the endless pursuit of one thing, we are prone to our own form of wind-suck addiction, where we try incessantly to inhale more of life than is possible in any one moment. While the rush of inhalation can be intoxicating, it can enervate us and malnourish us.

In addition to the press of hiding and avoiding, we tend to blame ourselves for the confusion we suffer. Yet, the truth is that we come in and out of various stages of clarity quite naturally. Much depends on whether the sea of circumstance we're in is turbulent or calm. Much depends on whether the sea inside is turbulent or calm. And there are those rare moments when the inner sea and the outer sea are both calm and we have heightened perception. The rise and fall of these moments have less to do with our fumbling and failings and more to do with the movement of inner and outer weather. When both align, we experience a clarity that we can make good use of until the sea gets choppy again. Yet no one is exempt from the convergence and dissipation of inner and outer weather. Rather than blame ourselves, we might better hone our skills in navigating the gathering and release of life's forces.

Being human, we are constantly asked to mend our breaks, to clear our confusion, and to continually grow. Let me speak to each.

In stitching a wound, you must thread a needle before you can sew what is torn. Then there is always a small puncture we must endure where the thread has to go. Withstanding the small puncture is necessary to close the wound. This is how truth makes way for love, how acceptance makes way for compassion. This is a natural progression of repair: thread, puncture, sew together. This is the work of all relationship, to perforate our coverings so we can stay connected. In this way, light threads the dark and, as birds thread the sky with their song, kindness and truth—thread and needle—stitch the places we are torn.

Inwardly, when things mend, they are stronger. When broken bones heal, they are twice as strong as before they were broken. And when trees stripped of their bark mend, they form a *callus roll,* a thick skin of new bark that covers the exposed trunk of the tree. Once the callus roll has formed, the tree is also twice as strong as before it was cut. Yet, if the new growth is too thick, it can, once again, keep us from life.

Consider, again, the life of a horse. When a horse has a serious cut, the connective tissue that grows over that wound can keep growing, more than is needed. When that happens, the excess of protective tissue is known as *proud flesh.* Likewise, when we over-protect our hurts, we inflame the wound out of pride and fear. Then, the excess of protective tissue can prevent healing and lead to a more lasting wound. The lesson here is that when healing from emotional and spiritual wounds, we must be careful not to thicken our walls too much. Then, we might develop our own form of proud flesh that will deepen our wounds instead of healing them.

Though no one can begin the healing process for us, we can't do it alone. A natural example of this is quartz, a mineral that forms in the Earth's crust. Quartz crystals typically grow straight up. However, when one breaks, it continues to grow but now it veers to join a stronger piece of quartz nearby. When a broken piece of quartz joins a stronger piece, they become what is known as a *mending quartz.* In just this way, when broken and true, we grow toward others nearby who are stronger. This is how we mend, by joining with others until we're strong enough to stand on our own.

Regarding confusion, there are two ways to clear confusion. We can *see through* confusion with our mind, which offers us clarity. Or we can sustain the presence of an open heart, so that our care can *disperse* confusion, the way the sun disperses a cloud. While seeing through confusion is helpful, it is not the same as dispersing confusion. Clarity of mind is the first step to living beneath confusion. But if we stop there, we are able to see each other but not touch or hold each other. Only when dispersing confusion with the warmth and light of our heart are we able to inhabit life without complication.

What this means is that we have to develop practices by which we can become skilled at both the clearing and dispersing of confusion. No one can discern what these practices will look like for you. But clearing and dispersing confusion are essential. They are like oars in the sea.

Once on the mend and clear of confusion, we are ready to grow, one more time. It's interesting that the word *rule* shares the same root with the word *trellis.* A trellis is a temporary latticework, screen, or piece of upright wood that a vine, plant, or sprouting tree is tied to, so it has something sturdy to lean on and grow alongside until it can grow on its own. Then, the trellis is removed. And so, the more helpful, original definition of a rule is not a confining restriction of behavior but a temporary structure that can help us grow. This is the enduring and healthy definition of a rule.

This notion is helpful in thinking about how to support our own growth and transformation. When trying to change or deepen our ways of being in the world, it helps to create some form of structure in our days that we can lean on until the new behavior takes hold.

Whatever the new behavior might be, what temporary structures can you implement that will help you incorporate the new practice into your life? We brush our teeth every day without thinking about it. Likewise, how might you set aside brief but concentrated windows of time in which to devote yourself to whatever ways you hope to grow? Until these new efforts are part of your daily routine, like getting dressed or walking your dog.

I confess that, for all I've learned, I am not exempt from this process of staying real and healing. Recently, I had a dream in which I followed the long walk through time to a clearing which was an outdoor theatre of sorts. There, an ordinary angel appeared who kindly waited for me to show my ticket. I wasn't sure what the ticket looked like or if I even had one. I began to explain, which led me to tell the story of my life, which landed me in complete silence.

It was then that the ordinary angel said, "Now what do you hear?" I started to listen with wonder and heard the birds and the rustle of the wind. I thought I could hear the light curl around the branches of the trees. I even began to hear the breathing of my ancestors. It made me smile with my whole heart.

It was then that the ordinary angel said, "Oh, now you may enter the clearing." When I woke, I was compelled to look up the history of the word *theatre,* to find that it has a Greek root, which means "the seeing place." So, at the end of all trial and story, we are asked to listen. For listening allows us to see.

Ultimately, we all struggle between the hidden life of avoidance and complication and the ways we can mend our breaks, clear our confusion, and continue to grow. No one is exempt from this push and pull of living. And crisis only heightens our opportunity to be real. Over the years, I have learned that surviving cancer or any life-threatening circumstance is not defined by how long we live, but by how open-hearted and loving we dare to be in each moment we are given.

From such deep trials, I can bear witness to how fragile and resilient we are at the same time. Facing what life brings us with both steadfastness and tenderness leads us into an intimacy with all things. Such intimacy empowers us to leave our narrow path of hide and seek and avoid and find. In those moments, our enduring kinship with all things reveals itself. When we dare love in the face of difficulty, when we dare to open after we have closed, we are guided into the Great Mystery we all drink from and which no one fully understands.

Being human, we are constantly asked to
mend our breaks, to clear our confusion,
and to continually grow.

Questions to Walk With

- In your journal, describe one way you want to grow and change. Then, imagine a steadying structure you can create in your days that will serve as a trellis or temporary rule you can grow alongside until the new behavior or way of being is strong enough in you to grow on its own. It might be taping a reminder on your mirror or setting aside a certain time every day to journal or meditate. Finally, take a first step in creating this trellis in your daily life.

- In conversation with a friend or loved one, describe a time when you avoided something life was bringing you. What made you avoid this and how did turning away from this aspect of life affect you? Then, describe a time when you faced something life was bringing you. What made you face this and how did facing this aspect of life affect you? Describe the impact of avoiding life and facing life and how they differ.

The Break that Leads
to Wisdom

The human spirit is like a small stubborn weed that,
against all odds, sprouts through the cracks in stone and
time—persevering through all we try to cover it with.

—MN

In the mid-1970s, Professor Dan Bar-On, of Ben Gurion University in Israel, went to Germany to ask children of the Holocaust to share their stories. But he didn't just ask the children of victims. He also asked the children of perpetrators. What he found was that Germany was a country that wanted to keep its past hidden, especially the history of its families. Still, there was a compelling need in some to have these stories surface.

Over five years, ninety Germans came forward and began a process of finding out the truth about their fathers, their uncles, and their grandfathers. He discovered that their families and neighbors grew angry at them for seeking the truth. Even if they could make it past everyone's disapproval, they themselves resisted the parts of the truth that forced them to re-configure their memories and, ultimately, their identities.

One young woman knew that her father had been killed at the end of the war. Her mother had always made him out to be a hero. But at thirty-eight, she began to feel the need to know more. As she searched for what actually happened, the story became unbearable. First she learned that her father, an SS officer, was captured by the Russians, tried, and executed for war crimes. She couldn't make war crimes fit with her memories of a loving father who tucked her in at night. Her mother denied everything she found and insisted on justifying her husband's role in the war.

Then the daughter learned that her father had been a commandant at a concentration camp for a year. Further, she discovered that the man who was commandant before him couldn't stomach the killing and was transferred. But her father assumed the post and systematically and efficiently killed thousands during his year of command. Learning this caused an earthquake in her identity. How could she come to terms with this side of her father who was so devoted and loving to her? And whatever allowed him to kill so efficiently—did it live in her?

Stories like this give us lessons that are transferable to our own lives. They tell us that it takes an inner vigilance to seek the truth and to reveal the truth in the face of those who grow aggressive to avoid it. And even surviving the disapproval of others, it takes an inner persistence to pursue and accept the complexity of truth when it undermines our nicely wrapped story of ourselves.

Dan Bar-On spoke with compassion about this. He noted how often, at first, we spit back pieces of truth too big to digest. Then, in order to avoid the disruption of our life story, we either demonize the brutishness of those who failed us or justify their trespasses. Either extreme distracts us from accepting the difficult complexity that the murderer is oddly lovable and the devoted lover is capable of murder.

The dynamic uncovered in Bar-On's work is potent. We can find it in our everyday life in more subtle forms. In my case, my mother, who is now gone, would withhold her love just when I least expected. Over time, it assumed a pattern. After each hurt, the question surfaced briefly within me, why was she so hurtful? My father discouraged my inquiries and made excuses for her. I was encouraged to decipher her moods, to note how kind she was to others, and to read between the cracks in our hearts.

Through the years of growing up, I went through the cycle that Dan Bar-On speaks of. I tried to make excuses for her coldness while avoiding her anger and waited eagerly for the few times her warmth would show itself. But somehow, I could not quell the need to know more of the truth. And though I never found out what made her the way she was, I moved through stages of demonizing her cruelty and then justifying her incapacities of heart.

Finally, in my forties, I saw her with my brother's child

and glimpsed a capacity of love in her that I had never experienced. In that moment, the whole truth of my mother jarred me as a contradiction that has since rearranged the story of my life. She wasn't a monster nor was she a victim of a world that wouldn't let her be loving. She just carried a woundedness, whose source is still a mystery, which made her wounding to anyone close.

That she was my mother has been a difficult riddle, which denying has kept me from my self, but which accepting has led me more squarely into my self. In a way, I mirror the daughter of the commandant, as I wonder how my mother could be so cold to me and so loving to others. Still, whatever allowed her to be so calculating and soft by turns, I'm frightened that it lives in me.

This is just one example. There are countless others. But whether we are scarred by the inexplicable anger of a mother or the incest of an abusive uncle or the war crimes of a dead father, there is an inevitable journey for those of us left behind. When we demonize those who have sorely failed us, or go to great lengths to justify their failings, either way we are pushing off the truth, so as not to have its contradictions touch us or rearrange us.

Inevitably, it takes courage to grow through the wounds we are given, in order to face and incorporate a larger sense of truth that is transforming. To do this, we are required to let truth and love inform each other, without having truth shut down our love or our love cloud what we need to know. Somehow, in doing this, we not only repair ourselves, but strengthen the very biology of community.

It takes an inner persistence to pursue and accept
the complexity of truth when it undermines
our nicely wrapped story of ourselves.

Questions to Walk With

- In your journal, identify a person in your life who has hurt you and describe a time in the history of your relationship when you have gone to great lengths to justify their failings and a time when you have condemned them for their failings. Explore a conversation in your journal between these two voices in an attempt to arrive at a more complete understanding of this person.
- In conversation with a friend or loved one, discuss "the difficult complexity that the murderer is oddly lovable and the devoted lover is capable of murder." How do you understand and experience this seed of human nature?

The Cavern of Soul

In Terence Davies's transcendent film *A Quiet Passion,* the inner life of Emily Dickinson and how difficult it was for her to stay in the world is movingly embodied by Cynthia Nixon. This struggle reaches a point of no return in the film when Emily's father dies. On the edge of her grief, she trembles and reflects inwardly, "When we reach into silence, there is no fear. For where there is nothing, there is God." While this expression deeply renders Emily Dickinson's worldview, the first sentence is nowhere to be found in her poetry and the second sentence belongs to the Irish poet William Butler Yeats.

Nevertheless, this unexpected realization reveals Dickinson's want to retreat from the difficulties of living, though we have no choice but to live in the world. This is a paradox that works us all. While we all need light, we can't live in the sun. While we all need water, we can't live underwater. Likewise, when we are forced by our suffering into the nothing that waits in the center of silence, that Bareness of Being, under all we aspire to and cling to, holds us, grief and all. Though we can't live in this bareness constantly, it is the cavern of soul to which we can retreat from the world—at least for a time.

Drinking there gives us the clarity that waits at the end of exhaustion where pain sometimes dissolves into acceptance. This is the center of silence that all the spiritual traditions point to, the place that we in our suffering search for and dream of—though it is as near as time's unravel and as fresh as birth.

Acceptance doesn't mean resignation or giving up. It is a more demanding art of perceiving life from that still point of being. It requires that we accept that all the fuss of our agitation and worry, understandable as it might be, will not help us. It requires us to let the dust of all our resistance and stubbornness settle in any given situation, so we can see more clearly things as they are. Then, we have access to the real choices that wait before us. Then, we can see what next steps are truly possible.

Humans have always tried to bypass or escape the trials of living. But everything we encounter is an initiation. Eventually, we use up what we want to accept who we are. Until surrender is cooperating with truth as we meet it. Then, acceptance is the hole in our tent that lets us see everything.

Some of us are born leaning into the world and are

drawn—like Emerson, Whitman, and Neruda—into the thousand forms of life to find truth in the aliveness of whatever is before us. But some of us are born leaning away from the world and need to retreat—like Dickinson, Thoreau, and Rilke—from the harshness of existence to find truth waiting underneath everything on the surface. Either way, we meet in the essence of what matters. For regardless of whether we make our way outwardly or inwardly, we all arrive at the same Bareness of Being.

But for gifted, sensitive beings like Emily Dickinson, there was an added, implicit weight in being a woman who was unseen, unheard, and unvalued, who needed her father's permission to write alone in the middle of the night. Like Kafka's hunger artist, who starved himself of outer experience in order to be free of the friction and pain of living, she found refuge in solitude and needed the freedom and safety that seclusion offered in order to hear her own voice and to see the architecture of the Universe. And, like all honest poets and steadfast pilgrims, what she found there helps the rest of us make our way in the world.

The poetry of Emily Dickinson bears witness to the fact that the depth the heart drinks from is unspeakable, and all we try to say is carried back into the deep like the fallen beat of a whale's thick tail across the plate of the sea. Repeatedly, all we feel rises and slaps the surface, only to sink as it vanishes. Yet the heart, like the whale, has no choice but to surface or else it will die. In truth, poetry rises from our endless attempt to break surface and speak.

Inevitably, as we enter that Bareness of Being, we all need to know how to come back into the world. Painful as that crossover may be, we can find our way in and out by admitting the truth of where we are. Time and again, it is the love of truth that allows us in, but it is the truth of love that allows us to find our way back out.

And while there are many things to fear along the way, we must not fear life itself. For hope is not how we turn from suffering, but how we move through suffering. When we can face our pain and come back to meet the world, it is the restorative power of truth that lets us see and feel how all things are connected. But it is the restorative power of love that lets us maintain and repair all the connections.

We all live between nothing and everything, between sorrow and joy, between the orchestrated chaos and the empty pause of silence that waits under everything. Along the way, our soul is the conductor of the thousand moods and emotions that rise from being human. When centered, our soul guides our heart in playing the unexpected symphony of our life—not controlling what comes forth, but enlivening it.

At times, different moods and feelings will have their solos. And one day, feeling their part so completely, anger or sadness or doubt will insist that they can take over and conduct our way in the world. Yet it is our inner work not to relinquish the soul's role as conductor to any one emotion, while letting them all play their very important parts.

Being human is not only *letting* the thousand moods play, alone and together, but *encouraging* them to do so. All the while, we keep being refined by God's friction known as the world. Until we know each other as a broken thing worn smooth.

Under it all, our strength comes from the depth of presence that lives below all names. Whether we willfully go there or are thrown there by loss and grief, we all need to dive like ancient fish, so the depths of being can reanimate our aliveness. But no one can escape the need to return to the surface. Like those magnificent whales and dolphins, we are compelled to give our all to the necessary breach back into the world.

> *Eventually, we use up what we want to*
> *accept who we are. Until surrender is*
> *cooperating with truth as we meet it.*

Questions to Walk With

- In your journal, describe a time when you went into the world and found truth in the aliveness of what was before you, and describe a time when you went inward and found truth waiting underneath everything on the surface. Which is more natural for you: going inward or going out into the world? What can you do to strengthen whichever effort doesn't come naturally to you?

- In conversation with a friend or loved one, discuss the notion that "surrender is cooperating with truth as we meet it." What does this mean to you? Describe a time when you cooperated with truth and how that impacted your life.

A Sensitivity to Other Life

*There are times when sympathy is as necessary
as the air we breathe.*

—Rose Pastor Stokes

The primatologist Frans de Waal has spent his life exploring the emotional life of animals. One of his breakthroughs was in discerning if elephants have some form of self-awareness. This had been proven in chimpanzees by observing their behavior in front of mirrors. Animals who exhibit self-awareness recognize some aspect of themselves in the mirror. They don't see their reflection as another animal.

For years, it was believed that elephants had no self-awareness because they did not register any recognition of themselves in the mirror. But de Waal, along with Josh Plotnik of Hunter College, realized that the mirrors used were too small for the elephants to see themselves completely. De Waal and Plotnik propped jumbo mirrors before the elephants and it quickly became apparent that they, indeed, have great self-awareness.

The first lesson here is that, before we judge or limit those around us, we need to make sure we are seeing as they see. Otherwise, we are the blind claiming there is no light or the deaf claiming there is no music. The second lesson is that loving another involves a commitment to empowering them to see themselves completely. This alone enables self-awareness.

Inevitably, when we put ourselves in the position of other life, we see with many eyes and hear with many ears. Then, the experience of felt awareness grows. Consider how a symphony can begin with a single note played by a piano. Then, the cello comes in, followed by the tympani and the horns until the entire orchestra swells in unison. This is how one soul being authentic can enable other souls to show up until the whole of humanity cries and sings at once. Through such felt awareness, truth and kindness are harmonious and far-reaching.

As radar measures range and velocity by how radio waves bounce between a sender and a receiver, our unfiltered sensitivity allows us to put ourselves in another's place and then return to our own life—integrating what we feel outside of us with what we feel inside of us.

Everything in the Universe carries an enduring sensitivity to other life, which we as humans call empathy. Indeed, as de Waal confirms, animals experience love and loss just like humans. Consider how a chimpanzee will carry the corpse of its infant for weeks. And how an elephant will return to the place where the bones of its dead rest year after year. Such sensitivity to other life is detailed and precise. De Waal reports that "In Thailand, where young elephants are often outfitted with bells around their necks to announce their presence to villagers, the elephants sometimes muffle the bell by stuffing grass inside."

We are no different than animals, just more developed in some aspects of our awareness, though access to our deep sensitivity is often blunted or blocked by the sheer mental noise we create and ascribe to. Our challenge, then, in the modern world, is to recover this sensitivity to other life and to let it be our guide.

As it is, we live behind a mental screen, assessing what's before us but seldom feeling it, seldom receiving it. How we recover and develop our sensitivity to other life determines how alive we will be while here. Inevitably, the journey churns us and thins us, the way weather disturbs and flattens the sea. In truth, struggle is the heart's exercise. It never leaves us. Given all this, perhaps Heaven is the chance to wake from all agitation—where we are—and try again.

I find that this struggle to inhabit Heaven where we are is all we have—staying on the journey with each other, admitting that no one knows how to do this. If blessed to awaken our sensitivity, we are engaged in life precisely—feeling everything with deep awe. Then, when we stumble, we help each other up and say, "Come. We will live and learn together."

Loving another involves a commitment to empowering them to see themselves completely.

Questions to Walk With

- In your journal, describe a time when opening your sensitivity to another's experience made you more sensitive to your own experience. In what ways has your sensitivity widened or deepened?
- In conversation with a friend or loved one, describe what being sensitive means to you and tell the story of someone whose sensitivity you admire. How can you practice what you admire?

To Sweep and Drop

Those who wake are the students.
Those who stay awake are the teachers.
How we take turns.

—MN

The above quote is my signature poem about teaching. How I came to it is a lesson in learning itself. The first two lines were originally the ending to a poem called "Unearthed Again." But thirteen years later, when I went to include it in my book *The Way Under the Way,* I realized it was incomplete without the final line, "How we take turns." Once discovering the final line, I could see that the three lines together were an important insight into the nature of learning and teaching.

In discovering the first two lines, I was a student. But it wasn't until years later, when I humbly discovered the final line, that I was, for the moment, a teacher. I needed to stay awake to discover the culminating line. I needed time to live in order to accept that we take turns being awake and staying awake. In truth, waking and staying awake are the DNA of learning. And so, we must hold all our conclusions lightly.

For seeing evolves, if we stay awake. We tend to think of sight as a momentary glimpse of reality, as if our heart and mind are digital cameras clicking away. But sight is ongoing, more than what is captured in any one moment. And so, the vow to keep looking, to stay committed to letting things unfold, which means we have to resist making conclusions too soon.

At best, we make temporary assessments of what's before us so we can keep growing. Otherwise, we deem the world gray before the clouds dissipate. Otherwise, we judge the worst of others before they have a chance to show their true kindness.

The truth is that we are always on the precipice of growth, teetering between all that is yet to be lived and our argument with life. At some point, we each have an argument or resistance to life as we meet it. We may find life unfair or harsh or random or even punitive. And while aspects of circumstance might, in fact, be all of these things, the greater tide of life keeps steering us into a deeper, more enduring practice of acceptance. All arguments, when broken of their grip, lead to acceptance. And acceptance, when taken in, leads to peace.

The work of staying awake always centers around our conversation between an old self and a new one. For to grow, by its very nature, means that there is something that has been useful that we are outgrowing. And since whatever we are outgrowing has been valuable, we are attached to it. It could be a person, a belief, a way of moving through the world, or a form of identity. But in order to grow, we often have to put down something that has mattered to us.

Being human, we don't let go of things easily. And so, our need to apprentice in the art of acceptance. At every turn, we are challenged not to stay captive of what has carried us this far and not to break it in order to move on. How can we honor what has carried us this far and keep growing?

Often, when we outgrow relationships, we tend to demonize the other in order to push off from the old into the new. Most of the time, this is unnecessary. Most of the time, running from change makes us cruel, while facing change makes us tender.

Regardless of the situation, we each face these dynamics of change as struggle points in our personal transformation:

- The need to change presents itself.
- Do we hear it?
- Do we accept it?
- Do we resist it? Mostly, we do until the cost is too great.
- How long do we weigh the costs?
- Even when accepting the need to change, we enter the war of *yes* and *no.*
- When do we inhabit the courage to change, despite our resistance that shows itself as fear?

- When do we start to integrate where we've been with where we're going?
- How do we stay open to this process happening again and again?

There are two other poems of mine that continue to be great teachers for me about the dynamics of change and growth. Let me share them:

BEING HERE

Transcending down into
the ground of things is akin
to sweeping the leaves that cover
a path. There will always be more
leaves. And the heart of the journey,
the heart of our awakening, is to
discover for ourselves that the
leaves are not the ground, and
that sweeping them aside will
reveal a path, and finally, to
fully live, we must take the
path and keep sweeping it.

PRACTICING

As a man in his last breath
drops all he is carrying

each breath is a little death
that can set us free.

The lesson from "Being Here" is that there is no end to clearing the path we are on in order to discover where we truly are. The covering and sweeping of paths is part of the endless nature of seeking and being that no one can avoid. It is humbling that we never fully arrive. We continually clear the way. If we can't accept the endless nature of holding on and letting go, life will feel defeating.

The lesson from the second poem "Practicing" is that, no matter how burdened or overwhelmed we may be, we can, in a second of quiet bravery, put everything down and begin again. When burdened, this seems impossible. But we can practice holding on and letting go, and picking up and putting down. Until we accept that we are more than anything we hold on to or carry.

Both of these poems offer an ongoing vow that we can turn to on the precipice of growth. The vow is to sweep and drop. When tangled and confused and unsure of the way, we can sweep the leaves of circumstance from our path and drop the very things we cling to. This is the daily practice that can help us move through the dynamics of change: to sweep and drop. These efforts are as natural and imperative as inhaling and exhaling. Sweep and drop. And begin again.

Seeing evolves, if we stay awake.

Questions to Walk With

- In your journal, explore what has energy for you right now. What keeps coming up, though you keep putting it down? What is changing? What is confusing? What is calling you to grow? What are you needing to attend but don't know how? What do you need to know now?

- In conversation with a friend or loved one, describe one thing you are holding on to that is preventing you from accepting change. What are the things in the way that you can sweep from your path? And what can you drop so your hands are free to hold what is new?

Being a Bridge

I wish you courage: to ask of everything you meet,
"What bridge are we?"

—MN

Visiting Lascaux

After twenty years of practice, a Jungian psychologist wanted to go to France to visit the caves at Lascaux in order to experience the early paintings which date back nineteen thousand years. Needing to limit the traffic in the caves, the French government had begun to require visitors to give a reason in writing for wanting to enter the caves.

This made the psychologist review her lifelong practice of listening to the struggles of others. Finally, she wrote that seeing and listening to the paintings of our prehistoric ancestors would help her tend to the souls of our day. She believed that whatever made these early seekers work so hard to scratch and paint their feelings on the walls of a cave might reveal a resource available to us all.

To her surprise, the French government accepted her request, writing back, "Of course! Please come!" So, she and her husband packed their bags and flew across the Atlantic. Once there, they were part of a group that was led to the mouth of the caves. By chance, or by some deeper timing beyond our understanding, the man who first discovered the cave paintings happened to be there.

On September 12, 1940, Marcel Ravidat was one of four boys exploring a fox hole into which their dog had fallen. Marcel was the first to slide all the way to the bottom where he found close to six hundred paintings etched and painted on the interior walls.

That moment changed his life. For Marcel has felt forever linked to those anonymous artists at work thousands of years ago. Through a translator, he told the group that he keeps returning to the caves. He can't help himself. Since that day as a boy, he keeps looking in the hills for the descendants of the deer and bison captured on those walls. He imagines the spirits of animals leaping from one generation into the next, all the way to today. He wonders if this happens with the souls of people. When he visits the caves, he feels the possibility of our wakefulness and wonders why he hasn't done more with his life.

The psychologist listened to the eager, anxious boy who found the paintings, though he was now in an old man's body. She came away with the affirmation that only following what feels true can connect us across time. And following what feels true—as exemplified by the effort to scratch drawings into stone in a cave—is the secret of resilience, enlivened within us and between us.

When she turned to leave Lascaux, she saw Marcel

peering into the mouth of the cave, yet again. She imagined him as his prehistoric ancestor coming upon the cave for the very first time, wondering what was inside. She imagined that prehistoric being not yet aware that he would start one of the first drawings in history.

That day in southwestern France changed her life. Once home, she again met with her clients, knowing that her visit to Lascaux was helping her care for others. Now, she sees each person as an unknown seeker needing to paint their struggles on the walls of their cave. She encourages them to hold nothing back in surfacing their story, then helps them to interpret it in an effort to find their place in the lineage of seekers across time. She now believes that we all live at the mouth of a cave, needing both shelter and to be in the world. She believes that our love, if given freely, flows from one generation to the next, like the one ancient deer forever leaping into life after life. How we want that for ourselves. Perhaps this is what that early seeker tried to capture by drawing that early deer in stone.

So, when we meet, be kind and try to listen, and I will, in time, bring you into my deepest cave where you can see the drawings of my dreams and pains scratched into the walls of my heart. Then, maybe you will show me yours. And we will be surprised how what begins as private quickly reveals itself as Universal. From this, we might get the strength to continue. Perhaps this is the reason for all art and therapy: to strengthen us when we come up into the world, and to help us remember that we are possible when the hardships of life make us forget.

Only following what feels true can
connect us across time.

Questions to Walk With

- Describe an unexpected moment of connection that has changed your life.
- In conversation with a friend or loved one, describe a marking on the wall of your heart and what it represents to you.

Our One Assignment

Buddha said that the origin of light came from within. The implication is that there is an inner plane of forces that mirrors the elements of the physical world. That as matter and gravity are the conduits for fire, water, earth, and wind, our wakefulness and love are conduits for the forces of inner light, which manifest as intention, care, compassion, and kindness. And while survival has us navigate the struggles of circumstance, the enduring way to meet and mitigate events is to express and pour the inner forces of light into the kinships that strengthen the Web of Life. In this way, light has migrated for eons through our suffering and delight into the world. This, then, is our one assignment: to make our humanness the lens through which light comes into the world.

Time and the misdeeds we perpetrate make ruin of

what we're given. And each generation takes its turn at restoring what has been broken, in each life and each era. As far back as the thirteenth century, the *Edda,* the source of Icelandic mythology, described God creating light by throwing embers into the darkness. This was an early archetype of our very flawed and human destiny: to find what has been lost and to remake what has been broken by throwing our care and ingenuity like embers into the darkness.

And so, despite the rise and fall of epochs, it is our vow to cast light into the dark that remains noble and enduring. In this, the French philosopher Albert Camus rightly sanctified the struggle itself, regardless of the outcome. Whether doomed or crowned, it is the lift of what is in the way that renews us. We must stay committed to the journey, regardless of what happens.

The fiercely tender American poet Chris Bursk revealed the heart of our journey when he said, "How many of us spend our lives traveling back and forth between the harm we inflict and the good we want to do?"

To act on love in real time is how we release our radiance, until more light remains than dark in every turn of the wheel.

This, then, is our one assignment: to make
our humanness the lens through which light
comes into the world.

Questions to Walk With

- In your journal, describe one act of care and ingenuity you can throw like an ember into the darkness you encounter. How might you begin to enact this gesture of love?
- In conversation with a friend or loved one, describe a struggle you have experienced over time and how it has been your teacher.

Giving Everything We Have

It was winter and I was in San Francisco to lead a workshop on the life of expression. I was planning to open the first morning by speaking about the Eternal Oneness that our wholehearted engagement opens us to. I was eager to offer the early Renaissance sculptor Lorenzo Ghiberti as a compelling example. Ghiberti was commissioned in 1401 to create a casting for the two main doors of the Baptistery adjacent to the great Duomo Cathedral in Florence. The young sculptor embarked on what would be twenty-one years of unfailing work in bringing alive his master work of bronze—the now legendary Doors of Paradise, named by Michelangelo upon first seeing the doors finished and complete. The ten panels depict scenes from the Old Testament in remarkable relief, as if the bodies and waves and mountains, exquisitely real, were dipped in gold and pinned to the doors. Each door is massive, more than sixteen feet high, each weighing more than a ton.

Such stories of devotion and effort endure in spite of the slow avalanche of history that covers and then later reveals these great artifacts and the stories behind them. A lifetime of work can be hidden or surfaced with the blink of a cosmic eye.

So, I was wandering the day before my workshop up and down the hills of San Francisco, a city I love. And there, along California Street, just past Taylor, I chanced upon Grace Cathedral. It was early and brisk. As I climbed the steps, I was amazed to see—*could it be*—Ghiberti's doors! I had no idea. And sure enough, six hundred years later, the entrance to Grace Cathedral held an exact replica of Ghiberti's master work.

I stood there—in awe—as I had before the original doors in Florence in 1981. The original doors had stood in Florence for centuries, their bronze glow slowly covered by the steady film of time, their brilliance hidden. Until, during World War II, Bruno Bearzi, the foundry master of Florence, supervised the taking down of the doors to hide them from the Nazis. The doors were sandbagged and hidden in a railway tunnel. While taking them down, ropes rubbed the grime away and their original gilding was discovered.

After the war, Bearzi returned to clean the doors completely and, before installing them in the Palazzo Pitti Museum in Florence, he made gelatin molds of the panels, from which he cast and finished exact replicas. It wasn't

long till Lawrence Kruse, one of Grace Cathedral's archi-
tects, learned of Bearzi's work and beseeched the congre-
gation to purchase the replica I stood before that February
morning in San Francisco. The trail across time is as pre-
carious and indelible as a cinder on the wind.

Sappho is another example of how what matters is
revealed, covered, and revealed again in the course of
time. It is believed that the great Greek poet of the seventh
century BC filled six papyrus rolls with more than two thousand of her lyrics. Centuries later, her poems, which were
housed at the Library of Alexandria, were destroyed with
many other works of antiquity when the library was burned
accidentally by Julius Caesar during his civil war campaign
in 48 BC. And Sappho was lost to us. Until bunches of the
half-burned papyrus rolls were found in an Egyptian trash
heap in the late 1800s. What we have of Sappho's work is
the small portion recovered from that trash heap.

Mozart is yet another example of how the life-force we
carry can appear with the force of a creative tornado, only
to vanish, leaving a path of beauty we can only marvel at.
In 1791, at the age of thirty-five, Mozart was failing with
a fever that made him delusional. Struggling to finish his
requiem, with only a few measures to go, he died trying.
He was placed in a common grave, the unfinished requiem
still on his desk alongside his magnificent Jupiter symphony. And within the year, the magnetic pull of Mozart's
creative force was still palpable to the Austrian composer
and conductor Franz Xaver Süssmayr, who felt compelled
to complete the last bars of Mozart's requiem.

We flare so brightly for such a short time. Yet the tragic side of life is bearable when we can honor the flare of Spirit that brings us alive through the giving of everything we have. All this to affirm that our devotion to expression is not to be *remembered* for Eternity, but so we can *experience* Eternity by giving ourselves completely to the life-force ever coursing within us and between us.

Give yourself, then, to anything that seems to be opening and it will open you. Give your heart to anything that stops you with its authenticity and you will be welcomed into the Bareness of Being that magnetizes all existence. Give your complete love of life to any sliver of unfiltered truth and the Mystery will place the song you were born with into the river of time—like a flower tossed by a god into the flow.

> *Our devotion to expression is not to be remembered*
> *for Eternity, but so we can experience Eternity.*

Questions to Walk With

- Give your complete attention to a small piece of nature or a piece of music or art or literature until its timelessness starts to appear. Through this piece of nature or art, feel your place in the flow of all time. In your journal, describe in detail this process of how care opens time and your experience of it.
- In conversation with a friend or loved one, do live research together and explore the history of

a piece of art or music that touches you both, detailing the circumstances of its creation and the place this piece of art held in the life of its creator, as well as the piece of art's journey since being created. What does this case study say to you about the relationship between the creator and the created?

The Jazz of Being Here

Working for what we want is often an apprenticeship for working with what we're given. It is how we learn to show up and apply spirit in an unpredictable world. This is akin to how a jazz pianist learns scales and chords in order to listen and improvise. Working for what we want is how we learn the scales and chords of being human. The real music appears live and unrehearsed when we meet life with our unfiltered heart in the jazz of being here.

Though we are hypnotized and driven in the modern world to think that our dreams will deliver us beyond our burdens and limitations, we inevitably arrive exactly where we are, the way roots and shoots labor tirelessly so a flower can break ground exactly where it is. For deeper than excellence and more lasting than achievement, our enormous efforts—at doing, building, creating, and repairing—are embodied preparations for the dance of who we are, alone and together.

While there is nothing wrong with working for what we want, it often serves as a practice ground for the real work that appears in our way. After many years, I've come to see that while desire has us seek endlessly, compassion leads us to give our all wherever we are.

We are constantly taught that life is better over there, while the joys and sorrows of being alive confirm, again and again, that the Wholeness of Life resides in the depth of where we are. We are encouraged to reach for things like stars and horizons, while peace only reaches us when we settle into the ground of being. This doesn't mean we should stop dreaming, growing, and reaching. Rather, that we need to see these efforts as paths to living fully in the one life we are given. For humbly, when we let go of what we want, we are often comforted by things we couldn't have imagined.

A great paradox in the journey of being human is that we are born with an urge to create, build, and repair outwardly, while also having an urge to empty and still ourselves inwardly. Outwardly, we want to go from here to there, to pick up what has been dropped, to gather what has been spilled, and to love what has been broken back together. The paradox is that for all the movement we are engaged in, the truth of our being arises when we stop and empty all that we gather until we accept that there is nowhere to go and nothing to do. For all our work and commitment, we are better off once we inhabit life rather than manipulate it. The mysterious constancy of being is the fire that burns our effort like wood, lighting everything around us.

As we negotiate the urge to build in the world while emptying all that is not essential, we fall down and get up repeatedly. And rising after falling is the calisthenic of heart that strengthens our being. All this led me to express this poem:

EARTHWARD

Under all our trouble, we drift
like flakes of snow, ever earthward.
Under all our pain and fear, we sink
softly like pebbles tossed by children
into the sea. After seventy-two years
of trying to get somewhere, life has
evaporated all I want. Now, like the
bottom of the ocean, I only wait to
receive. To go under all that gets in
the way and accept the stunning
beauty waiting in the ordinary.
Meet me there where everything
unfolds in slow motion, where
we sway like seaweed, where
our acceptance keeps us
from drowning.

Until we practice acceptance, it is impossible to remove what's in the way. And removing what's in the way is less about breaking impediments and more about taming the wolf of our mind until the bird of our heart can fly through the trees on the path.

All our designs are kindling for the fire of our aliveness. For *the call of the soul* is the pull of the nameless flame we call life-force that brings us ever closer to full living, while what we are drawn to do with this life-force is *our soul's calling*. Helping things grow may be the call of my soul, but my soul's calling, where I apply that, might be in becoming a gardener. Likewise, helping people grow may be the call of my soul, but my soul's calling, where I offer that in the world, might be in becoming a teacher or a therapist or a nurse.

Our ordinary destiny is to move ever forward into life, creating and emptying, while being worn of all that is extraneous. As erosion wears nature to its beauty, a lifetime of experience wears us down to our inner beauty. In this way, each of us is precisely worn over a lifetime until our patterned ways break down. This happens, again and again, until the soul is revealed in its fullness, regardless of what we accomplish or not.

When we build, we often fear we won't be seen for what we've created. And when empty, we often fear we will remain invisible. The truth is that while we think that being seen and heard will bring us alive, only living authentically will enliven us. Being seen and heard will make us feel loved and valued, but this is not the same as inhabiting our being, which restores our inner knowing that we are enough as we are.

A deep paradox colors our journey. For though everyone has been here, no one has felt what you feel or stood where you stand. So, reach for what has never been done, so you can land where everyone lands. The daily question is this: Despite whatever you have endured, how will you open yourself a little further? For life requires that we give a little more to keep coming alive.

Our gifts often appear when working with what we're given, rather than working for what we want.

Questions to Walk With

- In your journal, describe the difference between being seen and heard and feeling your own sense of worth that is not dependent on anyone else. How do you experience both? How does each enliven you?
- In conversation with a friend or loved one, describe a recent experience of your urge to create, build, and repair, as well as a recent experience of being still and emptying. As with the first question, how do you experience both? How does each enliven you?

Imparting Bliss

We must not meet fire with fire, but with light.

—MN

She was a kind and gentle woman who spoke softly near the end of a retreat I was guiding. She was moved to share a moment that changed her life. While crossing the street, she was hit by a car and was lying on the asphalt in shock, bleeding, in pain, disoriented. Waiting for the ambulance, she saw a patch of blue sky. Somehow, this patch of vastness lifted her from the scene of her trauma. She felt called to surrender to that patch of blue. It made her drop all the roles she had been carrying since birth. This feeling of surrender has stayed with her ever since. It has taught her that letting go is a never-ending process. Whenever lost or entangled now, she returns to that patch of blue. Yet, she worries, "How can I live in surrender and have hope for the future?"

In truth, surrender doesn't mean giving up the future, but giving up the assumptions, expectations, and conclusions we accrue along the way that keep us from living life directly. In this way, surrender is more like shedding the clothes that cover us in any moment than giving up the open road of life before us.

Whether it's a sudden patch of blue that trouble opens or a stillness at the end of pain, it is the unfettered clearing we are led to that imparts bliss. Still, we can't imagine how they do it, the tender, resilient souls who endure, only to tremble in the ordinary light. Like Francis of Assisi, giving everything away and loving everything. But as the lyrics of a song are lost in its echo, his vow of poverty has been sorely misunderstood. Radically, it was a vow of emptying, of putting aside all that is false and unnecessary. So there is nothing in the way. Then, we breathe air and, in our unencumbered center, it becomes love. This is the unimpeachable reward for removing everything in the way.

Yet, in our modern age, a growing segment of our society is suffering from having lost its direct connection to life. Without a foundation from which to navigate existence, we can become like trees without roots. Without the direct touchstone that love and suffering affirm for us, and with so many virtual and technological distractions, we can bounce between intensities that grab our attention and drain our energy. Without being grounded in what is real, we can mistake intensity for truth and stimuli for meaning, when they are only shiny objects blowing about in the storm of circumstance.

As in other times, the remedy is to restore our direct connection to life. This is what all the spiritual traditions have offered through the centuries. It sounds simple, but we must educate ourselves and our children, so that we can affirm that this is the ground we walk on and this is the air we breathe. Between earth and sky, we can compare our experience and offer many interpretations of what we go through. But that the earth and sky are our home is an indisputable fact.

A fish must accept that water is its home and we, as human beings, must accept that the days we move through are real and inescapable. Though, unlike fish, we must also accept that for us the water of experience is both life-sustaining and we can drown in it. Without a direct connection to life, we will never be able to discern the difference. Without a shared, grounded sense of reality, we will hurt each other quickly and deeply, as we are tossed about in storms of our own making.

So, how might we restore our direct connection to life? It always comes back to the engagement of our heart. For the heart is our greatest teacher, capable of foundational strength and delicate precision.

A simple example of this is present when I teach. I am often praised for being so well read and for having access to so many stories and voices. It is true. I carry a trove of allies with me. But I have not memorized any of them. Rather, they live in me. We are mistakenly taught in our modern world that to know by heart is to memorize. But, more deeply, to know by heart is to be so touched by something—a moment, a truth, a voice, a metaphor, or a story—that it is imprinted in our heart. Once touched in this way, the faces imprinted in my heart are always near, entreating me to bring them forward in a story or poem from which you can drink.

Nonetheless, I do forget and drift and lose my way, and find myself holding on to things that don't matter. So, when I need to let go of whatever is in the way, I enter this conversation with myself at a deeper level of being, often by journaling:

- The first effort I make is to accept that I am holding on or clinging in the first place. I can't let go if I don't admit that I am holding on.
- The second effort is to ask myself: What am I afraid of losing? What is at the heart of my clinging? What do I fear will be lost if I don't hold on?
- The third effort is to be in conversation with the paradox that stirs me with both the inevitable loss that I am facing in the world and the essence of what I'm afraid of losing as it lives in my spirit, which can never be lost. For example, I might be facing the loss of someone I love dearly, though I can never lose my capacity to love.
- Now, I can work with both sides of this paradox in the specific way it is confronting me. I can begin the hard work of accepting the loss in the world that is inevitable (i.e., losing someone

I love dearly). Then, I can touch into the place
where the essence of what I'm afraid of losing
lives in my spirit and drink from it (i.e., my capacity to love).

- Once establishing my inner stance of being, I
  can physically practice holding on and letting go.
  One way I do this is to squeeze a ball and release
  it, over and over, while saying, "I am holding on.
  I am letting go."

- Then, I can align my inhaling with the squeeze
  of the ball and my exhaling with the release of
  the ball, while saying, "Hold on, let go. Hold on,
  let go."

- Only when I have accepted the impending loss,
  can I find—through letting go—the pearl of
  peace as it settles under all my turbulence.

No one is free from this mysterious cycle of forgetting
and remembering, of drifting and returning, of holding on
and letting go. We each must discover our patch of blue.
We each must empty ourselves of all that is false and unnecessary until there is nothing in the way. Until we can
restore our direct connection with life. Until we can feel,
once again, our kinship with all things. Until we know the
world by heart, by what touches us, by what lets us know
we are alive.

This is a constant, unending challenge for each of us:
to enter the moment of living before us so thoroughly that

all of life presents itself. In this, animals are great teachers. For they cannot drift for long from their direct experience of life. And why is this return to direct experience so important? Because it is through our thorough living of the moment that we find the precise strength to meet what we are given.

Take, for example, the antelope. If we watch closely, we can see how an antelope scales a mountain without falling. The antelope does this by concentrating its entire being on the very next step. It foregoes squandering its attention ahead or behind. In truth, the antelope is predisposed to concentrate on the moment at hand. This is one of the hardest tasks for a human being. Yet, if we can forego all dream and memory when facing what is imminent, working with what is will keep us agile and grounded in the lift and fall of living. If you want to be skilled at falling down and getting up, be like an antelope.

This is a constant, unending challenge for each of us:
to enter the moment of living before us so
thoroughly that all of life presents itself.

Questions to Walk With

- In your journal, describe one aspect of your life you are holding on to. Why are you clinging to this? Describe what you fear in letting go and describe the pain in holding on. Then, close your eyes and practice holding on and letting go as you breathe steadily and deeply.

- In conversation with a friend or loved one, share a lesson about life that is imprinted in your heart. Tell the story of how you came to know this lesson by heart.

The Work of Flourishing

What a small flicker is given
To each of us to know.

—Naomi Shihab Nye

Being Opened

More than thirty years ago, I almost died from a rare form of lymphoma. One of the great lessons from that strident passage is that whatever opens us, whether harsh or loving, is never as important as what is opened in us. In truth, we often rail against the unfairness or injustice of what has brutally opened us, which can be true and legitimate. Yet, more than anything, our journey forward depends on how we meet and inhabit what has been opened.

Like it or not, everyone and everything changes and we are challenged to accept the change without being defined by the pain we encounter along the way. This doesn't mean that we minimize or deny our pain or stop working for justice, but that we meet our pain and move through it into the clearing that life has made within us. I know this is very difficult to take in and work with. All I can say is that being pried open by life has prepared me to keep a vow to stay open to life. And this has made a powerful and tender difference in the kind of life I have been able to live.

Being Broken

Being broken is never fun. No one seeks being broken. No one asks for it. But like erosion, being broken is a developmental phase of growth, not a deficiency. We have stigmatized being broken as a sign of damage or weakness. Yet mysteriously, it is being broken open that leads to all transformation. Rather than deny or resist this phase of growth—it is inevitable—we might better focus our efforts on mapping the new terrain on the other side of the break. What new way of thinking, feeling, or being are we being led to?

Consider the Grand Canyon, one of the largest broken open spaces on Earth. We save our money in hopes of traveling vast distances to peer into its great emptiness. Yet this natural wonder came into being precisely because the Earth at its core couldn't hold together. The Earth's plates split and wonder was the lasting result. So, too, with us, though it is, of course, understandable that this developmental phase of being broken is painful and hard to endure. Another reason we need each other: to help each other endure the breaking, to help each other enter the vastness opened by the break, and to marvel together at the wonder revealed.

Being Transparent

The question arises, "Is it a good thing to be transparent?"
That this is a question at all demonstrates how indoctri-
nated we are in the art of hiding. When someone says, "I
can see right through you," it has the connotation that we
are being exposed, that we are being revealed as a phony
or a charlatan. But life has taught me quite the opposite,
that there can be no growth or transformation or integrity of relationship unless we are transparent. In his poem
"Self-Protection," D. H. Lawrence poses the question: Is
the best self-protection hiding who you are or being who
you are? He goes on to point out that only the creatures
wholly and colorfully themselves have survived the centuries. Those who have been camouflaged have perished.

Of course, there are costs for being seen. We can be hurt,
misunderstood, rejected, or fooled. And each dismissal or
reprisal has its pain and grief that can't be minimized. But
I have found that the cost of not being who I am, of staying
hidden, is more corrosive and damaging to my soul and to
my very life-force. After all, whatever you wall out, you also
wall in. And the thicker the wall between us and life, the
more removed we are from being touched by life.

Being transparent allows us to be touched. It brings
us closer. It deepens our relationships. When hidden or
walled in, we can only reflect life. What approaches us
bounces off. When open-hearted, we receive and absorb
and are informed more thoroughly by life itself. When
transparent, we are warmed and illumined.

All this to say that I would rather be fooled than not believe. The hurts and slights and even embarrassment for being fooled are not pleasant to go through. But when we don't stay open to being touched by the smallest detail of life—letting it in—we shun the touch of angels along the way.

Being Vulnerable

Even if it takes years, it is important to heal the wounded places, so we can recover the full use of our heart. For the parts of our heart left wounded and unresolved remain preoccupied and not available for us to use in living. If unprocessed, the wounded places become dark and hard. Being vulnerable allows us to recover our heart, because being vulnerable and tender allows our wounds to soften and heal.

Anger, even when legitimate, will harden, if not processed and allowed to soften. Often, when I am angry, it is because I have been hurt. When I can let the anger subside, I discover a sadness beneath it that leads me to examine where I am hurt. When I stay angry, I never let the hurt place soften and so, it can never heal. When stuck in the anger, I keep feeling the hurt, though I can't locate and tend the hurt.

Untended, my heart becomes heavy where it is hard. Then, I walk around with a diminished heart that weighs me down with the wounded part unavailable to experience life. Staying vulnerable is both a cleansing and healing

agent that allows us to become whole again. As the ancient
sages all confirm, everything softens in time. If we want to
soften while still alive, we have to bring our hurt places
into the light.

Breaking Trail

There are a thousand reasons to come and go, to hold
and let go. But from our common depth of being, none of
them matters. All that matters is that we live in the open so
we can hold each other as long as possible.

Ultimately, every path holds the questions of those who
have walked it and every time we hold another in their pain
or joy, that embrace leaves its mark on all involved. The
reward for caring is that when present beyond our own
concerns, we are informed by the touch and questions of
others. When I stand long enough on the trail, I start to
hear the history of voices. When I hold you long enough,
the embrace transcends what brought us together and we
slip into the well of all touch.

Despite our want to be unique, breaking trail is not going where no one has gone before, but taking our turn at
finding the living center that we have in common with all
life by being opened, being broken, being transparent, and
being vulnerable. These are the daily practices that bring
us alive and keep us alive.

These are the spiritual aerobics that each of us must personalize, if we are to truly be here. Aristotle defined a virtue
as anything that helps us flourish as a human being, while a

vice is anything that impedes us from flourishing. Regardless of what others encourage or caution against, we must each discover what helps us flourish and what thwarts our growth, and then remain dedicated to the work of flourishing.

> *Breaking trail is not going where no one has gone before, but taking our turn at finding the living center that we have in common with all life.*

Questions to Walk With

- In your journal, describe separate moments when you experienced being opened, being broken, being transparent, and being vulnerable. How did these moments differ in their impact on you? What did these experiences reveal to you about your life?
- In conversation with a friend or loved one, begin to tell the story of your life as a trail you discovered along the way. Where has the trail of your life led you? What lessons have you learned about the art of breaking trail?

Full of Light

Finishing a book is like telling one more story around a campfire as the embers burn down. Soon, we will be breaking camp and making our way back into our lives. And all this talk makes me take in the view one more time. Where have we been? What have we learned? Where are we going? It seems the purpose of travel is not to arrive anywhere, but to unravel everything that doesn't contribute to life.

So, the final story goes like this. The yarn of dreams I've carried across my life has been cut up along the way, helping to stitch this and tie down that. And despite how we are taught to accumulate things, I've given almost everything away and this has left me full of light. I began this book wanting to explore how we fall and how we get up. Now, on the other side, after years of journeying with folks

like you, it is more deeply about giving so that the light we
carry can find its way into the world.

Without fail, life causes us to trip and fall but Spirit is
at the ready to help us find our footing and make our way.
And yes, every disruption is a storm of sorts, as well as a
clearing. The gentle Vietnamese monk Thich Nhat Hanh
spoke to this when he said:

> *Every time we survive such a storm, we grow a little.*
> *Without storms like these, I would not be who I am*
> *today. But I rarely hear such a storm coming until it*
> *is already upon me. It seems to appear without warn-*
> *ing . . . I know it must have been brewing a long time,*
> *simmering in my own thoughts . . . but when such a*
> *frenzied hurricane strikes, nothing outside can help. I*
> *am battered and torn apart, and I am also saved.*

We always seem to fight the storm, but welcome the
clearing. For falling down is always full of trouble and
pain. At first, it seems an assault but, on the other side,
we often thank the storm for its scouring. And thank each
other for the help in getting up. This is the work of friendship. It changes how we care. Not trying to avoid the fall,
but learning how to survive it.

I recently came upon this astonishing image. This is a
photograph of the library at Holland House in London,
after it was almost completely destroyed during the German bombing on September 27, 1940. That day, Holland

House was hit by over twenty incendiary bombs. Remarkably, the walls, stacked with rare and historic books, remained intact.

As the next day's light filtered through the smoke and rubble, ordinary souls wandered through the ruins to start over. The entire scene is the epitome of falling down and getting up. Though our roof may collapse, the light is still everywhere. And soon, one of us is looking, while one of us is reaching. Getting up always begins by following the light and clearing the rubble to discover a new path. Getting up always involves finding the fallen ladder, just waiting to be propped against something to climb, one more time.

There is something irrepressibly holy about such a scene of rubble and clearing, of ending and beginning. One could imagine this photograph as a portrait of a broken heart, or a life upended, having to dust itself off and begin again.

It brings to mind the great Nalanda library in twelfth-century India. That magnificent repository of knowledge had taken generations to assemble. Existing before the printing press, all the volumes were carefully copied on scrolls by hand. That one-of-a-kind library was set ablaze and destroyed in a single day in 1193 by marauding Turks. The fire was so deadly and the extent of manuscripts burning so vast that it took six months for the fire to smolder its way out. But legend has it that the wisdom of all those manuscripts, gathered and copied for generations, didn't disappear. Rather, it settled in the smoky ash that coated children's faces as they played. It settled into the innocent nostrils of cattle grazing. It caked itself on the spokes of wagon wheels clearing the rubble.

What matters can never be destroyed, only rearranged. This is the secret to falling down and getting up. So, clear the rubble in your heart and welcome the light now coming through your collapsed way of being. While nothing can minimize the pain and loss that comes from falling down, nothing can keep us from helping each other up. Our commitment to each other is that I will lift you when you are on the ground, if you help me sweep the debris from what I've built.

You see, falling down and getting up is an inevitable part of nature's cycle. Like leaves that go to mulch, only to seed somewhere else. Like nests that birds twig together, only to fly apart as straw once fledglings start their journey.

Like you and I meeting on the way and sharing stories of all we've been through around the earned glow of our heart. So, until next time, fall easy and find your footing. I will give you something soothing when we meet again. This is our ordinary destiny: to leave something life-giving on the path.

Gratitudes

I am deeply grateful to my publisher, Joel Fotinos, whose gentle insistence opened me to the life of this book. Joel kept being drawn to my work as a teacher and finally asked, "What kind of book would you write for those who are unable to participate in one of your teaching circles? What kind of journey would come closest?" What an invitation! From that moment, this book was born. And, like my other books, it quickly became *my* teacher.

I'm also grateful to my agent, Eve Atterman, for her deep company and care, and to James Munro and Fiona Baird and the WME team for their commitment through the years. And to Brooke Warner, my trusted friend, reader, and vision partner, for our many years of creating together. And to my publicist, Eileen Duhne, for representing me so well to the world.

Gratitude to my dear friends, each has helped me up

more than once. Especially George, Don, Paul, Skip, TC, David, Parker, Kurt, Pam, Patti, Karen, Paula, Ellen, Dave, Jill, Jacquelyn, Linda, Michelle, Rich, Carolyn, Henk, Elesa, Penny, Sally, and Joel. And to Jamie Lee Curtis for being such a steadfast example of resilience. And to Oprah Winfrey for being such a champion of the heart.

And to Paul Bowler for all we've been through together. And to Robert Mason for never having to explain what we know in our hearts. And to my dear wife, Susan, what is love, if not helping each other up one more time.

—MN

Notes

Epigraphs and poems without attribution are by the author.

p. ix, dedication: "The dirt that packs the plant . . ." from my poem "Under the Temple" in my book of poems *The Half-Life of Angels*.

p. xi, epigraph: "The Great Waters . . ." a poem in my book of poems *The Half-Life of Angels*.

The Depth of Life

p. xvii: "falling down and getting up . . ." I have been exploring this rhythm of experience my whole life and first wrote about it in the chapter "Falling Down and Getting Up" in my early book *The Exquisite Risk*, New York: Harmony Books, 2005, p. 127.

PART 1: THE WAY OF LEARNING

p. 1, epigraph: "When chickens or dogs . . ." Mencius, *The Four Chinese Classics*, translated by David Hinton. Berkeley, CA: Counterpoint, 2013, p. 524.

Our Conversation with Life

p. 3, epigraph: "We're with the push . . ." Robert Mason. By permission of the author.

My Life as a Teacher

p. 4: "In the eyes of the Ashkenazim . . ." Abraham Heschel, *The Earth Is the Lord's: The Inner World of the Jew in Eastern Europe*. New York: Jewish Lights, 1995.

p. 9: "students in China . . ." I was teaching for the Hailan Family Well-Being peer education institute. And I am indebted to Dr. Hailan and Joy Huang Xiaoyu for their impeccable care and for inviting me to teach and journey with their community, and to my dear friend Paul Ginter for introducing us. Please visit http://www.hailanxfj.com/.

As Time Unfolds
p. 12, epigraph: "What happens when people . . ." Haruki Murakami, *Norwegian Wood,* cited in *The Sun.* November 2021, p. 48.

No One Is Watching
p. 16: "no one is watching . . ." I first explored this topic in the chapter "As We Keep Searching" in my book *The Book of Soul.* New York: St. Martin's Essentials, 2020.

p. 16: " 'The Watcher' . . ." Jorge Luis Borges, *Selected Poems,* translated by Alastair Reid, edited by Alexander Coleman. New York: Viking Penguin, 1999.

p. 17: " 'The Music Beneath the Music' . . ." from my book *The Way Under the Way: The Place of True Meeting.* Louisville, CO: Sounds True, 2016, p. 15.

p. 21: "To teach is to create a space . . ." Parker J. Palmer, *To Know as We Are Known.* San Francisco: HarperSanFrancisco, 1993, p. 1.

p. 21: "Where We Need to Be . . ." from my book *The Way Under the Way: The Place of True Meeting.* Louisville, CO: Sounds True, 2016, p. 60.

p. 22: *Chatter: The Voice in Our Heads.* See Ethan Kross, *Chatter: The Voice in Our Heads.* New York: Crown Publishers, 2021. I'm grateful to my dear friend Rich Frankel for steering me to this book just as I was writing this chapter.

p. 24: "Drinking from Center . . ." This paragraph originally appeared as "Drinking from Center" in my book *Things That Join the Sea and the Sky.* Louisville, CO: Sounds True, 2017, p. 85.

Traveling Again
p. 32: "The Chinese word *hsien* . . ." Details of the root meaning of these words come from the glossary that David Hinton provides in his remarkable book of translation, *Classical Chinese Poetry.* New York: Farrar, Straus and Giroux, 2008, pp. 447–450.

Choice-Points

p. 41, epigraph: "I cannot think myself . . ." from *At Hell's Gate,* Claude Anshin Thomas. Boston: Shambhala, 2004. Cited from an excerpt in *The Sun,* Issue 346, Oct 2004, pp. 12–19. Claude Anshin Thomas is a Vietnam vet turned drug addict turned homeless person turned Zen monk.

To Speak What We Know to Be True
p. 50: "King George VI . . ." See the inspiring film *The King's Speech* (2010) for which Colin Firth won an Oscar. George VI was the King of England from 1936–1952.

p. 50: "as a child . . ." David Barrett tells us: "It was Pharaoh's daughter, Batyah, who found Moses and then adopted him as her own. [And] Miriam, Moses's sister, was at the river to watch him and asked Batyah if she wanted a woman to nurse him. When given a yes, she went and got Johevet, Moses's natural mother, to nurse him."

The Felt Realm In Between

p. 53: "There is an ancient story . . ." I am grateful to Desiree Alampi from Switzerland for introducing me to this story.

The Corridor of Aliveness

p. 66: "To Look or Not to Look . . ." For a more in-depth exploration of this archetype, please see the chapter "To Look or Not to Look" in my book *Surviving Storms: Finding the Strength to Meet Adversity,* New York: St. Martin's Essentials, 2022.

p. 71: "the work of Beethoven . . ." For an in-depth look at the life of Beethoven, please see the chapter "Seasons of Listening" in my book *Seven Thousand Ways to Listen.* New York: Atria Books, 2012.

The Anthem of Our Day

p. 73: "The Anthem of Our Day" Parts of this chapter first appeared in *Sufi: A Journal of Mystical Philosophy and Practice.* London: Khaniqahi Nimatullahi Publications, Issue 99, Summer 2020, as well as in my regular column in *Spirituality & Health Magazine,* May/June 2020.

The Truth and Grip of Our Feelings

p. 82: "I Go Among Trees" Wendell Berry, from *A Timbered Choir: The Sabbath Poems 1979–1997,* Berkeley CA: Counterpoint Press, 1999.

Stories About Learning

p. 93, epigraph: "[People] can starve . . ." Richard Wright, from *The Sun.* Chapel Hill, NC, Issue 512, August 2018, p. 48.

To Count and Compare

p. 94: "To Count and Compare" As with many themes I've explored through the years, my understanding deepens across time and throughout my books. This extended treatment draws on passages from earlier explorations, including: "Keeping Our Eyes Open" in *The One Life We're Given,* New York: Atria Books, 2016, p. 206, and "Cain and Abel" in *As Far As the Heart Can See,* Freefall Books, 2020, p. 175.

Images that Educate the Heart

p. 97, epigraph: "Art [is an attempt] to render . . ." Joseph Conrad, from *Narcissus and Other Stories.* Digireads.com, 2009. Originally published in 1897 by Joseph Conrad as the novella *Narcissus: A Tale of the Sea.*

Poetry and Education

p. 106: "Stop this day and night . . ." Walt Whitman, from "Song of Myself," #2, in *The Portable Walt Whitman,* edited by Mark Van Doren. New York: Viking, 1945, p. 71.

As We Go

p. 108: "As We Go" A version of this chapter was first published in *OMTimes,* August 2020.

p. 110: "I need no warrant for being . . ." Ayn Rand, from *Anthem.* New York: Plume Editions of Penguin, 2005, p. 94. The novel was first published in England in 1938.

p. 113: "What more mountain than the one that is" Cid Corman, from *Livingdying.* New York: New Directions, 1970, p. 2.

p. 116: "my lament [was] buried deep . . ." Pablo Neruda, from "Shyness" in *Isla Negra,* translated by Alastair Reid. New York: Farrar, Straus, and Giroux, 1982, p. 36.

p. 117: "For the first time . . ." Kahlil Gibran, from *The Madman: His Parables and Poems.* New York: Alfred A. Knopf, 1918, pp. 7–8.

p. 119: "I was walking lost in thought . . ." Rainer Maria Rilke, from *Rodin.* Salt Lake City, UT: Peregrine Smith, 1979, p. 97. Originally published as a monograph in March 1903 in Berlin for the art series *Die Kunst.*

p. 119: "It was walking with Seferis . . ." The three quotes here are from George Seferis in *A Poet's Journal: Days of 1949–1951,* translated by Athan Anagnostopoulos. Cambridge, MA: Harvard University Press, 1974, p. 59, 119, 123.

p. 127: "We shall not cease from exploration . . ." T. S. Eliot, from "Four Quartets," Boston: Houghton Mifflin, 1943.

The Arts of Liberation

p. 130, epigraph: "The Artist is no other . . ." E. E. Cummings, from *A Miscellany Revised,* New York: October House, 1965.

p. 131: "that keen observation . . ." Rachel Corbett, from *You Must Change Your Life: The Story of Rainer Maria Rilke and Auguste Rodin.* New York: Norton, 2016, p. 7–8.

p. 131: "What is Liberal Arts?" An earlier version of this passage first appeared in my book *As Far As the Heart Can See,* Deerfield Beach, FL: Health Communications Inc., 2011, p. 115.

Vessels of Learning

p. 137: "I was staying with friends on the edge of a canyon in Santa Fe, New Mexico . . ." These three paragraphs originally appeared in the chapter "The Mysterious Press of Oneness" in my book *The Exquisite Risk,* New York: Harmony Books, 2006, p. 241.

p. 138: "There are three errors to be avoided . . ." Jamgön Kongtrül Rinpoche, from *Cloudless Sky.* Boston: Shambhala, 1992, p. xi.

Freeing the Ox

p. 140: "Freeing the Ox" An earlier version of this essay appeared in my book of collected essays *Unlearning Back to God: Essays on Inwardness,* New York: Khaniqahi Nimatullahi Publications, 2006, p. 183.

p. 140: "We must not be afraid . . ." *The Illuminated Rumi,* edited by Coleman Barks & Michael Greene. New York: Broadway Books, 1997, p. 65.

p. 147: "[who we are] . . ." *Basic Writings: Chuang Tzu,* translated by Burton Watson. New York: Columbia University, 1964, p. 104.

p. 147: "Martin Buber's story" *Meetings,* Chicago, IL: Open Court Press, 1973, pp. 24–26.

Waking Close to the Bone

p. 151, epigraph: "Not too far . . ." Tao Ch'ien, from "Back Home Again Chant" in *The Selected Poems of Tao Ch'ien* translated by David Hinton. Port Townsend, WA: Copper Canyon Press, 1993, p. 33.

In the Awakened Flow

p. 172, epigraph: "The bee of the heart . . ." Kabir, from "The Swan" translated by Robert Bly, in *The Soul Is Here for Its Own Joy,* edited by Robert Bly. New York: Ecco Press, 1995, p. 86.

p. 172: "You can't tell . . ." William Stafford, from his last poem, "Are you Mr. William Stafford?" August 28, 1993, in *The Way It Is: New & Selected Poems.* Minneapolis, MN: Graywolf Press, 1998, p. 46.

Now You Must Choose

p. 181: "the Three Brushes of Ōbaku . . ." For a complete account of this story and its meaning, please see my chapter "Fire in the Temple" in my book *The One Life We're Given.* New York: Atria Books, 2016, p. 179.

PART 2: THE DEEPER TEACHERS

p. 185, epigraph: "Heroes didn't leap tall buildings . . ." Jodi Picoult, from *The Sun.* Chapel Hill, NC, Issue 501, Sept 2017, p. 48.

The Life After Tears

p. 187, epigraph: "Some things cannot be fixed . . ." Megan Devine, from the journal *The Sun,* January 2019, Issue 517, p. 48.

p. 188: "the Gnostic Gospels . . ." In 1945, fifty-two papyrus texts, including gospels and other secret documents, were found concealed in an earthenware jar buried in the Egyptian desert. These so-called Gnostic writings were Coptic translations from the original Greek dating from the time of the New Testament. Please see the remarkable book *The Gnostic Gospels,* by Elaine Pagels, New York: Random House, 1979.

Right-Sizing Our Pain

p. 199, epigraph: "Pain is knowledge . . ." Jerry Seinfeld, from *Comedians in Cars Getting Coffee,* Trevor Noah episode, Season 1.

p. 201: "an ancient, anonymous teaching story from India . . ." I tell an earlier version of this story in the January 15 entry, "How Does It Taste?" in my spiritual daybook, *The Book of Awakening*. Newburyport, MA: Red Wheel/Weiser, 2020.

p. 203: "I was on an examination table . . ." I first told this story in a longer piece called "Nothing As It Was" in my book *Surviving Has Made Me Crazy*. Fort Lee, NJ: CavanKerry Press, 2007, p. 11.

The Heart of Grief

p. 207, epigraph: "You don't need to know people . . ." Valarie Kaur, from *See No Stranger*. New York: One World Books, 2020, p. 59.

p. 216: "when I was in Prague . . ." This paragraph is from my journal from my time in Prague in 2009, which is part of my book *Where the HeartBeast Sings: Travel Journals 1998–2020*.

p. 217: "in the very center . . . inside everything." This sentence is a recast version of a stanza from my poem "Adrift" in my book *Inside the Miracle*. Louisville, CO: Sounds True, 2015, p. 217.

PART 3: THE JOURNEY TO WHERE WE ARE
All Things Are True

p. 221, epigraph: "All paths lead to the same goal . . ." Pablo Neruda, Nobel Laureate, 1971, from his Nobel Lecture, December 13, 1971. In *Nobel Lectures in Literature 1968–1980,* edited by Sture Allen. Singapore: World Scientific Publishing, 1993, p. 55.

Four Sages Find the Garden

p. 232: "a story in the Talmud . . ." See Peter Cole's introduction to *The Poetry of Kabbalah: Mystical Verse from the Jewish Tradition,* translated and edited by Peter Cole and Aminadav Dykman. New Haven, CT: Yale University Press, 2012, pp. x and 253, note 7.

Fidelity to the Journey

p. 240, epigraph: "Perhaps we'll find . . ." Wes Anderson, from his movie, *The French Dispatch.*

p. 243: "self-confidence." I first explored this deeper notion of confidence in the April 14 entry of my daybook *The Book of Awakening*. Newburyport, MA: Red Wheel/Weiser, 2000 & 2020.

Breathing Spell

p. 247, epigraph: "Faith is the willingness . . ." physicist Alan Lightman, from *The Accidental Universe: The World You Thought You* Knew. New York: Pantheon, 2014.

The Work of Integrity

p. 252, epigraph: "This is true alchemy . . ." Sparrow, from *The Sun.* Chapel Hill, NC, Issue 500, August 2017, p. 6.

Learning It All Again

p. 259: "Symeon the New Theologian (949–1022) . . ." from *The Enlightened Heart,* edited by Stephen Mitchell. New York: Harper & Row, 1989, pp. 159.

p. 259: "Kukai (774–835) . . ." from *The Enlightened Heart,* edited by Stephen Mitchell. New York: Harper & Row, 1989, pp. 163.

p. 260: "The first word, *Ah* . . ." Kūkai, from *The Enlightened Heart,* edited by Stephen Mitchell. New York: Harper & Row, 1989, pp. 36.

Grounded but Not Buried

p. 262, epigraph: "I take my time . . ." Tao Ch'ien, from "Returning to My Old Home" in *The Selected Poems of Tao Ch'ien* translated by David Hinton. Port Townsend, WA: Copper Canyon Press, 1993, p. 17.

p. 262: "I believe the ultimate . . ." Daniel Ladinsky, from "The Introduction" in *The Gift, Poems by Hafiz, The Great Sufi Master,* translated by Daniel Ladinsky. New York: Penguin/Arkana, 1999, p. 4.

p. 263: "'Your influence is' . . ." John La Farge to Okakura Kakuzō, in *The Book of Tea* by Okakura Kakuzō, introduction by Bruce Richardson. Danville, Kentucky: Benjamin Press. 2019, p. 38. John La Farge was an American painter and stained glass artist became great friends with the Japanese scholar and writer Okakura Kakuzō. Kakuzō published the legendary *The Book of Tea* in 1906, which is dedicated to La Farge.

p. 265: "'Open your eyes and look' . . ." Albert Schweitzer, from *The Sun.* Chapel Hill, NC, Issue 534, June 2020, p. 48.

Staying Clear and Authentic

p. 271: "Frankl saw three possible sources for meaning . . ." Harold S. Kushner, from his foreword to Viktor Frankl's *Man's Search for Meaning,* Boston: Beacon Press, 2006, p. x.

p. 272: "There are four soldiers . . ." From *The Yogavasishtha of Valmiki,* Book 1, Government of India Archives, translated by R. S. Gherwal. In the introduction to *The Concise Yoga Vasistha,* translated by Swami Venkatesananda (Albany, NY: State University of New York Press, 1984), Christopher Chapples tell us that "the Yoga-Vāsiṣṭha is a philosophical text attributed to Valmiki (a Sanskrit poet from the fifth century BC), but the real author is unknown. The complete text contains over twenty-nine thousand verses. The exact century of its completion is unknown, but has been estimated to be somewhere between the sixth century to as late as the fourteenth century, but it is likely that a version of the text existed in the first millennium."

The Endless Vows

p. 284: "From the Egyptian slave . . . between living things." This paragraph originally appeared as the poem "Into the Gap" in my book of poems *The Half-Life of Angels.* Freefall Books, 2023.

p. 289: "On January 25, 2011 . . ." "French Railway Formally Apologizes to Holocaust Victims" by Maia da le Baume, *New York Times,* https://www.nytimes.com/2011 /01/26/world/europe/26france.html.

p. 290: "In October 1992 . . ." "After 350 Years, Vatican Says Galileo was Right: It Moves" by Alan Cowell, *New York Times,* Oct 31, 1992, https://www.nytimes .com/1992/10/31/world/after-350-years-vatican-says-galileo-was-right-it-moves .html.

p. 290: "One more example . . ." I first explored the story of the Sahtu Got'ine elders and their pilgrimage to Japan in my book, *More Together Than Alone.* New York: Atria Books, 2018.

p. 291: "Maimonides offers . . ." Maria Popova, from her article "Repentance, Repair, and What True Forgiveness Takes" in *The Marginalian* in which she discusses the book *On Repentance and Repair: Making Amends in an Unapologetic World* by Danya Ruttenberg. Boston, MA: Beacon Press, 2022.

On the Precipice of Growth

p. 294, epigraph: "Bless what forces us . . ." Marge Piercy, from *The Art of Blessing the Day: Poems with a Jewish Theme.* New York: Alfred A. Knopf, 1999.

Mending Things

p. 295, epigraph: "When their knots are untied . . ." Abraham Abulafia (c. 1240 AD) was an eminent Spanish Jewish Kabbalist. This quote is from "Ginze Hokhmath Ha-Kabbala, #20," in *Major Trends in Jewish Mysticism,* Gershom G. Scholem. New York: Schocken Books, 1954, third edition, p. 131.

p. 302: "'the seeing place' . . ." For a more global exploration of this notion, please see the chapter "The Seeing Place" in my book *More Together Than Alone.* New York: Atria Books, 2018.

The Break that Leads to Wisdom

p. 304: "Dan Bar-On (1938–2008) . . ." was a remarkable man. He was professor of psychology at the Department of Behavioral Sciences at Ben-Gurion University in Israel and a pioneer in personal narrative and reconciliation work. Please see his books, *Legacy of Silence: Encounters with Children of the Third Reich*; *Fear and Hope: Three Generations of Holocaust Survivors' Families*; and *The Indescribable and the Undiscussable.*

p. 304: "Germany was a country that wanted to keep its past hidden . . ." In the decades since Professor Bar-On's study, the succeeding generations in Germany have bravely confronted their past. In an article for Time Magazine (Jan 27, 202), Jacob S. Eder writes: "There exists a broad consensus that the country has confronted its crimes and learned its lessons. Major cities boast impressive monuments, museums and centers dedicated to the study of anti-Semitism and the Holocaust. Germany's institutions illustrate a conscious and responsible approach to dealing with past sins. Some observers, like the American moral philosopher Susan Neiman, make the case that it's time for the rest of the world to begin 'learning from the Germans.'"

A Sensitivity to Other Life

p. 315, epigraph: "There are times . . ." Rose Pastor Stokes, from *The Sun*. Chapel Hill, NC, Issue 534, June 2020, p. 48.

p. 315: "The primatologist Frans de Waal . . ." Details are from "Not So Different After All," an interview with Frans de Waal by Mark Leviton in *The Sun*. Chapel Hill, NC, Issue 535, July 2020, p. 5.

To Sweep and Drop

p. 319, epigraph: "How we take turns . . ." from the poem "Unearthed Again" in my book of poems *The Way Under the Way: The Place of True Meeting*, Sounds True, 2016, p. 17.

p. 320: "our argument with life . . ." I first explored this notion in my book *The Endless Practice*. New York: Atria Books, 2014, p. 204.

p. 322: "there are two other poems of mine . . ." "Being Here" and "Practicing" are from my book of poems *The Way Under the Way: The Place of True Meeting*. Louisville, CO: Sounds True, 2016, pp. 198, 92.

Being a Bridge

p. 325, epigraph: "I wish you courage . . ." from the poem "Be a Circle" in my book *The Way Under the Way: The Place of True Meeting*. Louisville, CO: Sounds True, 2016, p. 287.

Our One Assignment

p. 330: "the origin of light came from within . . ." This and the Icelandic reference to the beginnings of light come from a remarkable history of light by Bruce Watson called *Light: A Radiant History*. Amherst, MA: Levellers Press, 2016, pp. xii, 10.

p. 331: "How many of us . . ." Chris Bursk, from his poem "Crisis Line" cited in *The Sun*. Chapel Hill, NC, Issue 549, September 2021, p. 28.

Giving Everything We Have

p. 334: "Bruno Bearzi . . ." Details of the history of the Grace Cathedral replicas of Ghiberti's Doors of Paradise are from gracecathedral.org.

The Work of Flourishing

p. 350, epigraph: "What a small flicker . . ." Naomi Shihab Nye, by permission of the author.

Full of Light

p. 357: "Every time we survive such a storm . . ." Thich Nhat Hanh, from *Fragrant Palm Leaves: Journals 1962–1966*. Berkeley, CA: Parallax Press, 2020.

p. 357: "the library at Holland House . . ." Holland House was one of the first great houses in the Kensington part of London, built in 1605 for Sir Walter Cope. During England's Civil War, it was occupied by Oliver Cromwell's army. After the bombing, the house remained in ruins until 1952 when parts were preserved. Today, the renovated parts of Holland House form an open-air theater. This photo was taken by Harrison for Fox Photos Limited, later acquired by Hulton Archive, subsequently purchased by Getty Images. The image was then released as a Crown Copyright by the Press and Censorship Bureau of the Ministry of Information of the United Kingdom and is now in the public domain.

p. 359: "the great Nalanda library . . ." For an in-depth discussion of the Nalanda library and its history, please see the chapter "The Seeds of Our Nature" in my book *More Together Than Alone*. New York: Atria Books, 2018, p. 106.

Permissions

About the Author

© Brian Bankston

With over a million copies sold, *MARK NEPO* has moved and inspired readers and seekers all over the world with his #1 *New York Times* bestseller *The Book of Awakening*. Beloved as a poet, teacher, and storyteller, Mark has been called "one of the finest spiritual guides of our time," "a consummate storyteller," and "an eloquent spiritual teacher." His work is widely accessible and used by many and his books have been translated into more than twenty languages. A bestselling author, he has published twenty-five books and recorded sixteen audio projects. He has received Life Achievement Awards from AgeNation (2015) and OMTimes (2023). In 2016, he was named by *Watkins: Mind Body Spirit* as one of the 100 Most Spiritually Influential Living People, and was also chosen as one of OWN's *SuperSoul 100,* a group of inspired leaders using their gifts and voices to elevate humanity. And in 2017 Mark became a regular columnist for *Spirituality & Health Magazine.*

Recent work includes *The Half-Life of Angels* (Freefall Books, 2023); *Surviving Storms* (St. Martin's Essentials, 2022); *The Book of Soul* (St. Martin's Essentials, 2020), a Nautilus Book Award winner; *Drinking from the River of Light* (Sounds True, 2019), a Nautilus Book Award winner; *More Together Than Alone* (Atria Books, 2018), cited by *Spirituality & Practice* as one of the Best Spiritual Books of 2018; *Things That Join the Sea and the Sky* (Sounds True, 2017), a Nautilus Book Award winner; *The Way Under the Way: The Place of True Meeting* (Sounds True, 2016), a Nautilus Book Award winner; *The One Life We're Given* (Atria Books), cited by *Spirituality & Practice* as one of the Best Spiritual Books of 2016; *Inside the Miracle* (Sounds True) selected by *Spirituality & Health Magazine* as one of the top ten best books of 2015; *The Endless Practice* (Atria Books), cited by *Spirituality & Practice* as one of the Best Spiritual Books of 2014; and *Seven Thousand Ways to Listen* (Atria Books), which won the 2012 Books for a Better Life Award. *The Exquisite Risk* was listed by *Spirituality & Practice* as one of the Best Spiritual Books of 2005, calling it "one of the best books we've ever read on what it takes to live an authentic life."

Mark was part of Oprah Winfrey's The Life You Want tour in 2014 and has appeared several times with Oprah on her *Super Soul Sunday* program on OWN TV. He has also been interviewed by Robin Roberts on *Good Morning America.* Mark devotes his writing and teaching to the journey of inner transformation and the life of relationship. He continues to offer readings, lectures, and retreats. Please visit Mark at: www.MarkNepo.com, http://threeintentions.com, live.marknepo.com, and https://www.harrywalker.com/speakers/mark-nepo.